Praise for

Miracles: Receiving the Miracles Prepared for You is a book that will increase and renew your desire for the supernatural by building your faith in the Word of God. Christians needs to release the Holy Spirit to do what the Scriptures teach that He does so that we can expect and receive the miracles God has prepared for us.

Pastor Frank Damazio is a man of faith who combines his personal experiences with a lifelong biblical understanding of miracles. I heartily recommend that you buy multiple copies of this book to inspire others, as well as yourself, and give God an opportunity to provide miracles for His people. Miracles are for us today!

—Dr. David Yonggi Cho
Senior Pastor, Yoido Full Gospel Church, Seoul, Korea

God is a God of miracles and the Bible is a book of miracles. In *Miracles: Receiving the Miracles Prepared for You*, Frank Damazio uniquely unlocks an understanding of our miracle-working God and His supernatural Book in order to release us into new dimensions of the miraculous.

—Dr. Dick Eastman
International President, Every Home for Christ

Pastor Frank has given us a long-awaited and much-needed pastoral look at the subject of miracles. With clarity and insight, he exposits the biblical principles of faith, prayer and fasting, explaining their relationship to the supernatural, and showing us how they work in real life. This is more than a teaching resource; it is a handbook for a life full of God's power.

—Ted Haggard
Senior Pastor, New Life Church, Colorado Springs, CO, U.S.A.

In *Miracles: Receiving the Miracles Prepared for You*, Pastor Frank Damazio chronicles his own church's journey into the realm of the miraculous. From his strong biblical foundation, Pastor Frank now leads us all from the basics of identifying the miracles—"capturing the miracles"—all the way to "expecting more"—actually receiving the miracles. This is a book to be read with a heart open to the Spirit and a pen in hand so that you don't miss a landmark on this miraculous journey of faith.

—TOMMY TENNEY
Best-selling author of The God Chasers *series*

In *Miracles: Receiving the Miracles Prepared for You*, Pastor Frank presents a fresh challenge to our faith. We often forget that only God can do miracles. Man cannot even heal, but only assist nature. Pastor Frank powerfully brings to our attention the fact that God has already laid up miracles that are waiting to be activated by our faith. This is a book that will inspire you to trust God for your healing and miracles. Once you start reading it, I doubt you will be able to put it down.

—DICK IVERSON
Chairman, Ministers Fellowship International

Frank Damazio is certainly right. God deeply wants to multiply miracles in the world today, but not through superstars and faith healers as much as through people like you and me. If you want to move into this exciting divine stream, Frank's incredibly practical book is for you!

—C. PETER WAGNER
Presiding Apostle, International Coalition of Apostles

This is a book for those who need a miracle. It is full of faith and hope for the hopeless. The whole Body of Christ needs to read this book.

—CINDY JACOBS
Cofounder, Generals of Intercession

Jesus said that signs would follow those who believe. As believers on a faith adventure, this book reminds us that we should not only expect God to do more miracles, but we should also contend for more of His supernatural power in everyday life.

—BRIAN HOUSTON
Senior Pastor, Hillsong Church, Australia

The combination of systematic teaching, powerful illustrations and the honest description of Frank Damazio's personal journey will challenge your mind-set and stir your faith and passion for miracles. This book will train you and your church to call forth a new day of signs, wonders and miracles. This day calls for ordinary people to boldly do extraordinary things because they know that they are connected to a supernatural God!

—RACHEL HICKSON
*Founder/Director of HEARTCRY Ministries
and M25 LONDON PRAYERNET, based in Britain.*

Frank Damazio has written a very important book with the potential to unlock the power of the supernatural in every believer's life. As followers of Christ, miracles are meant to be part of our everyday lifestyle. Everyone who wants to experience the fullness of God should read *Miracles*.

—PHIL PRINGLE
*Senior Minister of Christian City Church Oxford Falls, Sydney
& President of Christian City Church International*

As I read through the chapters of *Miracles*, I felt my faith grow. Every believer should read this book and start expecting miracles to become the norm in his or her life.

—CHÉ AHN
Senior Pastor, Harvest Rock Church

Miracles: Receiving the Miracles Prepared for You addresses one of the most important issues of a faith-filled walk with God. This important book reminds us that we should anticipate miracles, create an atmosphere for miracles to flourish in and allow our lives to be fueled with expectation for the miraculous. Put this book on your "to do" list. It will strengthen your life and ministry.

—JOE ALDRICH
President Emeritus, Multnomah Bible College

Miracles

RECEIVING THE MIRACLES
PREPARED FOR YOU

FRANK DAMAZIO

CITYBIBLE
PUBLISHING

Published by City Bible Publishing
9200 NE Fremont
Portland, Oregon 97220

Printed in U.S.A.

City Bible Publishing is a ministry of City Bible Church
and is dedicated to serving the local church and its leaders through the
production and distribution of quality materials. It is our prayer that these
materials, proven in the context of the local church, will equip leaders in
exalting the Lord and extending His Kingdom.

For a free catalog of additional resources from City Bible Publishing,
please call 1-800-777-6057.

First Edition, January 2004

Frank Damazio

All Rights Reserved
Printed in the United States of America

This book is dedicated to

my youngest daughter, Jessica,

who has taught me how to face the challenges of life

with a happy, positive and faith-filled attitude.

You're the miracle that hides in my heart waiting to be

finished. Remember our secret formula for life's crises:

T.C. —"temporary challenges" that pass in due time.

Table of Contents

God wants your need to collide with His power; He wants to intercept and capture you at His intersection in order to place a miracle in your path.

In the spirit realm, certain climates and environments work to either foster or frustrate miracles. You can learn the keys to creating an atmosphere for the miraculous.

You can begin today to pray through the 12 categories of miracles that each of us wants to intersect with our lives.

Because God is supernatural, we can expect that He will work according to His nature. It is normal for God to do the impossible, the supernatural. Make no small plans when you serve such a great God. Desire more!

Miracles, the supernatural, faith, healing, gifts of the Spirit—according to Scripture—these are yours. Don't let anyone talk you out of this faith position. Don't let anyone belittle or shrink or nullify anything that Scripture declares you already have.

Settling for less is a slow process of spiritual decline that usually involves comparing ourselves with our current environments and with what is normal around us—our friends, our family members, our churches.

To contend is to exert oneself without distraction to attain a goal. We are called to contend for the return of miracles and the supernatural in the Church of today.

Whether you are a well-taught believer who has already discovered, developed and now function in your spiritual gifts or a believer who is unsure about your gifts, you have gifts that God wants to supercharge with His miracle-working power.

God's power has not changed. He is the same yesterday, today and forever, and He has proven Himself to be a healing God!

Faith is a mysterious operation, and until we understand this fact, we can become very frustrated.

If we, the Christian community, are chosen to bring healing to broken and sick people, it is our responsibility to understand the mystery of suffering—yes, even the value of suffering. This world is a valley of tears that our technological genius has not been able to dry.

You have a place in this world where you can be used as a channel for God's miracles. God has chosen to work through your human weaknesses, flaws, shortcomings, doubts and fears—but you must be available.

God not only directs nations, but He also directs and cares for every single individual believer through personal involvement, plans his or her life, and provides for that person with masterful wisdom and love.

God is supreme, highest in authority, holding the highest place in all creation; He is unrestricted, not limited in any way or confined in any way! It's easy to believe in miracles when you understand the magnitude of our God. Yes, we are limited, confined, powerless and restrained, but with God these limitations are changed.

Foreword

THE COMMON DENOMINATOR of all I've ever seen Frank Damazio do is the uncommon dimension of seriousness and thoroughness he brings to the task. In his writing as a Spirit-filled leader, he consistently avoids the trite, trivial or triumphalistic, and cuts to the depth of the truths he explores and expounds. This work on the subject of miracles is another case in point: it is not only worthwhile, but it is also worthy of any reader's attention—and to our openness. We need to do more than study miracles; we're called to expect their possibility in our lives and ministries, as we partner with the sovereign grace that extends God's power-works.

—JACK W. HAYFORD
Chancellor, The King's College & Seminary
Founding Pastor, The Church On The Way

A Word from Albie

IN 1967-1968, A SOVEREIGN outpouring of the Spirit occurred. The Jesus People Movement was just beginning with a great youth harvest. I had no idea, however, that I would be part of it, because I was busy playing centerfield for the Los Angeles Angels—but Father God knew best. When I suffered a back injury that took me out of baseball, my wife, Helen, and I began a youth Bible study, not knowing the amazing fruit that would result from it.

It was a time of overwhelming visitation birthed through intercession. Joy abounded as we saw tumors disappear, deaf ears and blind eyes opened, and unclean spirits leave. In one instance a five-dollar bill floated into the window of a car doing 55 miles per hour for someone who needed gas. Miracles were daily occurences, and our expectation level grew continuously with the knowledge that tens of thousands of people were being birthed into the Kingdom. We personally baptized 300 kids in our own swimming pool. The Lord was moving on us, in us and through us as the gifts of the Holy Spirit were imparted. Helen and I had a minute part in that portion of Kingdom history, but the miraculous that occured all around us was even more mind boggling.

During that harvest, a 16-year-old young man appeared on the scene. He was to be one of the miracles in which the Lord would allow me to participate—the greatest miracle being a life birthed into the Kingdom. I am speaking, of course, about the author of this book, Frank Damazio. I saw the grace of God move on this young man with prophetic anointing almost immediately.

What a time! The prophetic grace of God was stirring and the nine gifts of the Spirit were moving through the lives of a generation. It was amazing then, but I believe what we were allowed to participate in was only a drop in the bucket compared to what God has begun in this generation.

Before you are pages written by Frank Damazio. I pray you will open up the eyes and ears of your heart, that faith may abound and hope be revealed. Get ready to run a race. God bless you as you hear and see what the Spirit is saying to the Church.

—Albie Pearson

Acknowledgments

MY DEEPEST GRATITUDE goes to these special people for their vital contribution to *Miracles*:

To my very special editor, Karen Kaufman, who worked under a serious deadline with grace, understanding and excellence. You're the best, Karen. Thank you, again.

To the faithful staff at City Bible Publishing: thank you all for your encouragement and help during this project.

To Cheryl Bolton, my secretary, who again corrected, footnoted and did anything and everything possible to communicate with editorial and me so that *Miracles* could happen on time. Thank you, Cheryl. Your reward will be in the lives of the people affected by this book.

To my wife, Sharon, for allowing me to spend many hours that I don't have on the writing of this book—it's her sacrifice that allows me to be an author. And thanks to my children, Nicole, Bethany, Andrew and Jessica, for understanding the importance of published works.

Finally, to the City Bible Church congregation. You were the ground I sowed this book into first. It is our journey of faith and frustration that made this material. You're awesome. I'm the richer for pastoring this church.

*O*pen my eyes, I want to see

beyond all I believe

By faith I open the door

To receive from the hand of the Lord,

I receive from the hand of the Lord.

Chorus excerpted from "How Very Great You Are." Words and music written by Sharon Damazio © 2002 Published by City Bible Music, Portland, OR.

Miracles

Introduction

THE DRIVE FROM RIVERSIDE TO Los Angeles was a couple of hours so we had a little time to talk about Kathryn Kuhlman. I asked Albie Pearson again, "Now who exactly is this woman and what does she do?" His reply was, "God uses her in signs, wonders and miracles. She prays for people and many are healed." The Shrine Auditorium was a very old facility in a poor location, yet as we approached it, we saw thousands of people lined up, waiting to get into the building. This was a very unusual sight for a 17-year-old kid who attended a small, half-empty Baptist church with more people waiting to get out than it had waiting to get in.

I was raised in and around church but had never experienced a real encounter with God. The things of the Holy Spirit—the gifts of healing or miracles—were not part of my world. I'd drifted away from the Lord and from church when I first met Albie Pearson. Albie had played for the Los Angeles Angels, but when a back injury prematurely ended his baseball career, he started reaching out to high schoolers with his testimony.

I heard about a bunch of youth who were meeting in a home so I went hoping to sell drugs, not to sing Christian songs and listen to an ex-major leaguer talk about the love and power of God. I was stunned by the number of young people responding to Albie's message and felt uncomfortable with the emotionalism of their responses. Nevertheless, through a series of events, I found myself on my knees on the golf course near Albie's house, asking God to make Himself real to me.

It happened. The powerful, invading presence of God enveloped me as I knelt on the fresh green lawn. I can still remember the smell of the grass, the gentle breeze and the tears coarsing down my face. I was having an encounter with God that would mark the beginning of a spiritual journey that would drastically change my life. No more drinking. No more drugs.

No more doing my own thing. I had been arrested by the power of God and was being directed in a brand new way.

During the next several months, hundreds of teenagers encountered Jesus at Albie's home. That time period in the early 1970s was the first wave of what the world would call "The Jesus People Movement." We began to see some unusual manifestations of God's power, things we'd never seen or experienced before. Many were filled with the Spirit and spoke in tongues. Miracles and healings were routinely occuring in our power-packed prayer meetings. Consequently, we were oblivious to the debates about whether or not Christians should speak in tongues and whether or not healing was for today. We just read the Scriptures and practiced what we read—pray, fast, lay hands on the sick and they will be healed.

We believed Jesus was the same yesterday, today and forever. Miracles were happening. Yes, there were some strange manifestations of God's power and presence, but we believed that this was the way it was supposed to be.

KATHRYN KUHLMAN AND THE SHRINE AUDITORIUM

As we approached the auditorium, Albie was admitted to a private parking area. We hastened through the back of the building and waited for Albie to meet with Kathryn Kuhlman. It was an old and decrepit looking place, run down with broken doors opening into empty offices and a jumble of boxes, papers and other unidentifiable objects scattered everywhere.

Then Kathryn entered, "Oh, Albie!" She was nothing like I had imagined a healing evangelist would be. She was demonstrative, yet sincere and open-hearted. She had a full laugh and spoke with intensity. What a unique woman! I liked her.

We finally made it into the meeting, where I was seated on the platform with Albie and about 40 other ministers and doctors. This was the first time I had attended a healing meeting in such a large auditorium with so many expectant people. The worship was simple but the Holy Spirit's presence was very heavy, so much so that the atmosphere was reflective of the biblical account of Jesus' presence as He worked miracles. That day I witnessed miracles that would forever change my faith and the way I would think about people in need of God's miraculous power.

I saw it. I touched it. It touched me. Today as I look back, I believe an impartation of that healing/miracle atmosphere was deposited into the depths of my heart. We had seen miracles happen in our prayer meetings at Albie's home, but in Kathryn Kuhlman's meeting we all saw another level of God's moving. Our faith was increased to believe for more healing and more miracles.

During the Jesus Movement in Riverside, California, many houses became mini-communes and mini-monasteries that were filled with newly saved young people who shared things in common—food, money, clothing, and ministry. I was part of one such house established by Albie Pearson in which we lived and from which we ministered to hundreds of young people. We were unlearned, but deeply sincere about God, prayer and evangelism.

Another group in Riverside called its house the "House of Miracles." We all believed miracles could happen at any time. We saw financial miracles, salvation miracles and physical-healing miracles—and we were miracles ourselves. That part of my foundation has pushed me toward contending for the supernatural and for the miracles that belong to us.

The book you hold is my personal journey of more than 30 years of contending for, hoping for and praying for miracles. It is not just my personal life story, but also my lifelong biblical understanding of miracles written with the hope that you will profit from what you read.

My wife, Sharon, and I pastor a church in the Northwest. This written account is our church's journey into contending for miracles, including several months of teaching on miracles, and the miracle journal we recorded as we dated and documented miracles in our midst. You will read about disappointments, heartbreaking stories of loss and the trying of our faith. You will read about cancer cases healed and those not healed.

This book is a journey shared to build your faith in the Word of God, not in our experiences or our results. Read it with a pen in your hand to mark it and make it your own. Look up the Scriptures and read them out loud. When I refer to prayers of healing or miracles, pray them audibly with me. Personalize, believe, contend for the supernatural. You were born for miracles!

1

Miracles Beyond You

WHEN YOU COME TO AN INTERSECTION while driving, you proceed with caution. Why? You don't want to collide with anyone or anything coming through that intersection. God's intersection, however, is just the opposite. As you move through life, God wants your need to collide with His power; He wants to intercept and capture you at His intersection in order to place a miracle in your path.

THE BOOK OF YOUR LIFE

Psalm 139:16-18 reads, "Your eyes saw my substance, being yet unformed. And in Your book they all were written, the days fashioned for me, when as yet there were none of them. How precious also are Your thoughts to me, O God! How great is the sum of them! If I should count them, they would be more in number than the sand; when I awake, I am still with You."

Notice that all the days are already ordained for you by God, days that have been written in heaven, days that have been written in God's book for your life. They are preordained, predestined pages of your life.

What size will your book be? How many of these pages will become reality, brought to earth by faith to be accomplished and fulfilled? Will you be a 16-page paperback or a 350-page hardback? Will you be a one-volume or a 10-volume person of destiny?

The apostle John wrote, "And truly Jesus did many other signs in the presence of His disciples, which are not written in this book" (20:30) and "there are also many other things that Jesus did, which if they were written one by one, I suppose that even the world itself could not contain the books that would be written" (21:25).

You are a book. Your life can be filled with divine surprises, supernatural happenings, miracles of every kind. Don't accept anything less than the full volume or volumes that God is writing for you, around you and through you. God has something prepared for you that is good, miraculous and life-changing. Believe right now that you are coming to a God-ordained intersection and that miracles are moving through that intersection to intercept you. Miracles are coming your way. Begin now, at this very moment, to cultivate a mind-set of faith: Yes, God can. God desires to. God is able and willing to work miracles through any person who has a heart to believe in His unlimited power and unlimited possibilities. Miracles are for you today.

MIRACLES AT GOD-ORDAINED INTERSECTIONS

Someone once said that a coincidence is a miracle that God doesn't want to take the credit for, and the following true story proves this point. A man got a sudden urge to do something very odd—go for a bike ride in the snow at 1:00 in the morning. He slipped, fell and lost his glasses in the snow. A young man, passing by, saw him crawling on his hands and knees and stopped to help. When they finally found the glasses, both men were cold, so they went into the young man's house to warm up with a cup of hot coffee. As they talked, the young man shared his desire to end his life, "Before I met you, I was on my way to the river to commit suicide."

What others would call a coincidence, that young man would call a

God-ordained intersection, a miracle in the form of a person riding his bike at 1:00 A.M. Miracles happen all the time.

Stop for a second and ponder these important questions: Are you living with an expectancy for miracles? When you get to an intersection in life, do you look to see what is coming to intercept you?

MIRACLES PREPARED FOR YOU

One definition of a miracle is a supernatural manifestation of divine power in the external world, a special revelation of the presence and power of God. Your life should be a place where God manifests His power in your external world. Your life should be characterized by the following words: miraculous, wonderful, surprising event, a marvel, phenomenon, a stunner, supernatural occurrence, unusualness, amazing, astonishing, astounding, awesome, extraordinary, fabulous, incredible, spectacular, superhuman, unbelievable, unimaginable, unreal, wonder working.

ATTITUDE OF EXPECTATION AND OPTIMISM

Let's develop an attitude of biblical optimism, an attitude that says nothing is impossible with God. Make pessimism and unbelief unwelcome in your mind and heart. Forbid them to trespass upon your thoughts. Don't live life with a low level of expectation. Lift the bar; raise the standard.

In his book *Weight of Glory*, C.S. Lewis (1898-1963) said, "Indeed if we consider the unblushing promises of reward and the staggering nature of the rewards promised in the gospel, it would seem that our Lord finds our desires not too strong, but too weak. We are half-hearted creatures. Like an ignorant child who wants to go on making mud pies in a slum because he cannot imagine what is meant by the offer of a holiday at the sea, we are far too easily pleased."[1]

Are you thinking, *Miracles? For me? Why me? After so many life disappointments, how can I expect great things from God? My dream has been ruined, and I'm not about to get knocked down again. Why would God want to waste a miracle on me?* I've heard all these questions and hundreds more. The enemy of our soul desires to rob us of the great Christian treasures of faith, hope and belief, and one of the ways he does so is by convincing us that God no longer intervenes in the affairs of His people.

> *Jesus is waiting for you to proclaim your faith in His ability to meet your need with a miracle.*

But Hebrews 13:8 says, "Jesus Christ is the same yesterday, today, and forever." This is Scripture, God's Word—and God doesn't lie! Will you accept something so simple? Jesus has not changed. He is the same every day. The same Jesus who worked all those miracles two thousand years ago is the same Jesus today.

In Luke 4:18 Jesus said, "The Spirit of the Lord is upon Me, because He has anointed Me to preach the gospel to the poor; He has sent Me to heal the brokenhearted, to proclaim liberty to the captives and recovery of sight to the blind, to set at liberty those who are oppressed." This same Jesus is waiting for you to proclaim your faith in His ability to meet your need with a miracle.

Please stop and make the following short, but powerful, proclamation:

The Holy Spirit is upon me to reveal the miracles that have been hidden, delayed or resisted.

Hidden Miracles

There are hidden miracles, miracles just below the surface, just out of your natural eyesight, just beyond your reach. They are real miracles and they belong to you. They are the hidden things God desires to release into your life physically, financially, socially, relationally, in your family and in your personal life. Don't give up because you can't see them. Faith believes in what it cannot see.

In Genesis 21, Hagar sat alone in the desert, crying in despair. Abraham had sent her away, her son was dying of thirst and she was helpless. Suddenly an angel of the Lord spoke to her and "God opened her eyes, and she saw a well of water" (Gen. 21:19). The well had always been there; the provision was right in front of her. She simply could not see it.

Whatever circumstance you are facing right now, don't sit down in the desert and give up. God has placed wells of provision for you. He may have prepared the well years ago for the need of today. It is there, waiting for your eyes to be opened to see it.

Delayed Miracles

Yes, there are delayed miracles. "Delay" means to put off, to slow, to stop, to detain or hinder for a time; to restrain motion. Other words used for delay are "impede," "hinder," "stop" or "obstruct." Our timing is certainly different from God's timing. We wait for minutes, hours or days and become discouraged because we see nothing. God is not affected by our sense of time. His promises find fulfillment in the fullness of time. His timing is not ours.

Permit me to illustrate. John 11:5-7 says, "Now Jesus loved Martha and her sister and Lazarus. So, when He heard that he was sick, He stayed two more days in the place where He was. Then after this He said to the disciples, 'Let us go to Judea again.'" Does Jesus' decision make sense to you? If you heard that a dear friend was dying and all he or she needed was a ride to the hospital, would you dawdle around waiting? There wasn't even anything serious for Jesus to wait for! He heard Lazarus was dying...and he delayed!

If I had been Lazarus, I would have seriously doubted the sincerity of my "friend's" love for me. Yet Jesus was simply waiting for the right timing. Not Lazarus's timing. Not Mary's timing. Not Martha's timing. God's timing. The result of delaying for God's timing? A miracle of resurrection life, a miracle beyond imagining. Do you think Lazarus regretted the delay after seeing the resulting miracle? Of course not.

No one likes delays—and I'm no exception. Near our house is a road that has been under construction for months. Since it is the only road to my house, every day I experience delay. I *endure* delay because I like getting home, not sitting in the car smelling gas fumes. I could try to take other roads that have no delays, but these roads will not lead me to my destination. Roads of destiny have delays. As my kids say at times, "Deal with it." Delayed miracles can be greater than immediate answers and delayed destinies can be more awesome than imagined.

Resisted Miracles

Some miracles are not just late or hidden, but they are also resisted by the evil powers of the dark kingdom. The mind-set of our enemy is to stop or resist all blessings sent from God to us. The evil one will use every tactic available, every weapon in his arsenal to resist a miracle that has been sent to a person who has been praying and believing. The devil is the resister of our miracles. Therefore, we must understand the nature of our enemy, put on the full armor of God, and having done all to exist, stand.

We stand our ground by faith in the Word of God (see Eph. 6:10-17). If we resist the devil, he will flee (see Jas. 4:7). Dig in. Resist. Stand your ground.

CAPTURING OUR MIRACLES

We can capture the miracles that are lying just beyond us, just out of reach to the natural mind and the natural hand, but we must do our part—we must contend for them. A key Scripture to personalize and stand on as you contend for and pursue miracles is 1 Corinthians 2:9:

> But as it is written: "Eye has not seen, nor ear heard, nor have entered into the heart of man the things which God has prepared for those who love Him." This is talk about God's Wisdom; thoughts, revelation — Not miracles

Some Christians assume that this verse is talking about heaven, but the context does not require that interpretation. The context certainly allows for the things God has prepared to be here-and-now miracles.

Let's take a closer look at that Scripture. First, we'll consider the following translations:

- *New English Bible*: "Things beyond our seeing, things beyond our hearing, things beyond our imagining, things God has prepared for those who love him."
- *J.B. Phillips*: "Things which eye saw not, and ear heard not, and which entered not into the heart of man, whatsoever things God prepared for them that love him."
- *The Amplified Bible*: "What eye has not seen and ear has not heard and has not entered into the heart of man, all that God has prepared (made and keeps ready) for those who love Him (who hold Him in affectionate reverence, promptly obeying Him and gratefully recognizing the benefits He has bestowed)."

Several things come to mind. First, let's discuss the eye. Then, we will explore the other components of this verse.

Eyes of the Spirit

To capture the miracles beyond us we must develop eyes of the Spirit. We're told in 1 Corinthians 2:10 that "God has revealed them to us through His Spirit. For the Spirit searches all things, yes, the deep things of God." When we have eyes of the Spirit, our capacity to perceive spiritual things is matured. We can see the hidden things of God by faith. We can see the miracles God has done, is doing and will do. Eyes of the Spirit cause us to look away from anything and everything else in order to see the supernatural.

Things Beyond Our Seeing

By the Spirit we begin to see with the spiritual eye that which the natural eye has not yet seen; we begin to see with new vision. We begin to see a new part of the vision that we have never seen before.

Things Beyond Our Hearing

Our natural ears have not yet heard, but we have a new set of ears. We are able to tune in to a new frequency. We have new plans, new strategies for our lives, our futures, our businesses, our ministries and our churches. They are new, never heard before.

Things Our Hearts Have Never Received Before

New passions are birthed. New dreams rise, new motivations awake. Things not received before, things God has held in reserve—these are the things that surpass the full comprehension of God's people. They are things that are infinitely beyond all that man can know or experience without the revealing power of the Holy Spirit. Enter into spiritual agreement with God's Word and God's will. Enter into spiritual alignment, beginning with a fresh surrender to God, to God's Word and to His delegated authorities. Bring your spirit into agreement through your attitudes, your confession and your prayers.

GOD IS BACK, LOOKING TO THE NEEDS OF HIS PEOPLE

Another scriptural promise we can take hold of and believe for today is Luke 7:16:

> Then fear came upon all, and they glorified God, saying, "A great prophet has risen up among us" and "God has visited His people."

The Message translation puts it like this:

> They all realized they were in a place of holy mystery and that God was at work among them. They were quietly worshipful and then noisily grateful, calling out among themselves, "God is back looking to the needs of His people!"

Can you hear the Holy Spirit speaking these words in your heart? God is back looking to the needs of His people! God is back working miracles! God is back healing the sick! We are standing on holy ground today, a place of holy mystery. God is certainly back among His people.

You've probably heard about all the visitations and outpourings of the Holy Spirit occurring around the world. China, Brazil, Argentina and other nations are experiencing great visitations, and the people are saying, "God is back, looking to the needs of His people." Whatever nation you are from or wherever you reside now, whatever city or state you live in, pray Luke 7:16 and believe for a new visitation of God.

RIGHTEOUS FRUSTRATION AND SATISFIED DISSATISFACTION

Maybe you feel somewhat like Gideon. I know I do at times. It's being in a place of righteous frustration with a satisfied dissatisfaction. I want more of all that I see in Christ and in the Scriptures—more salvations, more healings, more miracles, more freedom from bondages. Does Judges 6:13 sound a little familiar?

> Gideon said to Him, "O my Lord, if the Lord is with us, why then has all this happened to us? And where are all His miracles which our fathers told us about, saying, 'Did not the Lord bring us up from Egypt?' But now the Lord has forsaken us and delivered us into the hands of the Midianites."

Gideon's attitude abounds in America. We've had great revivals, awesome seasons of God's manifest power in signs, wonders and miracles. We have had—and do have—some of the world's greatest power ministries that fill the largest stadiums. Miracles happen.

And yet, what about many of the 330,000 churches in America that have never seen a single manifestation of God's power? What about the churches that have not seen a person walk down to the altar for salvation in years? What about the churches that have not seen a prodigal return or seen even the smallest of healings? What about those churches on a decline, with slipping attendance and decreasing offerings? What about the young people who are leaving while others sit at the back of the church whispering and laughing as they wait for the service to end?

WHERE ARE THE MIRACLES WE'VE HEARD ABOUT?

As in Gideon's day, the cry goes up, "Where are all the miracles we've heard about in the past? Where are the Kathryn Kuhlmans? Where are the Smith Wigglesworths? The John G. Lakes? The Oral Robertses? The A.A. Allens?" They were ministries with feet of clay that had their shortcomings, flaws and faults, but they also had God.

The past is not to be forgotten, nor is it to be a source of discouragement. Miracles and miracle ministries belong in every local church, not just in large stadiums. Miracles are not just for famous speakers, but they are also for you and me, for our friends and our families. They belong in America just as much as they do in Argentina or Brazil.

> *Miracles are not just for famous speakers, but they are also for you and me, for our friends and our families.*

The renowned R.A. Torrey (1856-1928), American Congregationalist evangelist, pastor, teacher, writer and shaper of a generation past, said, "The subject of divine healing is awakening an unusual interest in all parts of our country. Everywhere there is a most extraordinary interest in the subject." He observed that people were flocking by the thousands and tens of thousands to various cities to receive prayer. Miracles were happening.

If you resonate with what I am saying, and you, as a believing Christian, are part of a church in decline or a church in holy dissatisfaction, you have the opportunity to bend your knee and begin to cry out to God for a "Luke 7:16 happening," a God-visitation upon you and your church.

Just prior to the Civil War, Horace Bushnell (1802-1876), creator of America's first public parks, was one of America's leading theologians who believed in miracles and the great need for the supernatural. He believed Christianity was being disempowered and overshadowed by the growth of the modern era of science. He stated clearly that Christianity was imperceptibly being removed from the realm of faith and restricted to the domain of man's understanding. His prayer for the believer is still penetrating to the heart and encourages faith for the supernatural.

Let Him [God] now break forth in miracle and holy gifts, let it be seen that He is still the living God, in the midst of His dead people, and they will be quickened to a resurrection by sight. Now they see that God can do something still, and has His liberty. He can hear prayers, He can help them triumph in dark hours, their bosom-sins He can help them master, all His promises in the Scripture He can fulfill, and they go to Him with great expectations. They see, in these gifts, that the Scripture stands, that the graces and works, and holy fruits of the apostolic ages, are also for them. It is as if they had now a proof experimental of the resources embodied in the Christian plan. The living God, immediately revealed, and not historically only, begets a feeling of present life and power, and religion is no more a tradition, a second-hand light, but a grace of God unto salvation, operative now.[2]

Miracles are just beyond you. Look expectantly for God's intersection and plan to have your need collide with His miracle for your life.

Notes

1. C.S. Lewis, *The Weight of Glory* (www.CSLewisClassics.com). <http://www.cslewis-classics.com/ books/weight_of_glory-excerpt.html>. 23 December 23, 2002.
2. Horace Bushnell, *Nature and the Supernatural as Together Constituting the One System of God* (London: Alexander Strahan, 1867), p. 318.

2

Creating an Environment for Miracles

SCOTT AND PAULA WERE IN THE PROCESS of becoming believers. They were drinkers, pot smokers and drug users with a very bad reputation in our city. Like hundreds of other kids, they came to Albie's house to check out what was happening. Neither had any religious or church background, but that night they responded to the Holy Spirit and yielded their lives to God. Why?

During our prayer time, we offered to pray for anyone suffering with physical problems. Paula spoke up, "I have a tumor in the right side of my nose. Do you think God could do anything about that?" We prayed for a miracle, laying hands on her and agreeing for healing. First she screamed, then cried, then laughed semi-hysterically. The Lord healed her nose. Right in front of all those curious young people, God did a miracle. Though her nose had been hard on one side and discolored, after we prayed, it was soft and flesh-colored.

I still remember the atmosphere as if it was yesterday. God was back, looking to the needs of His people. We realized we were on holy ground, and we worshiped with joyful and expressive words. Many young people were saved because they had entered an environment rich with God's presence.

THE CLIMATE FOR MIRACLES

All living things need the appropriate environment in order to flourish. Orchids, for example, are among the most beautiful and exotic flowers. Amazing as they are, their chances of survival are slim. Only one or two orchid seeds out of hundreds of thousands will ever germinate. Orchid seeds must have precisely the right environment within the first year or they cannot survive. When scattered by the wind, they must land in a crevice that contains the perfect amount of moisture as well as a specific fungus. The seed establishes a symbiotic relationship with that fungus, feeding off the water and minerals that the fungus grows, in exchange for providing sugars from photosynthesis that the fungus needs. Without this precise environment, the orchid withers.

Similarly, in the spirit realm certain climates and environments work to either foster or frustrate miracles. The book of Mark tells us that Jesus found Himself in an environment that did not allow miracles. In chapter 5, Jesus raises a little girl from the dead. At the end of chapter 6, He feeds 5,000 people with five loaves and two fish. And yet, sandwiched between these chapters is Nazareth where there was not an environment for miracles and where "He could do no mighty work" (Mark 6:5).

WHEN MIRACLES MEET OBSTACLES

The miracle on its way will encounter fear, doubt, delays and adverse circumstances. C.S. Lewis once said, "The divine art of miracles is not an art of suspending the pattern to which events conform, but of feeding new events into that pattern."[1] We need to feed all our life challenges into God's world of miracles. God's will and purpose is to manifest His supernatural power in any and all areas of our lives, but we must choose to meet every obstacle with faith. We must be astounded by the greatness of our God by refusing to be confounded by our need.

Habakkuk 1:5 says, "Look among the nations and watch—be utterly astounded! For I will work a work in your days which you would not believe, though it were told you." Stop and ponder these words, putting your name into this Scripture.

> Be utterly astounded, (your name), for I will work a work in your day which you would not believe though it were told you!

Did you get that?! Be astounded. Shake that unbelief and discouragement from your spirit. Claim your miracle. Blaise Pascal said, "It is not possible to have a reasonable belief against miracles."[2] Jesus brought miracles to the rejected, the poor, the orphan, the widow, the lame, the dumb, the leper. If you are a person with great emotional, physical, mental, marital or social need, you are a candidate

We must be astounded by the greatness of our God by refusing to be confounded by our need.

for a miracle! (See Appendix A for a closer look at the biblical description of Christ's ministry.)

KEEPING A MIRACLE JOURNAL

One way to boost your faith is the tried and true process of keeping a miracle journal. Saint Augustine of Hippo (354-430) said, "It is only two years ago that the keeping of records was begun here in Hippo, and already, at this writing, we have nearly 70 attested miracles."[3]

George Fox (1624-1691), founder of the Quaker Movement, also kept a journal of miracles during his ministry. His journal, called *The Book of Miracles*, was lost sometime ago, but after Fox's death, Henry Cadbury began cataloguing all the books Fox had written. In the list of important lost books was *The Book of Miracles*. Although the book itself was missing, the catalogue cites the beginning and ending words of each miracle account. More than 150 miracles were recorded.

George Fox went about his seventeenth-century world preaching his fresh message of life and power. He had a remarkable healing ministry of diseases with the undoubted reputation of "miracle-worker." Fox and the early Quakers' faith spread rapidly because they preached the gospel with signs and miracles confirming the Word. Convincement, which was a logging of miracles to convince people of God's love and power, was a real phenomenon that went straight to the heart; the words were accompanied by the visible manifestation of the power of the Spirit. Early Quakers testified that Christ was actually present working in the same way He did in the New Testament. This living presence could be felt by those who were prepared to spend time waiting for the wind of the Holy Spirit to blow upon them. Here is just a short sample of the miracles Fox witnessed:

1652, July 6. The presence of the Lord went along with me, and in Derbyshire at a great market town called Chesterfield, His power was much manifested through me among some of their greatest professors. I was at a stand hearing them. They have a new gathered church, as they call it, but there was one of them that lay under the doctor's hand of a fever and I was made instrumental by the Lord. She was made well.

1653: And in bishopric whilst I was there they brought a woman tied behind a man that could neither eat nor speak and had been so a great while. And they brought her into the house to me at Anthony Pearson's. And I was moved by the Lord God to speak to her, that she ate and spake and was well, and got up behind her husband without any help and went away well.

1653: And after a meeting at Arnside where there was a many people, and I was moved of the Lord to say to Richard Myers amongst all the people, "Prophet Myers, stand up upon thy legs," for he was sitting down. And he stood up and stretched out his arm which had been lame a long time and said, "Be it known unto you all people and to all nations that this day I am healed!"[4]

When we at City Bible Church started journaling the miracles happening in and around our congregation, we discovered an amazing principle—the more you expect God to work, the more God works. More expectation, more miracles! No expectation, no miracles! Some entries in our miracle journal are as follows:

- Lisa asked for prayer for gastroparesis, diabetes, osteoporosis and chronic fatigue syndrome. On January 30 she got out of the bed she had been confined to for nearly four years and is now able to walk two miles. Her pain and medication have been greatly reduced.
- DeAnn had a growth on her tongue. We prayed for her the Saturday before she was scheduled for a biopsy and the growth disappeared.
- Michael was delivered and healed of methamphetamine addiction through the prayers of his cell group. Over time he married, has a new job, has restored his relationships and is a cell leader.
- On Sunday, February 17, Pastor Frank asked anyone needing healing in the right shoulder to stand up. A woman visiting the service had previously been unable to raise her hand because of an injury in a car accident. She received prayer, and her right arm and shoulder became mobile. She is no longer crippled by the injury and pain.
- Phil and his wife prayed for a financial miracle. Two weeks later Phil's employer gave him an unexpected bonus that met their need.
- In December 1998 Jennifer was diagnosed with a benign brain tumor on her pituitary gland. She needed medication daily to prevent it from growing. In February 2002 the

doctor said the tumor had completely disappeared and took her off all medication.

- Lynda suffered congestive heart failure about two years ago. At that time, doctors told her that very few people completely recover. During her last checkup, the doctor told Lynda with amazement that her heart has no damage and that she does not need to take medications to have a normal life.

- Alan lost his wedding ring while running errands. He and his family joined hands and prayed that the ring would be found. Alan re-traced his steps to a dumpster where he had been 20 hours earlier and found the ring sitting on top of some cardboard.

- Rick was hit in the eye with a Roman candle firework and lost 90 percent of his eyesight. He was put on disability because his eyesight was 20/800 (20/200 is considered legally blind). For a year Rick received prayer at every opportunity and his vision is back to 20/100.

- Augustin lost his job in November. After eight months of unemployment he decided to relocate to Arizona where some job opportunities were available. But the car broke down and delayed their departure. The day the car was repaired and the day before he and his family were to leave, Augustin received a new job here in town so they didn't have to move.

- A customer came into Lowell's store and mentioned that he was suffering from an eye condition diagnosed by doctors as a symptom of palsy. Lowell prayed and the man was healed.

I'd also like you to hear the following miracle of a man from our church because I think it will help you to expect God to do more in your life, your church, your world. Here is Peter del Val's testimony in his own words:

Becoming a firefighter is very difficult in my city, but after six months of tests, interviews and several supernatural hurdles, the divine help of God intervened. I was chosen to be one of the 40 hired out of 3,000 candidates.

The last stage of the hiring process required a three-hour visit to the doctor as he checked every imaginable body function.

I figured all I had to do was show up. What did I have to worry about? I had the fastest time in physical tryouts and endurance testing in the city, I was a 26-year-old in great shape.

The very last stage of my physical testing was a stress test. When it ended, the doctor, looking concerned, started asking some unexpected questions. In short, he informed me that he could not recommend that I be hired because of an abnormal heartbeat—which was either a serious problem or perhaps what is called an "athletic heart." Either way, I had to see a cardiovascular specialist for further tests. This was not what I wanted to hear because I had no insurance and I imagined the career of a lifetime fading away.

Our pastors and church body immediately went to prayer. They anointed me with oil and laid hands on me, earnestly praying for a miracle.

The first doctor I contacted spent 20 minutes looking over a ream of paper that showed my heartbeat and told me that the heartbeat on the paper was that of a 65-year-old with heart disease. Then he suggested we pray. So we knelt and asked God for a miracle.

The next doctor I went to see reaffirmed that I had a 65-year-old heart and added that I would be needing heart surgery within the next few months. He gave me the names of the three best doctors to see. I visited a specialist who reviewed all the previous test results and then scheduled one final test. That test revealed that the heartbeat on the first test did not match the second one. All of the pictures showed a healthy and strong heart. God had intervened in answer to the expectation of a body of believers.

Building Great Expectation

Great expectation saturates our church services. People simply come expecting God to do great things in their friends, in their bodies and in their marriages. They come expecting deliverance from eating disorders, alcohol and drug addictions, infirmities, diseases and demonic oppression. The Holy Spirit is respected and released to do what Scripture teaches that He does. He is the key to an atmosphere for miracles, and He is more than capable of working in our midst.

It is not by might nor by power but by the Spirit of the Lord that miracles occur in us, around us and through us. Listen to the way Romans 15:19 says it:

> In mighty signs and wonders, by the power of the Spirit of God, so that from Jerusalem and round about to Illyricum I have fully preached the gospel of Christ.

Miracles happen when the Holy Spirit is welcomed and faith is alive. The fact that the Spirit and faith are required is confirmed in Galatians 3:5, which says, "He who supplies the Spirit to you and works miracles among you, does He do it by the works of the law, or by the hearing of faith?"

The miracles God has for you are hidden in the Holy Spirit. Romans 14:17 explains that "the kingdom of God is not eating and drinking, but righteousness and peace and joy *in* the Holy Spirit" (italics added). The kingdom of God is in the Holy Spirit.

Creating an Environment for Miracles

Our expectations for miracles usually need some nurturing, reviving and strong encouragement. We can all find a multitude of reasons to become doubtful and discouraged when our answers don't manifest promptly. Maybe you are facing your own physical problems and desperately need a miracle, but it hasn't come—at least not on your timetable. Your need might involve a prodigal child, financial challenges, a new business, a crumbling marriage or a relationship that has gone bad.

Whatever is in your face, turn now and face God with these seeming impossibilities. Turn fear into faith and unbelief into believing. Begin today to create in your own mind and heart an atmosphere for miracles. Then move this atmosphere into your room, your apartment, your home, your car, and your workplace. Take this miracle-expecting atmosphere with you wherever you go and apply it to whatever you do (see Acts 5:12; 5:15,16; 8:6-8,13; 9:36-42; 14:3; 19:11,12).

A miracle atmosphere is nurtured by an attitude of expectation.

The attitude of expectation is the opposite of negativism or the "I'm not surprised that nothing happened" attitude. Expectation is a discipline of the believer's focus on Jesus and His Word. An expectant attitude can create an atmosphere charged with excitement and faith: God can; God has in the past. Let's pray together believing for a miracle in spite of how we feel. Maybe God will surprise us! Listen to the way Scripture says it:

Acts 3:5: So he gave them his attention, expecting to receive something from them.

Acts 28:6: However, they were expecting that he would swell up or
suddenly fall down dead. But after they had looked for a long
time and saw no harm come to him, they changed their
minds....

A miracle atmosphere is encouraged where an attitude of believing exists.

Believing is not based on a good or bad experience; it is based on the solid declaration of God's Word. If God has promised it, then you and I have the right and responsibility to reach for it. Our disappointment in unanswered prayer, or in watching people fail to receive their miracles when we think they should, may cause us to stumble and to allow a spirit of unbelief to settle upon our minds. We need not allow this to happen.

You and I can choose to believe. God is with us and He has not changed.

Saint Augustine once said, "Faith is to believe what we do not see and the reward of faith is to see what we believe."[5]

Jesus made believing a top priority:

Mark 9:23: "If you can believe, all things are possible to him who believes."

John 14:12: "Most assuredly, I say to you, he who believes in Me, the works that I do he will do also; and greater works than these he will do, because I go to My Father."

A miracle atmosphere is secured when we confess God's greatness.

The best way to confess the greatness of God is to read aloud His Word concerning the great things He has done. Read of the great acts of Creation, the miracles of the Lord working with His people, miracle bread, miracle water, healing the lepers, saving His people when they were facing insurmountable odds. God was great then and God is great now. Look at the way He provides for His people, answers prayer, protects, guides and works small and great miracles all the time.

> *Boldness means we go outside of our comfort zones and outside of our small prayers, asking boldly for miracles, for things that are humanly impossible and unlikely to happen.*

Memorize the following Scriptures:

Psalm 104:1,2: Bless the Lord, O my soul! O Lord my God, You are very great: You are clothed with honor and majesty, who cover Yourself with light as with a garment, who stretch out the heavens like a curtain.

1 Chronicles 29:11: Yours, O Lord, is the greatness, the power and the glory, the victory and the majesty; for all that is in heaven and in earth is Yours; Yours is the kingdom, O Lord, and You are exalted as head over all.

A miracle atmosphere is experienced in the presence of a living Christ.

We have the scriptural promise in Hebrews 13:8 that "Jesus is the same yesterday, today and forever." Jesus is alive today right now, in and through the power of the Holy Spirit. We experience the living Christ through the miracle of the Holy Spirit who abides in us and surrounds us as we pray and worship. To honor Jesus is to worship Him passionately and to recognize His powerful presence.

Ponder the following miracles, realizing that what Jesus did yesterday, He will do for you today.

> Mark 2:3,4,10-12: Then they came to Him, bringing a paralytic who was carried by four men. And when they could not come near Him because of the crowd, they uncovered the roof where He was. So when they had broken through, they let down the bed on which the paralytic was lying....He [Jesus] said to the paralytic, "I say to you, arise, take up your bed, and go to your house. "Immediately he arose, took up the bed, and went out in the presence of them all, so that all were amazed and glorified God, saying, "We never saw anything like this!"
>
> Mark 5:29,30: Immediately the fountain of her blood was dried up, and she felt in her body that she was healed of the affliction. And Jesus, immediately knowing in Himself that power had gone out of Him, turned around in the crowd and said, "Who touched My clothes?"

A miracle atmosphere is boldness without embarrassment.

In order to see more miracles today, we must ask for them often, pray for them specifically and declare they are here. Boldness means we go outside of our comfort zones and outside of our small prayers, asking boldly for miracles, for things that are humanly impossible and unlikely to happen. We ask. We ask boldly.

Matthew 20:30,31: And behold, two blind men sitting by the road, when they heard that Jesus was passing by, cried out, saying, "Have mercy on us, O Lord, Son of David!" Then the multitude warned them that they should be quiet; but they cried out all the more, saying, "Have mercy on us, O Lord, Son of David!"

Matthew 10:7,8: "And as you go, preach, saying, 'The kingdom of heaven is at hand.' Heal the sick, cleanse the lepers, raise the dead, cast out demons. Freely you have received, freely give." (See also Luke 9:1,2; Acts 4:29,30.)

A miracle atmosphere is cultivated by speaking God's Word.

The confession of the mouth is the heart speaking. Whatever fills your heart will eventually spill out of your mouth. Filling your heart with God's Word requires work and time. Spending time in church and devotional reading is not enough. You must set some memorization goals: a Scripture verse a day for five days per week, a chapter each month, whatever you desire. Why not start with the following:

Isaiah 55:10,11: "For as the rain comes down, and the snow from heaven, and do not return there, but water the earth, and make it bring forth and bud, that it may give seed to the sower and bread to the eater, so shall My word be that goes forth from My mouth; it shall not return to Me void, but it shall accomplish what I please, and it shall prosper in the thing for which I sent it."

Mark 11:23: "For assuredly, I say to you, whoever says to this mountain, 'Be removed and be cast into the sea,' and does not doubt in his heart, but believes that those things he says will come to pass, he will have whatever he says."

A miracle atmosphere is deepened through prayer and fasting.

Prayer and fasting is not the norm for most believers in America. Singing, eating, fellowshipping, church going, discussion groups and retreats—all of these are valuable in our religious culture. Prayer and fasting, however, are a powerful team for creating a miracle atmosphere. Jesus prayed and fasted. The apostles prayed and fasted. The First Church prayed and fasted. Scripture clearly teaches that God honors prayer and fasting and that special results come from this discipline. Let's get personal. How serious are you about creating an atmosphere for miracles? When is your next scheduled time for prayer and fasting?

Consider the following verses:

Isaiah 58:5,6: "Is it a fast that I have chosen, a day for a man to afflict his soul? Is it to bow down his head like a bulrush, and to spread out sackcloth and ashes? Would you call this a fast, and an acceptable day to the Lord? Is this not the fast that I have chosen: to loose the bonds of wickedness, to undo the heavy burdens, to let the oppressed go free, and that you break every yoke?"

Matthew 17:21: "However, this kind does not go out except by prayer and fasting."

CONCLUSION

Make up your mind today that you are going to establish a miracle-believing and miracle-expecting environment wherever you go. Express it in your attitude, your words and your actions. Look for those divine moments of opportunity when a miracle could be possible. In the office with your colleagues. Perhaps a coworker will confess that his marriage is on the rocks and that he is giving up. Bingo! Step in and change the environment from a "no-hope, no-future, no-answers" environment to a "God-hope, God-answers, God-has-a-future-for-this-situation" environment. Instead of shaking your head in sorrow, bow your head in faith and pray. Miracles are in you, around you and through you.

Notes

1. C.S. Lewis, *Miracles: A Preliminary Study* (London: Geoffrey Bles, 1947).
2. Robert Andrews; Mary Biggs; and Michael Seidel, et al, *The Columbia World of Quotations* (New York: Columbia University Press, 1996). <www.bartleby,com/48/1/13.html> 13 May, 2003.
3. Michael L. Brown, *Israel's Divine Healer* (Grand Rapids: Zondervan Publishing, 1995), p. 64.
4. Henry Cadbury, ed., *George Fox's Book of Miracles* (Philadelphia: Friend's United Press, 2000).
5. Augustine, "The Illustration Database: Faith," Bible Studies Foundation. <http://www.bible.org/illus/f>. 23 December, 2002.

3

Miracles in Twelve Categories

FOR MONTHS THE VILLAGE had been without rain. Crops were failing and the people were starving. Finally, the village leaders called for a day of prayer. Everyone in the village was to gather in the center of the town to pray for a miracle, to pray that the rains would come. On the appointed day, everyone had gathered, from the oldest to the youngest. The village elder stood in front of the people, looking out at the fear and desperation on their faces. He could read the questions in their eyes: What will happen if no rain comes? How long will we survive? Then his eyes looked into eyes of faith. They were set in the gaunt face of a little girl, so frail and thin that she looked as if a breath could blow her away. Among the fear-filled faces, she stood resolute and confident, the edges of a smile on her lips, faith in her eyes and an umbrella in her hand.

Do you have an umbrella in your hand? Do you have the excitement in your spirit that miracles are on the way? And what do we mean by miracle?

Greek Words for Miracle

In the New Testament, the word "miracle" is translated from several different Greek words. Two of the Greek words translated "miracle" are the words *semeion* and *ergo*. *Semeion* means an authenticating mark or token. *Vine's Expository Dictionary* tells us that the word is often used to refer to miracles and wonders as signs of divine authority. It refers to a miraculous sign and emphasizes the authenticity aspect of the miracle as an indicator that supernatural power is involved. *Ergon* means the energy of the Holy Spirit at work in a powerful way that produces miracles, mighty works, wonders, wonderful works.

The third Greek word translated "miracle" is dunamis. This Greek word literally means strength, power, ability, inherent power, power residing in a thing by virtue of its nature, power for performing miracles. It denotes both "power" and "miracle," which is a deed of power. Dunamis comes from a root word meaning power, emphasizing the miracle as a spontaneous expression of God's elemental power. Let's consider a few Scriptures where dunamis is used and translated "miracle" or "miracles."

- 1 Corinthians 12:10: To another the working of miracles (*dunamis*), to another prophecy, to another discerning of spirits, to another different kinds of tongues, to another the interpretation of tongues.
- 1 Corinthians 12:28: And God has appointed these in the church: first apostles, second prophets, third teachers, after that miracles (*dunamis*), then gifts of healings, helps, administrations, varieties of tongues.
- 2 Corinthians 12:12: Truly the signs of an apostle were accomplished among you with all perseverance, in signs and wonders and mighty deeds (dunamis). (See also Gal. 3:5.)

The *Dunamis* of God for the Believer

In the book of Acts, the word *dunamis* can refer to power, healing and miracles. Remember, we have been promised *dunamis* in Acts 1:8:

"But you shall receive power (*dunamis*) when the Holy Spirit has come upon you; and you shall be witnesses to Me in Jerusalem, and in all Judea and Samaria, and to the end of the earth."

The Amplified Bible reads:

"But you shall receive power (ability, efficiency, and might) when the Holy Spirit has come upon you, and you shall be My witnesses in Jerusalem and all Judea and Samaria and to the ends (the very bounds) of the earth."

When we believe the promise of Acts 1:8 personally and receive the baptism or infilling of the Holy Spirit, we receive the power that God uses to work miracles. We are people of the *dunamis*. We can believe and release this power as we minister to people all around us. Consider the following:

> *Take the miracles out of the New Testament, especially the Gospels and Acts, and little is left.*

- **Jesus affirmed by miracles:** Men of Israel, hear these words: Jesus of Nazareth, a Man attested by God to you by *miracles*, wonders, and signs which God did through Him in your midst, as you yourselves also know...(Acts 2:22,23).
- **Miracles of power:** So when Peter saw it, he responded to the people: "Men of Israel, why do you marvel at this? Or why look so intently at us, as though by our own *power* or godliness we had made this man walk?" (Acts 3:12).
- **The source of power:** And when they had set them in the midst, they asked, "By what *power* or by what name have you done this?" (Acts 4:7).

- **The apostles' witness with power:** And with great *power* the apostles gave witness to the resurrection of the Lord Jesus. And great grace was upon them all (Acts 4:33).
- **The power miracles of Stephen:** And Stephen, full of faith and *power*, did great wonders and signs among the people (Acts 6:8).
- **Miracles that cause amazement:** Then Simon himself also believed; and when he was baptized he continued with Philip, and was amazed, seeing the *miracles* and *signs* which were done (Acts 8:13).
- **The anointing of Jesus was power:** How God anointed Jesus of Nazareth with the Holy Spirit and with *power*, who went about doing good and healing all who were oppressed by the devil, for God was with Him (Acts 10:38).
- **Unusual miracles through Paul:** Now God worked unusual *miracles* by the hands of Paul (Acts 19:11).

We Are People of the Spirit

Please read the following prayer proclamation out loud and then pray it right now by faith:

The Holy Spirit is upon me to create an environment where miracles are welcomed, encouraged and received.

We have been born of the Spirit, worship in and through the Spirit, have gifts of the Spirit and pray in the Spirit. The Holy Spirit is our partner, our associate, our aide and our helper. Miracles happen when people honor and respect the Holy Spirit.

The Power Ministry of Smith Wigglesworth

One person who had great respect for the Holy Spirit was Smith Wigglesworth (1859-1947), a plumber in England who had a famous preaching and healing ministry. Wigglesworth speaks of Acts 1:8 as the key to his ministry and as the key to miracles:

> O the power of the Holy Spirit—the power that quickens, reveals and prevails! I love the thought that Jesus wanted all His people to have power, that He wanted all men to be overcomers. Nothing but this power of the Holy Spirit will do it—power over sin, power over sickness, power over the devil, power over all the powers of the devil (Luke 10:19).[1]

Smith Wigglesworth's ministry in the early 1900s witnessed many signs and wonders, restoration of hearing and sight, disappearance of cancerous growths, recovery of mental wholeness by the violently insane and the raising of several people from the dead. When praying for people, Wigglesworth would often hit or punch them at the place of the problem or illness, yet no one was hurt by this treatment. Instead, they were remarkably healed.

Miracles are the result of faith and cannot coexist with fear.

As great leaders of the past have demonstrated, we today may need more of the Holy Spirit working with us. I am certainly not suggesting that we start punching people, but we do need more boldness and aggressive praying to see miracles.

The Holy Spirit is upon you and me today, just as He was upon the believers in the book of Acts. We have the same *dunamis* promise that was given to the disciples: "you will receive power (*dunamis*)." Acts 2:39 says that "the promise is to you and to your children, and to all who are afar off, as many as the Lord our God will call." We are the children of this promise. We have been given the *dunamis* for the same purpose as the First Church, to see God work miracles that will confirm the preaching of the Word and to see multitudes saved (see Mark 10:7,8; 16:17; Luke 24:49; Acts 3:1-10; 14:3-8; 19:11,12).

And how did the Early Church grow? Miracles with the preaching!

Take the miracles out of the New Testament, especially the Gospels and Acts, and little is left. Many critics, however, have tried to discredit the evidential value of miracles; yet the fact remains that God made abundant use of miracles in giving Christianity a start in the world.

We Have a Supernatural God

Jesus had a supernatural conception, supernatural ministry, supernatural sacrifice and supernatural resurrection. Jesus started the Church with a supernatural experience and with a supernatural fire and wind. He caused the disciples to speak with supernatural tongues, a language above and beyond the natural understanding and ability. He caused supernatural signs and wonders to be wrought by the hands of the Church. God confirmed His Word spoken by the Church members with supernatural healings and miracles.

The supernatural should be expected—normal, not abnormal. The supernatural is anything above and beyond that which is natural. It is that which cannot be understood or explained by natural reasoning or human wisdom. The miraculous is an effect in the physical world that surpasses all known human or natural powers and is therefore ascribed supernatural.

If we believe God can speed up the laws of nature, supersede the laws of nature, bypass or override the natural laws, then our heart response should be, "You are the God of miracles and wonders. You still demonstrate Your awesome power." T. L. Osborne said in his book *Healing the Sick*, "The love of the miraculous is not a mark of ignorance, but rather reveals man's intense desire to reach the unseen God."[2]

God Desires that You Desire Miracles

Our desire is to let God be God, not to limit Him or hinder Him, but to release Him to be God in our midst. God has and will direct your path and mine to intersect with His miracles. Miracles will meet us on the way at prescribed times and places. He will fill our hearts with hope and an expectation for miracles now, today, in both our private and our work worlds. God will continually speak to us by allowing the Holy Spirit to nudge us into a place of divine providence that encounters the supernatural. To ignore divine impulses from the Holy Spirit could mean being at risk for missing the miracle that God is sending through your intersection of life.

It doesn't really matter what age you are, what your profession is, where you live or how bad your situation is. What matters is that God desires to work mighty signs and wonders in and through your life. God sustains our latter years to reveal some of His greatest miracles.

Corrie ten Boom, for example, spent the first 50 years of her life living peacefully with her father and sister above their watch shop in Haarlem, Holland. Her life was basically uneventful. Then, when World War II erupted, she and her family began hiding persecuted Jews. Corrie and her family were arrested and sent to concentration camps. There, God used Corrie's faith to release miracles of every kind. The greatest miracle of all is that God used an unknown woman in her 50s to change the world by captivating audiences with her message of faith and forgiveness through speaking engagements, books and movies.

No matter how late it is in your life, you can believe God for great miracles.

Scripture says in Luke 1:37 that "with God nothing will be impossible." In Mark 10:27, Jesus said, "But Jesus looked at them and said, 'With men it is impossible, but not with God; for with God all things are possible." God can and will bring miracles into your world, manifestations of His power. No matter who the agent is, the power is of God. Miracles are wrought by "the Spirit of the Lord" and in them is seen "the finger of God."

GREATER UNDERSTANDING OF MIRACLES

Herbert Lockyer (1886-1984), pastor and author in both England and the United States, defines a miracle as "a work wrought by a divine power for a divine purpose by means beyond the reach of man."[3] C.S. Lewis defines a miracle as "an interference with nature by supernatural power."[4] And J.I. Packer (1926–) says a miracle is "an observed event that triggers awareness of God's presence and power."[5]

Miracles are acts beyond human power. They are occasional, visible acts of power beyond the ability of human experience to account for, or for human faculties to accomplish, although they are sometimes wrought through human agency. Miracles are something we usually do not understand because they transcend our experiences and lie beyond the scope of the laws of nature.

Unfortunately, many people think that miracles are the result of a prayer formula—they're not. Miracles are the result of faith and cannot coexist with fear.

"Your adversary would love for you to fear the worst about your situation. He would enjoy seeing you heave a sigh and resign yourself to feelings of depression. However, it's been my experience that when God is involved, anything can happen. The One who directed the stone between Goliath's eyes and split the Red Sea down the middle and leveled that wall around Jericho and brought His Son back from beyond takes delight in mixing up the odds as He alters the inevitable and bypasses the impossible."[6]

TWELVE MIRACLE CATEGORIES WE SHOULD EXPECT

God can and desires to bring miracles into your life, family and ministry. Expect miracles. The following are at least 12 categories of miracles you can begin to pray through each day. Perhaps one or two of the 12 may directly apply to you now. Read these Scriptures and bring them into your present situation.

1. Miracles of Divine Provision

Have faith in God to provide supernaturally in spite of the natural, physical and economic realm. God can supply miracles of provision when there seems to be no possible way for the provision to come to us. In the story of Elijah being fed by the ravens, we see the miracle of God overriding the natural law of nature to provide. Miracles happen when natural resources end. We usually move into our miracle of provision when all normal resources have been exhausted.

> Genesis 22:14: And Abraham called the name of the place, The-Lord-Will-Provide; as it is said to this day, "In the Mount of The Lord it shall be provided."
>
> Psalm 78:23-25: He had commanded the clouds above, and opened the doors of heaven, had rained down manna on them to eat, and given them of the bread of heaven. Men ate angels' food; He sent them food to the full.
>
> (Read also Deut. 8:3; 1 Kings 17:1-16; Phil. 4:19.)

2. Miracles of Divine Providence (Intervention)

Providential miracles work within the framework of natural laws but absolutely involve the activity of God. God can and does work in situations, causing many things to come together in a special sequence and timing that otherwise would not have happened. We would call these miracles, even though God is working within natural laws. An example would be a person applying for a job that providentially comes together. As William Temple (1881-1944), 98th Archbishop of Canterbury, said, "When I pray coincidences happen and when I don't, they don't."[7]

> Zephaniah 2:7: The coast shall be for the remnant of the house of Judah; they shall feed their flocks there; in the houses of Ashkelon they shall lie down at evening. For the Lord their God will intervene for them, and return their captives.
>
> Genesis 18:13,14: And the Lord said to Abraham, "Why did Sarah laugh, saying, "Shall I surely bear a child, since I am old?" Is anything too hard for the Lord?
>
> (Read also Gen. 18:10-14; 2 Kings 6:5,7.)

3. Miracles of Divine Protection

In an age of multiplied and complex problems that range from terrorism to rare diseases, people are living on the edge of fear. Life is very stressful and the future is uncertain, so we are seeing a natural upsurge of anxiety. People need reassurance and a renewal of their faith in a God who can and will protect them. We need to pray for and walk in the miracles of divine protection.

A missionary couple were living in China during the 1930s conflict with Japan. As village after village was bombed, this couple simply trusted in Psalm 91:7, "A thousand may fall at your side, and ten thousand at your right hand; but it shall not come near you." One morning they gathered their children and headed for the market. Flagging down a passing cart, the husband began to dicker for the price of a ride. Frustrated with what he considered an unreasonable price, the missionary told his wife to take the children back home because they weren't going. That very day, at the exact time they would have been crossing, the ferry was bombed and thousands were killed. Was it a coincidence that the price for a ride that day was too unreasonable for the missionary to pay? Or was it a miracle of divine protection?

> Psalm 91:11: For He shall give His angels charge over you, to keep you in all your ways.
>
> Matthew 4:6: And said to Him, "If You are the Son of God, throw Yourself down. For it is written: 'He shall give His angels charge over you,' and, 'In their hands they shall bear you up, lest you dash your foot against a stone.'"
>
> Mark 4:39: Then He arose and rebuked the wind, and said to the sea, "Peace, be still!" And the wind ceased and there was a great calm.

4. Miracles of God's Sovereignty

God is all-powerful. That is, He can do anything at any time, anywhere, because He is God. God controls the laws of nature and can, at His choosing, intervene within the natural laws to work out His will according to His own power. When Jesus turned the water into wine (see John 2:11), He revealed His power over the chemical processes of nature. With one word, He accomplished the transformation that a wine requires several months to produce. This was a miracle of His sovereignty over nature and all natural laws.

Acts 17:26: "And He has made from one blood every nation of men to dwell on all the face of the earth, and has determined their preappointed times and the boundaries of their dwellings."

Nehemiah 9:6,7: You alone are the Lord; You have made heaven, the heaven of heavens, with all their host, the earth and everything on it, the seas and all that is in them, and You preserve them all. The host of heaven worships You. You are the Lord God, who chose Abram, and brought him out of Ur of the Chaldeans, and gave him the name Abraham.

5. Miracles of the Marketplace

God is interested and vitally involved with those who work in the marketplace and with those who own and operate businesses. Author and evangelist Ed Silvoso said, "To be anointed for business is to be set aside by God for service in the marketplace. Once anointed, we are to use our job as a ministry vehicle to transform the marketplace so that the gospel will be preached to, heard by every creature in our sphere of influence." God desires to work miracles in the marketplace as much as, if not more than, in the church services.

Our church sponsors a business leaders group called "Business With A Purpose." The group members recognize their God-given callings and giftings to do mighty works in the marketplace. Whatever marketplace you are in—construction, farming, ranching, banking, education, sales, medical, social services—wherever you are, you are in a place where God desires to work miracles. Faith is not believing that God can, but that God will. Remember what He did for Joseph:

Genesis 41:41-44,49,55-57: And Pharaoh said to Joseph, "See, I have set you over all the land of Egypt." Then Pharaoh took his signet ring off his hand and put it on Joseph's hand; and he clothed him in garments of fine linen and put a gold chain around his neck. And he had him ride in the second chariot which he had; and they cried out before him, "Bow the knee!" So he set him over all the land of Egypt. Pharaoh also said to Joseph, "I am Pharaoh, and without your consent no man may lift his hand or foot in all the land of Egypt."... Joseph gathered very much grain, as the sand of the sea, until he stopped counting, for it was immeasurable.... So when all the land of Egypt was famished, the people cried to Pharaoh for bread. Then Pharaoh said to all the Egyptians, "Go to Joseph; whatever he says to you, do." The famine was over all the face of the earth, and Joseph opened all the storehouses and sold to the Egyptians. And the famine became severe in the land of Egypt. So all countries came to Joseph in Egypt to buy grain, because the famine was severe in all lands.

6. Miracles of Serendipity

A serendipity is a blessing, a break, fortunate find, happenstance, happy chance, stumbling upon, tripping over. There are no accidents in a true believer's life. As Marcus Aurelius said, "God overrules all mutinous accidents, brings them under the laws of fate and makes them all serviceable to His purpose."

God often works in our lives without our ever really knowing or acknowledging it. He is at work bringing together small and large miracles for you. They are coming through your intersection. Remember the story of George Müeller (1805-1898), the great man of faith who built orphanages in Bristol, England? He needed a miracle because there was no milk and no money and he had made a commitment to ask God rather than man for his needs. Later that morning, a milk truck broke down right in front of the orphanage, providing the much-needed milk for the breakfast of the hungry children.

And let's not forget about Christopher Columbus (1451-1506) who had trouble with his ship. His response was, "I recognized that our Lord had caused me to run aground at this place so that I might establish a settlement here. And so many things come to hand that the disaster was a blessing in disguise."

> Romans 8:28, 29: And we know that all things work together for good to those who love God, to those who are the called according to His purpose. For whom He foreknew, He also predestined to be conformed to the image of His Son, that He might be the firstborn among many brethren.
>
> Psalm 84:11: For the Lord God is a sun and shield; The Lord will give grace and glory; no good thing will He withhold from those who walk uprightly.

7. Miracles of Healing

It may be you, a family member or a dear friend who is in need of healing. The need may be simple like the flu or a sports injury, or it may be life threatening such as cancer, organ failure, heart disease or AIDS. Whatever the challenge, the potential for a genuine miracle of healing is present and your responsibility is to pray, believe and ask for the healing. Jesus created the human body and knows how to heal it of any complication. God may heal by using the laws of medication, diet, healthy eating and exercise, or He may heal without any natural laws at work. It is not our job to tell God how to perform the miracle, only to believe that He will.

> Isaiah 58:8: Then your light shall break forth like the morning, your healing shall spring forth speedily, and your righteousness shall go before you; the glory of the Lord shall be your rear guard.
>
> Jeremiah 33:6: "Behold, I will bring it health and healing; I will heal them and reveal to them the abundance of peace and truth."
>
> (Read also Mal. 4:2; Matt. 4:23; Luke 9:11.)

8. *Miracles of Restored Relationships*

Do you suffer from a broken relationship or relationships? Do you feel lonely, isolated, disillusioned, fearful and in constant emotional pain? Unhealthy individualism and fear of intimate relationships are symptoms of emotional brokenness. God wants to restore your broken heart and the broken relationships in your world beginning today. Sometimes He does so by showing us where we have developed a wrong belief about ourselves or the way we think people look at us. He may have to change us from the inside out.

I am aware, of course, that some relationships require miracles to happen in another person before reconciliation can take place. Child abuse, spousal unfaithfulness, addictions, extreme manipulation—all these and more require the miracle of personal choice changes in the other person to make it possible for restoration, but God can change the heart. God can restore the prodigal child, but we may have to allow some gone-wrong attitudes to be purged first.

Samson's parents had to wait until the end of their son's life to see the miracle of his destiny fulfilled, but it happened. Leave the timing of the miracle in God's hands and trust Him with your relationships.

Psalm 51:12: Restore to me the joy of Your salvation, and uphold me by Your generous Spirit.

Isaiah 42:22: But this is a people robbed and plundered; all of them are snared in holes, and they are hidden in prison houses; they are for prey, and no one delivers; for plunder, and no one says, "Restore!"

(Read also Jer. 30:17; Joel 2:25,26; Gal. 6:1.)

9. *Miracles of Dreams Fulfilled*

We are people of the Spirit. We have an inner ear, eyes, mind, will and emotions. The Holy Spirit visits each one of us to illumine the dreams that He desires to share with us, our visions for the future. Seeing spiritual visions is the art of seeing with the hidden eyes of our spirit. Vision and dreams are what give us a sense of direction, a discipline for living, a dynamic fulfillment in life. Maybe you have a dream that has been delayed or destroyed, a dream that seems impossible to fulfill. God has in the past worked for people who had dreams and no possible way to see them come to pass: Joseph, Moses, David, Jesus, Paul. No dream is ever too small. Walt Disney said, "If you can dream it, you can do it!" Disney was not even a born-again believer, so just imagine what you could do with God intervening on behalf of your faith. There are miracles especially made just for your dreams—miracles of providence, provision and surprise!

> 1 Kings 3:5,15: At Gibeon the Lord appeared to Solomon in a dream by night; and God said, "Ask! What shall I give you?"... Then Solomon awoke; and indeed it had been a dream. And he came to Jerusalem and stood before the ark of the covenant of the Lord, offered up burnt offerings, offered peace offerings, and made a feast for all his servants.
>
> Psalm 126:1: When the Lord brought back the captivity of Zion, we were like those who dream.
>
> (Read also Gen. 37:5-10.)

10. Miracles of Victory in the Valleys

Psalm 23:4 says, "Though I walk through the valley of the shadow of death, I will fear no evil; for you are with me; Your rod and your staff, they comfort me." As long as you are living on this planet, you will at times walk in the valleys of life. And in those valleys you may experience some of your greatest miracles. First Peter 4:12 says, "Beloved, do not think it strange concerning the fiery trial which is to try you, as though some strange thing happened to you."

We must rid ourselves of clichés such as "because you are a Christian, your valley experience will absolutely be solvable" or "all your valleys are clearly addressed in the Bible." Some valleys bewilder us.

Some have no explanation—but we *can* look for hidden miracles while we are in the valley. Remember Hagar in Genesis 21? She was sent out into the wilderness to die with her son. A very unjust punishment was placed upon her—a valley experience she did not deserve and that she thought would be the death of her. But Genesis 21:19 says, "And God opened her eyes, and she saw a well of water. And she went and filled the skin with water, and gave the lad a drink." A miracle hides in the valley, waiting for you. Open your eyes. Look up in faith. It may be the greatest miracle you will ever receive.

> Acts 20:19: Serving the Lord with all humility, with many tears and trials which happened to me by the plotting of the Jews.
> James 1:2: My brethren, count it all joy when you fall into various trials.
> (Read also 1 Sam. 2:14; 2 Cor. 12:9; 1 Pet. 1:6; Rev. 3:10.)

11. Miracles of Answered Prayer

Billy Graham said, "A miracle is an event beyond the power of any known physical law to produce. It is a spiritual occurrence produced by the power of God, a marvel, a wonder."[8] Some prayers ask for things that God can put into our hands by using our friends, families, jobs, neighbors, spouses or even animals. We may not consider the answer to our prayer an absolute miracle of God because He didn't have to work outside of natural laws to perform it, but we can and often do perceive the ordinary as a miracle.

"Many, many years ago, Felix of Nola was escaping his enemies, and he took temporary refuge in a cave. He had scarcely entered the opening of the cave before a spider began to weave its web across the small opening. With remarkable speed, the insect completely sealed off the mouth of the cave with an intricate web, giving the appearance that the cave had not been entered for many weeks. As Felix's pursuers passed by, they saw the web and didn't even bother to look inside. Later, as this godly fugitive stepped out into the sunlight, he uttered these insightful words: 'Where

God is, a spider's web is a wall; where He is not, a wall is but a spider's web.'"[9] God used an ordinary spider to meet an extraordinary need.

Look for God in the ordinary to find the miracle of your answered prayer.

> 1 Kings 8:28,29: Yet regard the prayer of Your servant and his supplication, O Lord my God, and listen to the cry and the prayer which Your servant is praying before You today: that Your eyes may be open toward this temple night and day, toward the place of which You said, "My name shall be there," that You may hear the prayer which Your servant makes toward this place.
>
> Psalm 4:1: Hear me when I call, O God of my righteousness! You have relieved me in my distress; have mercy on me, and hear my prayer.
>
> (Read also Pss. 39:12; 143:1.)

12. Miracles of Prophetic Words Fulfilled

I have personally experienced numerous miracles of prophetic words fulfilled. One I'd like to share happened while I was teaching at Portland Bible College and getting ready to pioneer my own church. I hadn't discussed my plans for pioneering a church with anyone but my wife because I was looking for direction from the Lord. My natural inclination was to go to Santa Barbara, California, where I had previously lived, but I didn't know how to discern the leading of the Lord in that situation. Then, I received a prophetic word that caused me to take notice. The word basically said, "You will not choose your own city, but the Lord will send a person to you and that person will have a need for a church." At first, nothing happened. Still frustrated, I began a seven-day fast. Then, on the fourth day of the fast, I was stunned by a visit from the father of one of my students. He drove up from Eugene not knowing my desire to plant a church. "I'm inviting you to our city," he said, "and I think you should consider praying about it. We need you." With that, he left and I prayed. The rest is history. God fulfills the prophetic words He gives.

Psalm 105:17-19: He sent a man before them—Joseph—who was sold as a slave. They hurt his feet with fetters, he was laid in irons. Until the time that his word came to pass, the word of the Lord tested him.

Proverbs 16:1: The preparations of the heart belong to man, but the answer of the tongue is from the Lord.

Proverbs 19:21: There are many plans in a man's heart, nevertheless the Lord's counsel—that will stand.

ANSWERING GOD'S CHALLENGE

J. Hudson Taylor said, "The prayer power has never been tried to its full capacity. If we want to see mighty wonders of divine power and grace wrought in the place of weakness, failure and disappointment, let us answer God's standing challenge, 'Call unto Me, and I will answer thee, and show thee great and mighty things which thou knowest not!'"[10] The Lord is calling you to do more than just accept a doctrine of supernatural ministry. He calls you and me to the risk of its dynamic, the risk of living in constant availability to His miracle presence. God has called all of us to be a people of expectancy, a people of power who are moving wholeheartedly into whatever manifestations of His Spirit He desires to give. We must put a demand on our faith and a demand on the anointing. We must contend for miracles.

Notes

1. Smith Wigglesworth, *Experiencing God's Power Today* (New Kensington, PA: Whitaker House, 2000), p. 137.
2. T.L. Osborne, *Healing the Sick* (Tulsa: T.O. Publications, 1959).
3. Herbert Lockyer, *All the Miracles of the Bible* (Grand Rapids: Zondervan Publishing, 1961).
4. C.S. Lewis, *Miracles* (San Francisco: Harper, 2001).
5. J.I. Packer, et al, *The Kingdom and the Power* (Ventura, CA: Regal Books, 1993).
6. Charles Swindoll, *Tale of the Tardy Oxcart* (Dallas, TX: Word Publishing, 1998), p. 263.

7. Lane Adams, "I'm in Big Trouble," www.Christianity Today.com. <http://www.christianitytoday.com/moi/2001/006/dec/5.5.html> 7 March, 2003.

8. Mark Water, ed., *Encyclopedia of Christian Quotations* (Grand Rapids: Baker Book House, 2001), p. 674.

9. J. Hudson Taylor, "The Illustration Database: Prayer" (Bible Studies Foundation). <http://www.bible.org/illus/p>. 23 December, 2002.

10. Charles Swindoll, *Perfect Trust* (Nashville: J. Countryman, a division of Thomas Nelson, 2000), p. 14.

4

Miracles Desired with Passion and Determination

I HAD ALREADY GRADUATED from Portland Bible College, taught there for five years and pioneered a church in Eugene, Oregon, when I decided to enroll in some seminary classes. After taking some classes at Fuller Seminary, I eventually enrolled in the Masters of Divinity program at Oral Roberts University (ORU) where I graduated in 1991. Oral Roberts University was a first-class, state-of-the-art campus, and being there—sitting in the chapels, attending the classes and learning from the professors—was one of the highlights of my life.

Oral Roberts had been healed of tuberculosis and a lifetime stuttering problem as a youth. From that experience, he took the message of healing and miracles to the world. His simple, yet profound, slogans are still imbedded in the minds of millions:

- Turn your faith loose.
- Create a point of contact.

- Sow a seed of faith.
- Make God your source of total supply.
- Expect a miracle.
- Something good is going to happen to you.

THE SURPRISE REBUKE

I respected Oral (1918-) as a man of faith and vision and admired the fact that his healing ministry was so profoundly impacting upon the nations. So when I was invited to dine with Oral and Evelyn Roberts just before I graduated, it was like living a dream. Here I was, right in the middle of his vision, his campus, his spirit and attitude. I knew someone had given Oral my book, *The Making of a Leader*, and to my surprise, he had read it, all 349 pages. We were sitting at a dinner table with a few other leaders when Oral realized that I was the author of the book.

Oral turned to me and said, "I read your book. It is very well written. I am impressed." I could feel my heart swell—and perhaps my head, too. Just think, Oral Roberts was giving me a compliment, affirming me as a leader.

Then came the bombshell. "Frank, can you explain to me how a man can write 349 pages about how to make a leader and not mention miracles or healing the sick or moving in the supernatural?"

My heart plummeted. I was speechless, embarrassed and pinned to the floor. His words hit me hard, but even more penetrating than his words was the conviction of the Holy Spirit. Oral was right. How could I have become so lukewarm toward the supernatural? The answer was easy. I had allowed my desires for the supernatural part of Christ's ministry to become a fringe part of my whole ministry emphasis. After all, I had become a teacher, a preacher and a pastor and was learning all the important skills of linguistics, oratory, exegesis and Bible knowledge. What place did the supernatural ministry of Christ have in my own life? In my own prayers? In the weekend services at our church? Not much!

That night changed my focus. Miracles, healing and breaking spiritual bondages off people's souls would become a priority for me and my house. What had changed? Desire. A deep craving began to grow in the depth of my soul for God to do the impossible. I had a new appetite, a new aspiration and a new love for wanting the miracles of Christ to become the miracles for today. This newly aroused passion would not be satisfied laying dormant in my heart; it had to find powerful expressions in my world.

THE DESIRE FOR THE SUPERNATURAL IS RIGHT

Desire. Appetite. Attraction. Craving. Eagerness. Hunger. Passion. Thirst. Urge. Yearning. Petition. Covet. Do you feel it? What is the level of your desire for the supernatural? What longings do you have wrapped up inside of you when I mention the words "miracles," "healings," "deliverance"?

The desire for the supernatural is biblically right for every believer. It is not just for ministers or missionaries, but for all—the housewife and the professional, the blue-collar worker and the white-collar worker, the young and the old, the educated and the uneducated, the new believer and the mature believer. This desire is right for anyone!

Because God is supernatural, we can expect that He will work according to His nature. It is normal for God to do the impossible, the supernatural. Make no small plans when you serve such a great God. Desire more!

Desire begets desire. Desires can be changed by the right influence in the right atmosphere. The desires we have for more of God can be deepened through prayer and fasting. E.M. Bounds said, "How vast are the possibilities of prayer! How wide its reach! It lays its hand on Almighty God and moves Him to do what He would not do if prayer was not offered. Prayer is a wonderful power placed by Almighty God in the hands of His saints, which may be used to accomplish great purposes and to achieve unusual results. The only limits to prayer are the promises of God and His ability to fulfill those promises."[1]

Three Reasons to Believe in Healing

Certainly there are many reasons to believe for, and expect, healing miracles today. Numerous books have been written on the subject, but I want to give you three simple and basic facts to stand upon as you believe for your miracles.

1. **God is unchangeable.** God healed the sick in the past, and He will heal the sick in the present. Hebrews 13:8 says that "Jesus Christ is the same yesterday, today and forever." The God who healed in the past is the same God who heals today. (See also Mal. 3:6.)

2. **The Holy Spirit is the same.** The same Holy Spirit who worked within Christ, the apostles and the Early Church to provide miracles and healings is still working today! The Holy Spirit who stirred within Peter as he spoke to the lame man at the Gate Beautiful is the same Holy Spirit who resides in you. The Holy Spirit who moved through the disciples with power in signs and wonders is the same Holy Spirit who moves through you.

3. **Christ's last command includes healing.** As Jesus stood on the mount to leave His disciples, He gave them a last command, the Great Commission. That commission includes healing the sick. The last words a dying man gives to his family are usually the most important. He knows this is his final opportunity to impart his desires and he shares the things that are most significant to him. As Jesus stood on the mountain, preparing to ascend to heaven, He spoke these important words from Mark 16:17,18: "And these signs will follow those who believe: In My name they will cast out demons; they will speak with new tongues; they will take up serpents; and if they drink anything deadly, it will by no means hurt them; they will lay hands on the sick, and they will recover."

Clearly, Jesus desires to see you desire miracles.

What do you desire most in life? No matter what the answer, your desire can be changed, transformed and deepened. Let's see what Scripture has to say about your desire:

- **The desire of the humble:** Lord, You have heard the desire of the humble; You will prepare their heart; You will cause Your ear to hear (Ps. 10:17).
- **The heart's desire:** May He grant you according to your heart's desire, and fulfill all your purpose (Ps. 20:4).
- **The fulfillment of desire:** You have given him his heart's desire, and have not withheld the request of his lips (Ps. 21:2).
- **The open hand of God satisfies desire:** You open Your hand and satisfy the desire of every living thing (Ps. 145:16).
- **The blessing of desire satisfied:** Hope deferred makes the heart sick, but when the desire comes, it is a tree of life (Prov. 13:12).
- **The desire of our soul:** Yes, in the way of Your judgments, O Lord, we have waited for You; the desire of our soul is for Your name and for the remembrance of You (Isa. 26:8).

> *Desires can be changed by the right influence in the right atmosphere.*

We see that Jesus recognizes each person's greatest desire and responds accordingly when He says in Matthew 15:28, "'O woman, great is your faith! Let it be to you as you desire.' And her daughter was healed from that very hour." This woman was not ashamed to ask big, even though as a Samaritan she did not deserve the same benefits given to the Israelites. Her desire pushed embarrassment out of the way and pushed doubt and fear aside. Her desire pushed ahead asking for the crumbs from the table of God—just the crumbs! Her response to Jesus was, "I'll take even the crumbs." Her desire would not be denied and her desire moved the hand of God!

Desire in the New Testament

The word "desire" in the New Testament Greek is *epithumia*. It means a deep craving or a longing; it is translated as a word for strong lust, either a good lust or an evil lust. This word speaks of passions, affections, intense desire and inward impulse. It means to reach or stretch out, signifying the mental effort of stretching oneself out to grab something. It is to have zeal toward a thing.

Here are some New Testament Scriptures about desire:

- **A fervent desire:** Then He said to them, "With fervent desire I have desired to eat this Passover with you before I suffer" (Luke 22:15).
- **A requesting desire:** "If you abide in Me, and My words abide in you, you will ask what you desire, and it shall be done for you" (John 15:7).
- **A serious and focused desire:** But earnestly desire the best gifts. And yet I show you a more excellent way (1 Cor. 12:31).
- **A desire that blesses others:** Pursue love, and desire spiritual gifts, but especially that you may prophesy (1 Cor. 14:1).
- **A desire for spiritual activity:** Therefore, brethren, desire earnestly to prophesy, and do not forbid to speak with tongues (1 Cor. 14:39).
- **A desire to give:** But now you also must complete the doing of it; that as there was a readiness to desire it, so there also may be a completion out of what you have (2 Cor. 8:11).

Four Decisions to Increase Your Desire

You can develop a right desire to renew and increase the supernatural power of God in your life and your world by making the following four right decisions.

Decision 1

Cultivate a strong desire and unbending determination to discover and practice all that Christianity was meant to be. True Christianity as seen in the book of Acts demonstrates the way church was meant to be! Read it for yourself and desire it.

Acts 5:12: And through the hands of the apostles many signs and wonders were done among the people. And they were all with one accord in Solomon's Porch.

Acts 5:15,16: So that they brought the sick out into the streets and laid them on beds and couches, that at least the shadow of Peter passing by might fall on some of them. Also a multitude gathered from the surrounding cities to Jerusalem, bringing sick people and those who were tormented by unclean spirits, and they were all healed.

Acts 6:8: And Stephen, full of faith and power, did great wonders and signs among the people.

Acts 8:6,7: And the multitudes with one accord heeded the things spoken by Philip, hearing and seeing the miracles which he did. For unclean spirits, crying with a loud voice, came out of many who were possessed; and many who were paralyzed and lame were healed.

Acts 9:33,34: There he found a certain man named Aeneas, who had been bedridden eight years and was paralyzed. And Peter said to him, "Aeneas, Jesus the Christ heals you. Arise and make your bed." Then he arose immediately.

Acts 9:40: But Peter put them all out, and knelt down and prayed. And turning to the body he said, "Tabitha, arise." And she opened her eyes, and when she saw Peter she sat up.

Acts 14:3: Therefore they stayed there a long time, speaking boldly in the Lord, who was bearing witness to the word of His grace, granting signs and wonders to be done by their hands.

Acts 14:8-10: And in Lystra a certain man without strength in his feet was sitting, a cripple from his mother's womb, who had never walked. This man heard Paul speaking. Paul, observing him intently and seeing that he had faith to be healed, said with a loud voice, "Stand up straight on your feet!" And he leaped and walked.

The First Church in the book of Acts saw the ongoing contemporary occurrence of signs and wonders, confirming the proclamation of Christ and the gospel as a continuation of the signs and miracles of God seen in the ministry of Jesus.

Decision 2

Decide to make whatever paradigm and practice shifts are necessary to move into a ministry with supernatural, spiritual power.

The Church is not a manmade institution. It does not exert or exist on normal laws or religious forms. The life of a true believer operates on spiritual laws and functions in the supernatural. Power is not in political prestige, secular position, wealth or fame. It is in the power and demonstration of the supernatural ministry of the Holy Spirit.

A.B. Simpson (1843-1919), founder of the Missionary Alliance denomination, gave high priority to the supernatural, healings and miracles. Many Alliance churches began with great healing ministries. What happened?

The Church of the Nazarene had powerful healing ministries in the early years, as did the Quakers and the Mennonites. What happened?

They made paradigm and practice shifts that eliminated the supernatural, miracles and healing experiences. George Fox (1624-1691), founder of the Quaker movement and Friends Church, was used powerfully in the working of miracles and healings. An essay written by Edmund Goerke called "The Gift of Healing in the Life of George Fox" states:

At the age of nineteen he began his ministry and for nearly forty-five years his labors were in gathering people to Jesus Christ. During his lifetime he visited Scotland, Ireland, Holland, Germany, the West Indies and some of the British Colonies in North America. He requested that after his death his own Journal should be printed along with his *Doctrinals, Epistles* and *Book of Miracles*. All but the latter were published and, except for a catalogue of the miracles, this piece has never been found by modern scholars. However from his other works, and Journals of other Friends, many of these divine healings and revelations can be reconstructed. In all, there are about one hundred and seventy of them.

There can be no doubt that spiritual healings did manifest themselves in a remarkable way through George Fox and others in ways very similar to those found in the Acts. Wherever they came they sounded the Day of the Lord, that Christ has come to teach His people Himself. Their labor was not to form another sect or denomination or to reform those that were established through a revival of pietism, but to call out and gather all to Him who baptizes with the Holy Ghost and fire and forms His own righteous community. By 1690, the Friends, or Quakers as they were sometimes called, were as large as the largest of all the non-conformist groups in Great Britain. There was also the possibility that the British Colonies in North America might move in this direction as large segments of the country from North Carolina to New England were inhabited by these people.[2]

Decision 3

Decide to develop a strong sense of daring to take whatever risks are necessary to launch forth into unfamiliar territory. This means you must move out of your comfort zone. You can't walk on water unless you get out of the boat. You can't see miracles of faith unless you are willing to take risks, and sometimes you must take big risks. To see a great catch of fish, Peter had to cast his nets on the other side of the boat. He had to launch out into the deep. Hudson Taylor once said, "Unless there is an element of risk in our exploits for God, there is no need for faith."[3]

Aimee Semple McPherson, founder of the Foursquare denomination, preached the foursquare gospel: Jesus Christ our savior, our baptizer with the Holy Spirit, our healer and our soon-coming king. Her meetings packed the largest indoor arenas from New England to the Pacific Coast—and her church, Angelus Temple, which seated 5,000, was filled to capacity three to four times each Sunday. She was a daring woman of God. She did things that were not the norm in her day. Her services were filled with dramatic performances, handbell ringers, harpists, girl buglers, male quartets and child soloists. Her services bulged with high enthusiasm, cheering, clapping, rejoicing, altar calls, praying for the sick. Ambulances were allowed to bring people directly into the meetings. She dared! She stepped up and out to do something different, something bold. She organized 24-hour prayer for months and years in the "watch tower," a small room built on the top floor of Angelus Temple where intercession was made all day by women, and all night by men. A continuous fire of intercession burned upon the altars of the Almighty.

Aimee Semple McPherson served the Jesus of today, the Jesus of the "now." Listen to her words and be provoked to dare, to move into new territory:

> Is Jesus Christ the great "I am" or is He the great "I was"? Pastors, leaders, churches tell the multitudes eloquently, instructively. "We will tell you of the wonderful power Christ used to have, the miracles He used to perform and the sick He used to heal. Wonderful, marvelous was the power that used to flow from the great "I was."[4]

You may never travel the world or build a 5,000-seat auditorium where the miraculous happens in the midst of thousands, but you can see miracles in you, around you and through you. You can be a dispenser of hope, faith and love. You can expect God to do the impossible for your friends, your family and your coworkers. Step out of the boat. Dare. Allow the Holy Spirit to give you new thoughts, new ideas and new strategies.

Faith comes by hearing the word of God, both the written Word and the *rhema* (Spirit-inspired) word. God desires to quicken new thoughts in you that will be the beginning of a new miracle in your world. A new thought might be doubted at first, but don't dismiss it until you know whether or not it is a "God thought." Be willing to change, to leave what is familiar to you. Leaving behind the familiar means doing things differently. You know that if you keep doing what you've always done, you'll keep having what you've always had, so if you want different results, you need new ideas.

Oral Roberts, in his book *Still Doing the Impossible*, says, "We operate from the ideas that God gives us. I call it ICI—ideas, concepts and insights. Everything begins with an idea. God had an idea to create the world. He had an idea to create man. He had an idea to send Jesus. Everybody does what they do with an idea. God begins pouring an idea out of heaven. Then it becomes a concept. Once the concept becomes a way of life, God gives you insight or wisdom in how to apply the idea."[5]

We must move out of our old ways of thinking about things and move into some new God-ideas. How do we see the miraculous touch many thousands of people in these days of modernism, pessimism, dead churches and empty souls? We must fill our souls with a new vision of Jesus doing the unusual and the impossible in our homes, our schools, our cars, our streets and our marketplaces. Let's not limit God to our church buildings or our religious gatherings. Kathryn Kuhlman said, "Think big, talk big, act big because we have a big God." Wherever we find the presence of the Holy Spirit, we will always find the supernatural because He turns the natural into something super!

Decision 4

Decide to be patient with yourself and with God as you learn to move into the supernatural. "Frustration" and "discouragement" are two familiar words to those who seek to invent new things, write new songs, find new medical breakthroughs, solve complex humanitarian problems and see the supernatural happen in today's world. The more I desire, the more I stir my faith and passions, the more I seem to run head on into the wall of frustration.

I remember a time when two women in our church were diagnosed with cancer—one a behind-the-scenes person, the other very prominent and effective in ministry. My wife, Sharon, and I cared deeply about both of these people. We had prayed with all of our hearts for them, believing they would both be healed. To our amazement, the obscure woman lived but the other woman did not. I cannot tell you how upset people were with the outcome of our prayers. Many people took offense, saying that we had not extended enough faith, or fasted enough, or engaged in enough warfare. I realized then that the Lord looks at the whole picture, not the effectiveness of a life—and He is God no matter what the outcome of our prayers. We don't pray in order to control God; we pray to partner with His will—even when we don't like it. Does it hurt? Of course. But love must always take the risk of being hurt. As a couple, we've shed many tears over the disappointments of others.

Why? Why do I feel so deeply when people are not healed, marriages not saved, addictions not broken? Why? Because I have chosen to put myself and my emotions on the line with the challenge. I have positioned myself in a place of uncertainty where I can win or lose, where I can be very excited about a breakthrough or very saddened by a loss or a setback.

> We don't pray in order to control God; we pray to partner with His will—even when we don't like it.

I could protect my feelings and guard my emotions. I could build a hedge around my heart so that I am not affected deeply. To me, this is a coward's approach to the supernatural, not a Christlike approach. Jesus wept when He was standing in front of Lazarus's grave. He felt deeply. He allowed His heart to be touched.

Be patient with God and with yourself as you learn the supernatural. Allow the broken world to penetrate your inner world. Feel the pain, shed some tears, begin to open up to the challenge. We see miracles happen often in our quest, but we also live with the losses, the lack of healing, the discouragement that comes when a long battle ends in something other than a supernatural breakthrough.

Be patient. God will teach you how to stand in the gap and leave the results to Him. No matter how you reason, argue or request, God is God and we are His servants. God is the righteous judge, the compassionate God, the God who works all things after the counsel of His will. He sees things from eternity to eternity. He is not affected by time, death or any other human parameters.

Be patient, but keep pursuing. First Samuel 30:8 says, "David inquired of the Lord saying, 'Shall I pursue this troop? Shall I overtake them?' And He answered him, 'Pursue for you shall surely overtake them and without fail recover all.'"

"Pursue" means to follow after, run after, chase, attend closely upon, pursue ardently, aim eagerly and securely. "Overtake" means to reach, take hold upon, attain to, stretch out, overcome the obstacles (see Heb. 3:16,14,18; 4:14; 10:23). "Recover" means to snatch away, remove, save, pluck out of the enemy's hands, take back.

As you read these words, I believe the Holy Spirit wants to permeate your heart with a fresh new spirit of pursuing, overtaking and recovering. Let go of yesterday's disappointments. Let go of the questions you have not answered or the feeling that you were somehow at fault. Let go of the thoughts that if only you would have fasted more, if only you would have had more faith, if only you had prayed more powerful prayers, then God would have returned your prodigal child, healed your ailing son or daughter, rescued your spouse from a long and painful battle with a terminal disease.

Stop! Right now, let go of all the "if onlys," because these things happened for reasons you are not supposed to understand right now. Stop! Believe! Accept that God is always in control and that His ways are beyond your finite reasoning. Pursue again your desire to see the supernatural. Reach out and overtake your challenge, recovering some lost time, lost prayer and lost hope.

In 1 Samuel 30:18,19 we read that "David recovered all that the

Amalekites had carried away, and David rescued his two wives. And nothing of theirs was lacking, either small or great, sons or daughters, spoil or anything which they had taken from them. David recovered all."

Sometimes our recovery is finished here on earth, in this lifetime. Other times total recovery will not happen until we are in eternity. Either way, we win, now or then. So pursue. Do so with patience.

Notes

1. E.M. Bounds,"The Illustration Database: Prayer" (Bible Studies Foundation). <http://www.bible.org/illus/p>. 23 December, 2002.
2. Edmund Goerke, *The Gift of Healing in the Life of George Fox* (Quakerinfo.com). http://www.Quakerinfo.com/healing1.shtml. 22 February, 2003.
3. Paul Borthwick, *Leading the Way* (Colorado Springs: Navpress, 1989), p. 153.
4. Aimee Semple McPherson, *This Is That* (Los Angeles, CA: Foursquare Publications, 1923), pp. 704-705.
5. Oral Roberts, *Still Doing the Impossible* (Harrisburg, PA: Destiny Image, 2002), p. 13.

Miracle
Faith Position Secured

A STORY IS TOLD OF A LITTLE GIRL who desperately wanted a circle of glistening white pearls in a pink foil box. The girl saved and saved until she finally had $1.95 to purchase the plastic necklace. Oh how Jenny loved her pearls. They made her feel beautiful and special. She only took them off when she went swimming or had a bubble bath because her mother warned that they would make her neck turn green.

Jenny had a loving daddy who read her a story each night before tucking her into bed. One night, however, when he finished the story, he asked Jenny, "Do you love me?"

"Oh, yes, Daddy. You know that I love you."

"Then give me your pearls."

"Oh, Daddy, not my pearls. But you can have Princess—the white horse from my collection. The one you gave me. She's my favorite."

"That's okay, honey. Daddy loves you. Good night." And he brushed her cheek with a kiss.

About a week later, after the story time, Jenny's daddy asked again, "Do you love me?"

"Daddy, you know I love you."

"Then give me your pearls."

"Oh, Daddy, not my pearls. But you can have my brand new baby doll, the one I got for my birthday. You can even have the yellow blanket that matches her yellow sleeper."

"That's okay. Sleep well. God bless you, little one. Daddy loves you." And as always, he brushed her cheek with a kiss.

A few nights later when her daddy came in, Jenny was sitting on her bed with her legs crossed Indian-style. As he entered the room, he noticed her chin was trembling and one silent tear rolled down her cheek.

"What is it, Jenny? What's the matter?"

Jenny didn't say anything but lifted her small hand up to her daddy. And when she opened it, there was her little pearl necklace. With a little quiver, she finally said, "Here, Daddy. It's for you."

With tears gathering in his own eyes, Jenny's kind daddy reached out with one hand to take the dime-store necklace, and with the other hand he reached into his pocket and pulled out a blue velvet case with a strand of genuine pearls and gave them to Jenny. He had had them all the time. He was just waiting for her to give up the dime-store stuff so he could give genuine treasure.[1]

Like Jenny, we often settle for the ordinary, or even the counterfeit, when if we would only expect the unexpected, God would give us the real thing—the supernatural thing, the thing that Christianity is meant to be.

Are you determined to experience all that Christianity is meant to be, and to see in your day a return of the authentic power of God resulting in supernatural manifestations in all areas of life?

We serve the God of the supernatural. Since God is supernatural, it is to be expected that He will work according to His nature. It is normal for God to do the supernatural. Acts 26:8 asks, "Why should it be thought incredible by you that God raises the dead?" Why shouldn't we have a faith position that expects God to do the impossible, to work beyond our natural reasonings and beyond our natural laws? We all desire a faith that sees the supernatural world of God. We desire a faith that sees the miracles of God released in people's lives, miracles of every kind, including the miracles of healing. We desire to see the supernatural power of God in all 12 of the categories surveyed in Chapter 3.

It Is Right to Believe for the Supernatural

It is right to encourage you, my friend, to develop a faith attitude and to encourage you to learn how to stand on the Word of God and a Word-of-God confession. It is right for you as a believer in God, in Scripture and in the Holy Spirit to expect more than you have been expecting and to reach out and lay hold of the supernatural. The supernatural is not just for ministers or missionaries—it is for everyone.

Miracles, the supernatural, faith, healing, gifts of the Spirit—according to Scripture—these are yours. Don't let anyone talk you out of this faith position. Don't let anyone belittle or shrink or nullify anything that Scripture declares you already have. In Christ's day, the Sadducees did not believe in angels, spirit, the Resurrection or any hope of supernatural manifestations. They rejected Christ's teachings, Christ's miracles and Christ's prediction of the Resurrection. They were the modernists of Jesus' day.

The Sadducees: There is no supernatural.

Today's books, magazines and seminaries convince us that there are still plenty of Sadducees to go around. They are the modernists who doubt the validity of Scripture and take away the hope of miracles, removing all the gifts of the Spirit from today's Church. They are like the locusts to which the prophet Joel refers. They strip the land. Everywhere they go they leave barrenness, no crops and no fruit, just barren land. Do not be duped or deceived by these modern-day Sadducees.

The Pharisees: The supernatural is not for today.

Jesus also encountered the Pharisees. They were a little different but just as devastating as the Sadducees. The Pharisees believed in miracles, angels, the Resurrection and the supernatural as it was done in the days of Moses, in the ancient past, but never for their day. Yes, those things happened in the Old Testament with Moses, Elijah, Elisha—and they happened in the New Testament with Jesus and the apostles, but they don't happen today. They are gone, part of the past.

This group has no need for miracles, healings or the gifts of the Spirit, because they believe we have Scripture so nothing else is required. The problem with their viewpoint is that Scripture teaches, encourages and—in my humble estimation—demands that we preach the Word with signs following. We pray for the sick with the expectation that they will be healed. Clearly, Scripture teaches that God has not changed and that we are the recipients of His great power.

God Has Not Changed

Psalm 77:14 says, "You are the God who does wonders; You have declared Your strength among the peoples." Jeremiah 32:17 relates, "Ah, Lord God! Behold, You have made the heavens and the earth by Your great power and outstretched arm. There is nothing too hard for You." And Mark 16:17 heralds the message that "these signs will follow those who believe: In My name they will cast out demons; they will speak with new tongues." Of course, Hebrews 13:8 is probably the most basic of "faith position" Scriptures, "Jesus Christ is the same yesterday, today, and forever."

> *We often settle for the ordinary, or even the counterfiet, when if we would only expect the unexpected, God would give us the real thing—the supernatural thing.*

Most of us don't have a problem with the God of yesterday, the God of the Old Testament, the Christ of the first century. Yesterday's God was powerful and did many mighty works. He created the heavens and the earth. He created man. He opened the Red Sea. He provided food in the wilderness and brought water from a rock. Yes, the God of yesterday is awesome.

I believe in the Jesus of yesterday. Of course He healed the sick, raised the dead, multiplied the bread and the fish and rose from the dead. I have no problem believing that!

Do I believe in the God of yesterday? Yes, of course. And do I believe in the God of the future, the God of eternity? The God who made a real heaven with no sickness or sin, no death, no devil and no demons? Yes, absolutely! The God of eternity is awesome, and I can't wait to get into heaven. What an awesome God!

What about the God of today? Hebrews 13:8 says, "Jesus is the same yesterday, today and forever." We seem to have no problem believing in yesterday's God and in tomorrow's God. What about today's God? Our God is a today God, a God of the now, a God who inhabits this moment, right now.

Wherever you are, whatever you face, whatever your challenge, your God is a now God. Don't push all of your faith into the past or into the future. Activate your faith for today. Our confession should be, "Jesus is the same yesterday, today and forever. He still has compassion. He still has power. He still heals, delivers and saves people. There is nothing too hard for Him. God has not changed!" Hebrews 10:23 enjoins us to "hold fast the confession of our hope without wavering, for He who promised is faithful."

John Adams (1735-1826), second president of the United States, says it this way:

> The great and Almighty author of nature, who at first established those rules which regulate the world, can as easily suspend those laws whenever His providence sees sufficient reason for such suspension. There can be no objection, then, to the miracles of Jesus Christ.[2]

The Holy Spirit is upon you to establish a faith position in the Word, the work of the cross of Christ and the power of the Holy Spirit.

Let us be people of the Word of God, people who love His Word, who spend time in His word and who live our lives by His Word. Let us also be lovers of the Cross and its power to save the unsaved. As Charles H. Spurgeon so eloquently put it, "If sinners be damned, at least let them leap to Hell over our bodies. If they will perish, let them perish with our arms about their knees."[3]

Let us be hungry for the supernatural. Let there be a driving hunger that will not let us settle for an ordinary life. We are not called to be ordinary; we are called to be followers of Christ and to obey His Word—today.

Our Faith Position Is *In* and *On* the Word of God

The Bible is the revelation of God's will and purpose to humankind (see Gen. 1:1; John 1:1-3). Behind and beneath the Bible, above and beyond the Bible, is the God of the Bible. The Holy Scriptures are a revelation of God that come from God and flow through one person to another. The Scriptures are the only inspired and infallible revelation ever given to the human race and are the supreme authority in all matters of faith and morals. First Corinthians 15:3 states, "For I delivered to you first of all that which I also received: that Christ died for our sins according to the Scriptures." (Read also Rom. 15:4; Acts 18:28; 1 Pet. 3:16.)

The Scriptures define for us the God we serve, pray to and believe in to do miracles. Our view of God must be scriptural so that our faith in God begins with His Word, not with our own thoughts, reasonings or experiences. Notice how some children wrote letters to God that show how they view Him:

Dear God, in Sunday School they told us what You do. Who does it for You when You're on vacation?

Dear God, please put another holiday between Christmas and Easter. There is nothing good in there now.

Dear God, maybe Cain and Abel would not kill each other so much if they had their own rooms. It worked with me and my brother.

Dear God, did You mean for the giraffe to look like that or was it an accident?

Dear God, did You really mean "do unto others as they do unto you?" Because if You did, then I'm going to fix my brother!

Dear God, thank You for the baby brother, but what I prayed for was a puppy.

Dear God, I bet it is very hard for You to love all of everybody in the whole world. There are only four people in our family and I can never do it.

HATH GOD SAID?

From the beginning, the number one goal of the devil was to get humans to doubt and disbelieve God's Word. He tried it in the Garden and he tries it today. Genesis 3:1 explains,

> Now the serpent was more cunning than any beast of the field which the Lord God had made. And he said to the woman, "Has God indeed said, 'You shall not eat of every tree of the garden?'"

The devil has tried to keep the Bible out of the hands of people, or to blind their minds when they read it. Second Corinthians 4:4 warns that "whose minds the god of this age has blinded, who do not believe, lest the light of the gospel of the glory of Christ, who is the image of God, should shine on them." (See also 2 Cor. 11:3 and 2 Tim. 2:26.)

Jesus used the Scriptures to battle against the devil. In Matthew 4:4 He tells the devil, "It is written, 'Man shall not live by bread alone, but by every word that proceeds from the mouth of God.'" (See also Matt. 4:7 and 4:10.)

Before this generation sees the miracles recorded and promised in Scripture, a new level of faith in the Scripture will be required. Unfortunately, our modern educational system undermines students in order to remove the power of God's Word. A lack of faith in the Word of God will result in a lack of miracles in today's world. Listen to what university students from various campuses have said about the Bible:

"I don't think the Bible is true. I think the stories were put in there to teach lessons. I study a lot of mythology. It all relates."

"It sounds to me like a legend that's been passed down from generation to generation. I think, as is the case with any legend, things get exaggerated, and things get distorted."

"I think it is fascinating. I think it's beautiful. I think there is a lot of truth within it. I think there's a lot of history within it. I think there's a lot of fiction within it. I think there's a lot of culture within it."

"We are pretty safe saying the Bible is true to some extent."

"I don't think it is true for everybody, and I don't think it ever could be."

"In the context that the Bible was written in [it is true]. When you introduce science and things like that, some of it does become, let's say, dated—not necessarily untrue, but dated."

"You can't take the Bible word-for-word verbatim. You have to learn how to read it, read between the lines, and get the message out of what they were trying to say."

"I have read parts of the Bible, and I really enjoy it. I don't really have very much time to do any recreational reading aside from school work, and I don't read the Bible in my spare time."[4]

Their perspective is much different than that of Isaac Newton (1642-1727), one of the greatest minds from the past, "If all the great books of the world were given life and brought together in convention, the moment the Bible entered, the other books would fall on their faces as the gods of Philistia fell when the ark of God was brought into their presence in the temple of Dagon."

When the great British missionary David Livingstone (1813-1873) started his trek across Africa, he and his companions carried 73 books in 3 packs, weighing 180 pounds. After the party had traveled 300 miles, Livingstone was obliged to throw away some of the books because those carrying his baggage were so fatigued. As he continued on his journey his library grew smaller and smaller, until he had but one book left—his Bible.[5] That the youth of today would cherish the Bible that much!

Believe Every Word of the Bible

Our first and foremost rock to stand on is the Word of God, the Scriptures. Our faith position is as sure as the Word, as big as the Word, as lasting as the Word. Our first battle, however, is with our own thoughts and reasonings, which might not agree with the Word of God. We have to cast down any thoughts or imaginations that try to negate God's Word (see 2 Cor. 10:3,4).

Look with me at Mark 9:23,24:

Our faith position is as sure as the Word, as big as the Word, as lasting as the Word.

Jesus said to him, "If you can believe, all things are possible to him who believes." Immediately the father of the child cried out and said with tears, "Lord, I believe; help my unbelief!"

Does this plea resonate with you? Are there times when you believe but you are praying, "O God, help my unbelief"? We move from doubt to believing by moving into and onto the Word of God. Hebrews 4:2 says, "For indeed the gospel was preached to us as well as to them; but the word which they heard did not profit them, not being mixed with faith in those who heard it." The mixing of faith plus the Word equals profitable results.

To mix the right ingredients together while baking a cake is very important if you want the cake to taste good. Leave out the eggs or the sugar or another key ingredient and your cooking will not have a "profitable" result. So it is with the mixing of the right ingredients of faith and the Word to achieve the right results in the kingdom of God.

Charles Spurgeon (1834-1892), one of Britain's greatest preachers ever, said, "I would recommend you either believe in God up to the hilt, or else not believe at all. Believe this Book of God, every letter of it, or else reject it. There is no logical standing-place between the two. Be satisfied with nothing less than a faith that swims in the deeps of divine revelation; a faith that paddles about the edge of the water is poor faith, and is not good for much. Oh, I pray you, do believe in God, and His omnipotence!"[6]

OUR FAITH POSITION IS *IN* AND *BUILT UPON* THE WORK OF CHRIST

You cannot—by yourself and by your own willpower—work up or manufacture this thing called "faith." God Himself must impart faith to you through the person and work of the Holy Spirit. It is through the work of the cross of Christ, His redemptive work of atonement, and the reconciliation between God and man provided by Christ's life, Christ's sinless character, death and resurrection. When we come to Christ, we come to salvation, not by the works we do nor by our own righteousness, but by identifying with Christ's work, His sinless sacrifice, His authority to cover my sinfulness and redeem my life from destruction.

My faith is in Christ and His work on the cross. My faith is in His provision. My faith receives from and builds upon Him. Isaiah 53:4,5 says, "Surely He has borne our griefs and carried our sorrows; yet we esteemed Him stricken, smitten by God, and afflicted. But He was wounded for our transgressions, He was bruised for our iniquities; the chastisement for our peace was upon Him, and by His stripes we are healed." Moffat translates this last phrase, "The blows that fell to Him have brought us healing."

The gospel of Matthew 8:16,17 affirms, "When evening had come, they brought to Him many who were demon-possessed. And He cast out the spirits with a word, and healed all who were sick, that it might be fulfilled which was spoken by Isaiah the prophet, saying: 'He Himself took our infirmities and bore our sicknesses.'" First Peter 2:24 reiterates that this work on the Cross affects those who call on the name of the Lord and find salvation and healing in Christ "who Himself bore our sins in His own body on the tree, that we, having died to sins, might live for righteousness—by whose stripes you were healed."

Isaiah 61:1-4 says, "The Spirit of the Lord God is upon Me, because the Lord has anointed Me to preach good tidings to the poor; He has sent Me to heal the brokenhearted, to proclaim liberty to the captives, and the opening of the prison to those who are bound; to proclaim the acceptable year of the Lord, and the day of vengeance of our God; to comfort all who mourn, to console those who mourn in Zion, to give them beauty for ashes, the oil of joy for mourning, the garment of praise for the spirit of heaviness; that they may be called trees of righteousness, the planting of the Lord, that He may be glorified. And they shall rebuild the old ruins, they shall raise up the former desolations, and they shall repair the ruined cities, the desolations of many generations."

Then, in Luke 4:19-21 Jesus said He came "to proclaim the acceptable year of the Lord." Then He closed the book, and gave it back to the attendant and sat down. And the eyes of all who were in the synagogue were fixed on Him. And He began to say to them, 'Today this Scripture is fulfilled in your hearing.'"

These two passages of Scriptures give us a biblical description of Christ's ministry both in the New Testament and this present time. As the Body of Christ today, we, the Church, have the same ministry. This eight-fold description of Christ could be called the mission statement of every believer and of every church:

- To heal the brokenhearted
- To deliver the captives

- To heal the blind
- To set free the bound
- To proclaim God's truth
- To comfort the mourning
- To give beauty for ashes
- To give the garment of praise for the spirit of heaviness

The cross of Christ is foundational to the healing and miracle ministry of Christ and the Church. Isaiah 53:5 says it is because of His crucifixion that we are healed: "But He was wounded for our transgressions, He was bruised for our iniquities; the chastisement for our peace was upon Him, and by His stripes we are healed." (See also Exod. 15:26.)

Our faith position is in the finished work of the Cross. This finished work has provided for us in body, soul and spirit. Christ has forgiven my sins and His Spirit has intertwined my spirit, resulting in a new spiritual birth. I am born again. I am an eternal possession of Christ's work on the cross. Christ also transforms my soul. My mind, my will and my emotions now belong to Him. They are bought by His shed blood. My mind can be healed, my will can be softened and redirected into God's will, and my emotions—however tangled and damaged before my salvation—can now be cleansed, healed and restored to a right working order.

Christ's work on the cross also provides healing for my physical body. One of the names used for the Lord in the Old Testament is Jehovah Rapha, meaning "The Lord my healer." My faith position is settled in the finished work of the Cross.

Sometimes, however, we are similar to the poor European who wanted to emigrate to the United States. After years of saving his money, he was able to get enough together to pay for steerage passage on a ship to America. To sustain himself on the long journey, the man bundled up food that would not spoil. While the other passengers were eating in the dining room, he would go off by himself and eat his bread and cheese. Near the end of the trip he was tired of this fare, and the smells drifting from the dining room were causing his stomach to rumble. So he stirred up his courage to ask one of the ship's stewards how much it would cost to get a hot meal. The steward looked at him and said, "You have a ticket, don't you?"

"Well, yes," the man answered.

"Then you can eat whatever you want. Your meals are included in the price of your ticket."

Think of all this poor man had missed simply because he did not know the benefit that belonged to him, the provisions that had already been bought and paid for! Let us not overlook any of the benefits our Lord purchased for us on the Cross.

Our Faith Position Is *In* and *Through* the Work of the Holy Spirit

Andrew Murray (1828-1917), the great South African pastor and writer, said, "Divine healing is the work of the Holy Spirit. Christ's redemption extends its powerful workings to the body, and the Holy Spirit is in charge of transmitting it to us and maintaining it in us."[7] The work and power of the Holy Spirit is part of our salvation package. We are saved by the grace and power of the Holy Spirit working in us. The Holy Spirit drew us to the Lord to receive our salvation. We didn't have the heart or the motivation; it was the working of the Holy Spirit in us and upon us.

The Holy Spirit was the source of all of Jesus' power during His earthly ministry. Jesus accessed no power of or by Himself. We today can expect to do the same or greater things than Jesus did because we have been given access to the same power source, the Holy Spirit. Kathryn Kuhlman was once asked, "What is the secret to the power in this ministry?" Her answer was, "The secret is found in the person of the Holy Spirit. I have chosen to accept the gift that Jesus left for me and you will never regret it if you accept His gift too."[8]

Miracles and healings take place wherever the Holy Spirit has freedom to work in power. Romans 14:17 says, "The kingdom of God is not eating and drinking, but righteousness and peace and joy in the Holy Spirit." Let's take out the middle phrase and read it this way, "The kingdom of God is in the Holy Spirit." All of God's promises are made alive by and in the Holy Spirit. As we see in the following Scriptures, it is the Holy Spirit who quickens the Word of God to us and through us (italics added):

> 1 Corinthians 12:4: There are diversities of gifts, but the *same Spirit*.
>
> 1 Corinthians 12:9: To another faith by the *same Spirit*, to another gifts of healings by the *same Spirit*.
>
> 1 Corinthians 12:11: But one and the *same Spirit* works all these things, distributing to each one individually as He wills.

Notice the repetition: "by the same Spirit," and "Spirit works all these things." All the gifts work by the Holy Spirit's power to use human vessels. He uses our minds, our emotions and our wills, but the power source and the content of the gifts are in the Holy Spirit. Our faith position for seeing the supernatural is a faith in the power and working of the Holy Spirit. Will you trust Him to work the supernatural in and through you?

Notes

1. Alice Gray, ed., *Stories From the Heart*, taken from "The Treasure" by Alice Gray (Sisters, OR: Multnomah, 1997), pp. 147-148, adapted.
2. John Adams, "John Adam's Diary: March 2, 1756" (The Constitution Society, 7793 Burnett Road #37, Austin, Texas; www.constitution.org). http://www.constitution.org/primarysources/ adamsdiary.html. 10 May, 2003.
3. "Revival Resource Center," Watchword.org. http://www.watchword.org/fire_from_the_altar_of_prayer.htm. 17 April, 2002.
4. R.C. Sproul, *Ultimate Issues* (Grand Rapids: Baker Books, 1996), pp. 3,9.
5. "Today in the Word," April 1989 (www.sermonillustrations.com), 25 April, 2003.
6. Charles Spurgeon, *Is God in the Camp?* (www.spurgeon.org). http://www.spurgeon.org/sermons/2239.htm.
7. Andrew Murray, *Divine Healing* (New Kensington, PA: Whitaker House, 1983).
8. Kathryn Kuhlman, *Heart to Heart* (Gainesville, FL: Logos Publishers, 1988).

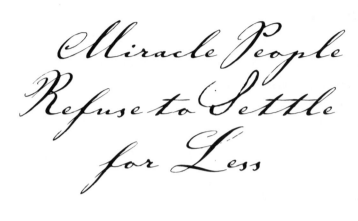

6

Miracle People Refuse to Settle for Less

SETTLING FOR LESS OF ANYTHING is usually the wrong way to live. Settling for a lower level of personal health can be very costly later in life. Settling for a lower level of integrity on your job or in your business can eventually catch up with you, resulting in a potentially embarrassing demotion or the loss of business respect.

The "settling for less" attitude happens gradually. It begins with a heart change, a decrease in motivation, and a weariness in pursuit of excellence. You may become satisfied with less of God, less prayer, less Holy Spirit fire, fewer answered prayers, fewer miracles, less witnessing. If this acceptance of "less" is allowed for a lengthy period of time, you and I can become satisfied with less of anything and everything. A life habit settles in and a lifestyle is in the making.

Revelation 3:17,18 says that "because you say, 'I am rich, have become wealthy, and have need of nothing'—and do not know that you are wretched, miserable, poor, blind, and naked—I counsel you to buy from Me gold refined in the fire, that you may be rich; and white garments, that you may be clothed, that the shame of your nakedness may not be revealed; and anoint your eyes with eye salve, that you may see." The deceiving attitude is, "I have need of nothing. I'm all right. Everything is working out fine. There's nothing wrong with me or with my spiritual passions." We may say, "I attend church, teach a class, lead a small group, sing in the choir, work with the children. How could you think I have settled for less?"

We may need to stop here for a quick moment of silent prayer and ask,

Dear God, am I this person? Don't let me think I have need of nothing. Anoint my eyes with the eye salve of the Holy Spirit so that I may see clearly my condition.

Settling for less is a slow process of spiritual decline that usually involves comparing ourselves with our current environments and with what is normal around us—our friends, our family members, our churches. We may be comparing right now and concluding that we are normal. Maybe you have begun to accept less because you are subject to a lesser spiritual environment and people of lesser spiritual passions. Maybe you have adapted yourself to the wrong level of spiritual life.

Second Corinthians 10:12 warns us not to compare ourselves:

For we dare not class ourselves or compare ourselves with those who commend themselves. But they, measuring themselves by themselves, and comparing themselves among themselves, are not wise.

The Message translation reads, "We're not, understand, putting ourselves in a league with those who boast that they're our superiors. We wouldn't dare do that. But in all this comparing and grading and competing, they quite miss the point."

Let's pause right now for a prayer confession:

> The Holy Spirit is upon me to stir me to a higher level of faith that refuses to settle for less.

Would you, if possible, say this three times out loud as if you and I are agreeing together? Now let's add some Scriptures to this prayer that you can use to read and plow into your spirit and mind.

Philippians 3:14: I press toward the goal for the prize of the upward call of God in Christ Jesus.

Zephaniah 1:12: And it shall come to pass at that time that I will search Jerusalem with lamps, and punish the men who are settled in complacency, who say in their heart, "The Lord will not do good, nor will He do evil."

Zephaniah is speaking to those who have become like wine stored overlong, those who are satisfied with their hardened lifestyles, those who are stagnant in spirit and those who are settled in complacency. The Holy Spirit is our lamp, our search light for our inner world. He will expose any and all of these potential problems if we will allow Him.

Would you right now simply give the Holy Spirit freedom to penetrate your inner world? Ask the Holy Spirit to open up new thoughts, new insights for you that you may successfully deal with anything and everything in your life.

Isaiah 49:20 says that "the children you will have, after you have lost the others, will say again in your ears, 'The place is too small for me; give me a place where I may dwell.'" This is the prayer of those who feel spiritually cramped, limited, hedged in and will not settle for less. Cry out! Pray! Do not live in a narrow place. God doesn't want less for you; He wants you to experience more. The Scriptures do not teach less. Push out the walls of your spiritual world.

Exodus 16:17 says, "And the children of Israel did so and gathered, some more, some less." The Lord provided more than enough manna for everyone to gather all they needed. Some people gathered more and some people gathered less. Commit yourself to reach out and gather more from all of God's abundant provisions, not less. Gather enough for your friends, for your family and for your future. Gather all you can when God provides.

Don't Settle for Reduced Benefits

Psalm 103:1-5 says, "Bless the Lord, O my soul; and all that is within me, bless His holy name! Bless the Lord, O my soul, and forget not all His benefits: who forgives all your iniquities, who heals all your diseases, who redeems your life from destruction, who crowns you with lovingkindness and tender mercies, who satisfies your mouth with good things, so that your youth is renewed like the eagle's."

Benefits speak of His gracious acts for us and to us, anything contributing to an improvement in our present condition and circumstance. When the preacher R.C. Chapman was asked how he was feeling, he replied, "I'm burdened this morning!" His happy countenance contradicted his words. So the questioner exclaimed in surprise, "Are you really burdened, Mr. Chapman?" "Yes, but it's a wonderful burden—it's an overabundance of blessings for which I cannot find enough time or words to express my gratitude!" Seeing the puzzled look on the face of his friend, Chapman added with a smile, "I am referring to Psalm 68:19, which fully describes my condition. In that verse the Father in heaven reminds us that He 'daily loads us with benefits.'"[1] Psalm 116:12 says, "What shall I render to the Lord for all His benefits toward me?" These benefits need to be identified one at a time and appreciated individually.

"Forgives all your iniquities"

We ought to live under the constant flow of grace and forgiveness. We are like bad trees, which cannot bring forth good fruit. Our roots have been contaminated by sin and by our sin nature. Our life is sadly marred by transgressions and by shortcomings. We need repeated forgiveness, multiplied pardons—and God graciously bestows them upon us. No blessing is greater in scope for us poor sinners, nor any gift that is so entirely undeserved as the forgiveness that freely comes from God.

"Heals all your diseases"

All of the mortal ills, the infirmities, the sicknesses that try to attach themselves to our redeemed bodies can be healed by Jehovah Rapha, the Lord our healer (see Exod. 15:26; Deut. 29:22). Corruption and disease have a spiritual origin. All material corruption was preceded by spiritual corruption. All diseases were, and are, spiritual to begin with. The divine art of healing, therefore, lies in the forgiveness of our sins and iniquities and in the breaking of the power of corruption that works against our bodies. The ultimate healing will be a redeemed, immortal body that carries no sicknesses or infirmities of any kind. What a wonderful future! A perfect body, no pain, no deformity, no sickness (see Mark 4:7: 1 Cor. 15:20-28; 15:41-48)!

"Redeems your life from destruction"

God redeems our lives from the pit of hell, from the grave and from all powers that seek to bring ruin. The Lord redeems the soul from sin and from the penalty of sin: spiritual and eternal death. God will ransom our redeemed bodies and souls from the power of the grave and will endow us with endless and blessed lives. All the destructive powers of the devil work against humankind until an individual is brought under the cross of Christ through salvation. John 10:10 says, "The thief does not come except to steal, and to kill, and to destroy. I have come that they may have life, and that they may have it more abundantly." We are redeemed from destruction. Don't settle for anything less than full recovery!

"Crowns you with lovingkindness and tender mercies"

We are crowned with the love of God that is saturated with mercy. The love of God not only delivers us from sin and its destructive influence, but also from sin, disease and death. This is mercy. Because He loves us, He heaps upon us what we do not deserve and renders to us abundant riches. The crown is woven out of God's lovingkindness and compassion, His mercy is at work in us and upon us. Though humiliation may be rightly deserved, God bestows on His people the largesse of His favors, whereby He makes us feel like kings on their day of enthronement.

"Satisfies your mouth with good things"

God and God alone can satisfy the deep needs of the human soul. Outside of God, the wants and desires of the soul can never be truly satisfied. Our satisfaction comes as we find Christ and as our souls are brought into covenantal relationship with the living God. The Lord we serve forgives, redeems, sustains and fully restores all the covenantal benefits. Even though sin has breached these benefits, the Scriptures promise us that God's presence and grace will fill us with true satisfaction and our mouths will speak of His great work. Our mouths will speak the "good things" that God has done, for out of the heart our mouths speak (see Ps. 63:5; Isa. 55:1,2).

"Renews your youth like an eagle"

The eagle is used here because it is symbolic of vigor and strength. The comparison of an eagle's going through its annual molting and the renewing of its plumage is a metaphor for the renovation of our spirits and souls by the grace and power of God. The molting of the eagle's plumage periodically gave new strength and new energy. We renew our spiritual strength through constantly abiding in Christ, evidenced by our living in the Spirit and in prayer.

DON'T SETTLE FOR LIVING IN THE BOAT

Matthew 14:22-33 provides the historical account of the well-known story of Peter getting out of the boat and walking on the water. Let's read this portion together as a reminder of what actually happened.

Immediately Jesus made His disciples get into the boat and go before Him to the other side, while He sent the multitudes away. And when He had sent the multitudes away, He went up on the mountain by Himself to pray. Now when evening came, He was alone there. But the boat was now in the middle of the sea, tossed by the waves, for the wind was contrary. Now in the fourth watch of the night Jesus went to them, walking on the sea. And when the disciples saw Him walking on the sea, they were troubled, saying, "It is a ghost!" And they cried out for fear. But immediately Jesus spoke to them, saying, "Be of good cheer! It is I; do not be afraid." And Peter answered Him and said, "Lord, if it is You, command me to come to You on the water." So He said, "Come." And when Peter had come down out of the boat, he walked on the water to go to Jesus. But when he saw that the wind was boisterous, he was afraid; and beginning to sink he cried out, saying, "Lord, save me!" And immediately Jesus stretched out His hand and caught him, and said to him, "O you of little faith, why did you doubt?" And when they got into the boat, the wind ceased. Then those who were in the boat came and worshiped Him, saying, "Truly You are the Son of God."

Peter activated a spirit of faith to arise and leave his comfort zone, his place of safety and security. Peter, like all of us, had to get up, step up, step over and step out of the boat. Don't settle for living inside your "boat" of human limitations. Get up, step up, step over all the obstacles—beginning with your own reasoning and excuses. Step out.

> *You cannot discover new oceans unless you have the courage to lose sight of the shore!*

Hudson Taylor, the great man of faith who founded the China Inland Mission, integrated faith and risk. He said, "Unless there is an element of risk in our exploits for God, there is no need for faith."[2] "One of the reasons why mature people stop growing and learning," says John Gardner, "is that they become less and less willing to risk failure."[3] To risk means to get up from where you are, to step over the side of the boat, to step over all the obstacles and to step out on the water. I may sound somewhat repetitious, but I want you to understand that you cannot discover new oceans unless you have the courage to lose sight of the shore! Think outside of the box. Live outside of the box. Don't settle for a life lived in the boat. Jean-Claude Killy didn't.

Jean-Claude Killy was part of the French national ski team in the early 1960s and he prepared to work harder than anyone else to be the best. At the crack of dawn he would run up the slopes with his skis on, an unbelievably grueling activity. In the evening he would lift weights, run sprints—anything to get an edge. But the other team members were working as hard and long as he was. He realized instinctively that simply training harder would never be enough. Killy then began challenging the basic theories of racing technique. Each week he would try something different to see if he could find a better, faster way down the mountain. His experiments resulted in a new style that was almost exactly opposite the accepted technique of the time. It involved skiing with his legs apart (not together) for better balance and sitting back (not forward) on the skis when he came to a turn. He also used ski poles in an unorthodox way—to propel himself as he skied. The explosive new style helped cut Killy's racing times dramatically. In 1966 and 1967 he captured virtually every major skiing trophy. The next year he won three gold medals in the Winter Olympics, a record in ski racing that has never been topped.[4]

First Corinthians 2:14 cautions that "the natural man does not receive the things of the Spirit of God, for they are foolishness to him; nor can he know them, because they are spiritually discerned."

DON'T SETTLE FOR A RESTRICTED FUTURE

A study was conducted involving famous and exceptionally gifted people to determine what produced such greatness. The conclusion was that virtually all of them, 392 out of 413, had to overcome very difficult obstacles in order to become who they were. These were people who would not allow their situations to box them in or limit what they could accomplish.

Hebrews 11:1,2 explains that "faith is the substance of things hoped for, the evidence of things not seen. For by it the elders obtained a good testimony." Faith is what we have and is what we use to break out and enlarge our borders. Faith resists the restrictions the enemy tries to impose on us. Faith demolishes the negative thought patterns that seek to restrict our God-given futures. Faith faces the forces that restrict our visions, our hopes and our dreams.

To settle for less is to live a restricted life and to forfeit a faith-filled future. God is not going to give us wings to fly away from pressure. Stand up, face the troubles of life (see Ps. 55:4-8). God does not take us out of the world to keep us from trouble. We are to overcome the world by the Word of faith (see John 17:15; Rom. 5:17). First John 5:4 says, "This is the victory that has overcome the world—our faith."

Don't settle for a restricted future! Faith looks past the immediate circumstances to the ultimate fulfillment of the promise. Faith believes in the impossible, even when the mind speaks differently. Don't settle for living in the boat. Don't settle for less than a faith-filled life. You will never experience the supernatural hand of God opening and closing doors, providing all you need for the dream, conquering your enemies and doing things only God can do if you settle for less than living by faith.

Faith is not moved by the five natural senses of hearing, seeing, smelling, tasting and touching. Faith is moved by the Spirit of the living God. Matthew 9:29 can be prayed and applied right here and right now. "Then He touched their eyes, saying, 'According to your faith let it be to you.'" Job 8:7 says, "Though your beginning was small, yet your latter end would increase abundantly." Claim this for your life, your children and your ministry. No matter how small the beginning seems, if God is your partner it won't stay small. It will grow, increase mightily and become a miracle!

Jeremiah 29:11 says, "I know the thoughts that I think toward you, says the Lord, thoughts of peace and not of evil, to give you a future and a hope." Many of us can identify with Jabez who did not accept the limitation put on his life and his future. The prayer of Jabez in 1 Chronicles 4:9,10 has recently become a famous prayer in both the Church and the secular world. It is a prayer of faith, the prayer of a dreamer. Let's read it together:

> Now Jabez was more honorable than his brothers, and his mother called his name Jabez, saying, "Because I bore him in pain." And Jabez called on the God of Israel saying, "Oh, that You would bless me indeed, and enlarge my territory, that Your hand would be with me, and that You would keep me from evil, that I may not cause pain!" So God granted him what he requested.

No restricted future. Live beyond the limits. Live outside the fence. Unclaimed blessings are waiting for you. Live beyond your pain and discouragement. God's blessings are limited only by our wrong choices and lack of faith, not by His resources, power or willingness to give. Refuse any obstacle, person or opinion that restricts your future! Faith sees the invisible, believes the incredible and receives the impossible. Let us never limit our God like those referred to in Psalm 78:41, "Yes, again and again they tempted God, and limited the Holy One of Israel."

Don't Settle for a Religion Without Power

Our commitment is to refuse to settle for anything less than the God of the Bible. Nothing less will satisfy us or the spiritually hungry world in which we live. We are committed to contending for the return of God's supernatural power in today's Church. We must not settle for a religion without the true power of God at work in a mighty and obvious way. If good preaching alone were the answer, we would have seen a different America, or any other nation, a long time ago. If good gospel music, radio programs and plush sanctuaries were the key to revival, we would know it by now!

Second Timothy 3:5 warns about those, "having a form of godliness but denying its power. And from such people turn away!" They have a form, a mere resemblance or appearance of godliness but they deny its power source (see 1 Tim. 2:2; 3:16; 4:7,8). These people and churches lack spiritual dynamite. They have empty lives and empty souls. Psalm 62:11 claims, "God has spoken once, twice I have heard this: that power belongs to God." First Chronicles 29:11,12 reiterates this truth, "Yours, O Lord, is the greatness, the power and the glory, the victory and the majesty; for all that is in heaven and in earth is Yours; Yours is the king-dom, O Lord, and You are exalted as head over all. Both riches and honor come from You, and You reign over all. In Your hand is power and might; in Your hand it is to make great and to give strength to all."

We need the fresh and authentic power of God in the Church today as we pray for the sick and for those in need of a supernatural touch from God. Like Jesus, we need to be filled with the power of God (see Luke 4:14; Acts 1:8; 6:8).

Watchman Nee presents a great example of the power of God, not dead religion but a power-filled religion that confronts the power of the enemy.

Watchman Nee went with a team to an island on the South China coast. The island was fairly large, containing about 6,000 homes. Preaching seemed quite fruitless on the island, and Nee discov-ered it was because of the dedication of the people there to an idol they called Ta-wang. They were convinced of his power because on the day of his festival and parade each year the weather was always near perfect.

One of the team members, Brother Wu asked, "When is the procession this year?" "It is fixed for January 11th at 8 in the morning," was the reply. "Then I promise you that it will certainly rain on the 11th." The crowd cried out, "If there is rain on the 11th, then your God is God!"

The Christians earnestly began to pray. On the morning of the 11th, there was not a cloud in the sky, but during breakfast, sprinkles began to fall and these were followed by heavy rain. Worshipers of the idol Ta-wang were so upset that they placed it in a sedan chair and carried it outdoors, hoping this would stop the rain. Then the rain increased. After only a short distance, the carriers of the idol stumbled and fell, dropping the idol and fracturing its jaw and left arm.

A number of young people turned to Christ as a result of the rain coming in answer to prayer, but the elders of the village made divination and said that the wrong day had been chosen. The proper day of the procession, they said, should have been the 14th. When Nee and his friends heard this, they again went to prayer, asking for rain on the 14th and for clear days for preaching until then. That afternoon the sky cleared and on the good days that followed there were 30 converts. The 14th broke with another perfect day. As the evening approached they met again at the appointed hour and began to pray. His answer came with torrential rain and floods as before.

The power of the idol over the islanders was broken; the enemy was defeated. Believing prayer had brought a great victory.[5]

Our God is a miracle-working God who has power over all the forces of evil. Allow the following Scriptures to saturate your soul:

Exodus 15:11: Who is like You, O Lord, among the gods? Who is like You, glorious in holiness, fearful in praises, doing wonders?

Psalm 136:4: To Him who alone does great wonders, for His mercy endures forever.

Acts 2:22: Men of Israel, hear these words: Jesus of Nazareth, a Man attested by God to you by miracles, wonders, and signs which God did through Him in your midst, as you yourselves also know.

Acts 2:43: Then fear came upon every soul, and many wonders and signs were done through the apostles.

Acts 4:30: By stretching out Your hand to heal, and that signs and wonders may be done through the name of Your holy Servant Jesus.

Romans 15:19: In mighty signs and wonders, by the power of the Spirit of God, so that from Jerusalem and round about to Illyricum I have fully preached the gospel of Christ.

Don't Settle for a Bible That Doesn't Work Today

If the Scriptures are not working for you, it's not because they don't have the power to work. The Scriptures in the hands of the people of the Spirit bring alive the Word of God. Mark 7:13 warns that you and I can be guilty of "making the word of God of no effect through your tradition which you have handed down." Any person or group of people who nullify the living Word of God by elevating their own traditions or rituals will not see the miracles and the supernatural works of God. Jesus had to deal with this destructive attitude and behavior in the Pharisees who continually enthroned their traditions and dethroned the Word of God.

> *We must honor what Scripture clearly teaches and, if need be, rid ourselves of human traditions that make the Word of no effect.*

We face the same battle today, exalting men's opinions and denying the authentic revelation of the Word by doing things that are against it. The power of God finds its release in and through the Word of God and the Spirit of God. We must honor what Scripture clearly teaches and, if need be, rid ourselves of human traditions that make the Word of no effect.

In Matthew 22:29, "Jesus answered and said to them, 'You are mistaken, not knowing the Scriptures nor the power of God.'" And 2 Timothy 3:16 reveals that "all Scripture is given by inspiration of God, and is profitable for doctrine, for reproof, for correction, for instruction in righteousness."

The close connection between believing in the Word of God and seeing the supernatural work of God in healing and deliverance is evidenced in Psalm 107:20, which tells us that "He sent His word and healed them, and delivered them from their destructions."

A close look at Hebrews 4:12 reveals to each person just how powerful the Word of God is and should be in our lives. Let's look at it in several translations:

- *New King James*: For the word of God is living and powerful, and sharper than any two-edged sword, piercing even to the division of soul and spirit, and of joints and marrow, and is a discerner of the thoughts and intents of the heart.
- *Amplified Bible*: For the Word that God speaks is alive and full of power [making it active, operative, energizing, and effective]; it is sharper than any two-edged sword, penetrating to the dividing line of the breath of life (soul) and [the immortal] spirit, and of joints and marrow [of the deepest parts of our nature], exposing and sifting and analyzing and judging the very thoughts and purposes of the heart.
- *The Message*: His powerful word is sharp as a surgeon's scalpel, cutting through everything, whether doubt or defense, laying us open to listen and obey. Nothing and no one is impervious to God's word. We can't get away from it—no matter what.

Gipsy Smith (1860-1947) told of a man who said he had received no inspiration from the Bible although he had "gone through it several times." "Let it go through you once," replied Smith, "then you will tell a different story!"[6]

One New Year's Day, in the Tournament of Roses parade, a beautiful float suddenly sputtered and quit. It was out of fuel. The whole parade was held up until someone could get a can of gas. The amusing fact was that the float represented Standard Oil Company. With its vast oil resources, its truck was out of gas.[7] With all the resources in the Word of God, we can act like that float, not connected to our power source. Believe what the Scriptures say about our God while pondering the following:

Deuteronomy 7:21: You shall not be terrified of them; for the Lord your God, the great and awesome God, is among you.

Deuteronomy 10:17: For the Lord your God is God of gods and Lord of Lords, the great God, mighty and awesome, who shows no partiality nor takes a bribe.

Deuteronomy 10:21: He is your praise, and He is your God, who has done for you these great and awesome things which your eyes have seen.

Don't Settle for a Survival-Thinking Mind-Set

Survival simply means the continuation of life or existence. A survivalist is one who views survival as a primary objective. As a believer in God and His Word, my primary objective is not just to survive, but to surpass and accomplish great things for God and with God. My attitude is not just to endure, to hang in there, to exist, to hold out, keep afloat or tough it out until the end. No, this kind of thinking is wrong to the core. We are not to settle for a "living in the boat" mentality, which is the opposite of believing and living for and with a miracle-working God.

Author Irving Stone (1908-1989) spent a lifetime studying greatness, writing biographies of such men as Michelangelo, Vincent van

Gogh, Sigmund Freud and Charles Darwin. Stone was once asked if he had found a thread that runs through the lives of all these exceptional people. He said, "I write about people who sometime in their life...have a vision or dream of something that should be accomplished...and they go to work. They are beaten over the head, knocked down, vilified and for years they get nowhere. But every time they're knocked down, they stand up. You cannot destroy these people. And at the end of their lives they've accomplished some modest part of what they set out to do."[8] These people didn't have a survival mentality, but an overcoming mentality.

The great musician Quincy Jones said, "A person's age can be determined by the degree of pain he experiences when he comes in contact with a new idea."

Scripture says we are overcomers, more than conquerors, and that our weapons are powerful in the spirit realm. We are not to allow a survival attitude to influence our thoughts or to rule our visions. Dee Hock, the leader of VISA said, "The problem is never how to get new, imaginative thoughts into your mind, but how to get the old ones out. Every mind is a room packed with archaic furniture. You must get the old furniture of what you know, think and believe out before anything new can get in. Make an empty space in any corner of your mind and creativity will instantly fill it."[9]

Make room in your mind and spirit for new Holy Spirit thoughts about everything—your job, your marriage, your education, your ministry to the poor, your prayers for the lost, your prayers for miracles. Break out into the new.

The great musician Quincy Jones (1933-) said, "A person's age can be determined by the degree of pain he experiences when he comes in contact with a new idea."[10] I am willing to put myself through almost anything. Temporary pain or discomfort means nothing to me as long as I can see that the experience will take me to a new level. I am interested in the unknown and the only path to the unknown is forged through by breaking barriers! Hebrews 11:6 says, "But without faith it is impossible to please Him, for he who comes to God must believe that He is, and that He is a rewarder of those who diligently seek Him."

Don't Settle for Small Prayers

Among those in the court of Alexander the Great (356-323 B.C.) was a philosopher who found himself in deep financial need. Unable to fix the problem himself (and before the days of chapter 11 bankruptcy), the man approached Alexander asking for financial help and was told to draw whatever he needed from the imperial treasury. Taking Alexander at his word, he went to the treasurer and asked for an amount equal to $50,000. The treasurer refused to give it to him, stating he needed to verify that such a large sum was authorized. When the treasurer asked Alexander, the ruler replied, "Pay the money at once. The philosopher has done me a singular honor. By the largeness of his request he shows that he has understood both my wealth and generosity."[11]

Do you understand both the wealth and generosity of the God you serve? If you knew God was as generous as Alexander the Great, would you not enlarge your prayers and raise the standard of your request? Consider the words of Jesus in John 4:10:

Jesus answered and said to her, "If you knew the gift of God, and who it is who says to you, 'Give Me a drink,' you would have asked Him, and He would have given you living water."

Do you know who is offering you all the resources of heaven? If you knew, would you not ask for more than just a drink of water? I believe you would ask for miracles—not little bitty, inconsequential, meager, microscopic miracles; not modest miracles; not pint-sized miracles; not pocket-sized miracles. You would ask for huge miracles. You would pray colossal prayers, gargantuan, humongous prayers! The God who created the heavens and the earth is ready to listen to your prayers. Make your request huge, not small. Don't insult God. Don't limit Him to be God. First

Kings 2:20 says, "Then she said, 'I desire one small petition of you; do not refuse me.' And the king said to her, 'Ask it, my mother, for I will not refuse you.'" And 1 John 5:14 explains that "this is the confidence that we have in Him, that if we ask anything according to His will, He hears us." God can work out anything, big or small. Let us make our requests a little larger.

Dr. Helen Roseveare, author, medical pioneer and missionary to Zaire during the 1960s, told the following story:

> A mother at our mission station died after giving birth to a premature baby. We tried to improvise an incubator to keep the infant alive, but the only hot water bottle we had was beyond repair. So we asked the children to pray for the baby and for her sister. One of the girls responded. "Dear God, please send a hot water bottle today. Tomorrow will be too late because by then the baby will be dead. And dear Lord, send a doll for the sister so she won't feel so lonely." That afternoon a large package arrived from England. The children watched eagerly as we opened it. Much to their surprise, under some clothing was a hot water bottle! Immediately the girl who had prayed so earnestly started to dig deeper, exclaiming, "If God sent that, I'm sure He also sent a doll!" And she was right! The heavenly Father knew in advance of that child's sincere requests, and five months earlier He had led a ladies' group to include both of those specific articles.[12]

Our answers are directly linked to our level of expectation. Second Kings 13:18,19 illustrates the importance of refusing to settle for less:

> Then he said, "Take the arrows"; so he took them. And he said to the king of Israel, "Strike the ground"; so he struck three times, and stopped. And the man of God was angry with him, and said, "You should have struck five or six times; then you would have struck Syria till you had destroyed it! But now you will strike Syria only three times."

How many times will you strike the ground of faith? These are sad words, "so he struck three times, and stopped." Stopped! Cut short! Pulled up too soon! Quit too soon! Don't stop your request. Don't shrink your spirit and start asking too little. Don't settle for small prayers!

To get just a small idea of God's creative power, let us consider our universe.

We live on one of nine planets that revolve around the sun. As the dominant light of our solar system, our sun gives off far more energy in one second than all humankind has produced since Creation. With a diameter of approximately 860,000 miles, the sun could hold 1 million planets the size of Earth, yet our sun is only an average-size star. Our sun is just one among 100 billion stars in our galaxy, the Milky Way. The Pistol Star gives off 10 million times the power generated by our sun, and 1 million stars the size of our sun can fit easily within its sphere. It takes 100,000 light-years to travel from one side of the Milky Way to the other. (One light-year is 5.88 trillion miles or the distance light travels in one year.) Our galaxy is moving through space at a phenomenal speed of 1 million miles per hour! If the Milky Way were compared to the size of the North American continent, our solar system would be about the size of a coffee cup! Yet our Milky Way is not a huge galaxy. One of our neighbors, the Andromeda Spiral galaxy, is 2 million light-years away and contains about 400 billion stars. No one knows how many galaxies there are in the universe, but scientists estimate that there are billions of them.[13]

Wow! Think about your prayers and your faith for miracles when you consider the God you are praying to! Jeremiah 32:17-19 says, "Ah Lord God! Behold, You have made the heavens and the earth by Your great power and outstretched arm. There is nothing too hard for You. You show lovingkindness to thousands, and repay the iniquity of the fathers into the bosom of their children after them—the Great, the Mighty God, whose name is the Lord of hosts. You are great in counsel and mighty in work, for your eyes are open to all the ways of the sons of men, to give everyone according to his ways and according to the fruit of his doings."

Settle in your heart that God is a miracle-working God yesterday, today and forever. Settle in your heart that God has miracles for you according to His promises in His proven Word. The promises may be hidden, delayed or resisted by the enemy, but they won't be stopped.

Open up your miracle door by faith. Settle in your heart that you serve a great God who can do anything at anytime and that you have enough to release great things. Settle in your heart that you are loved. You are accepted in Christ. You have a unique, God-given destiny. You have miracles coming your way right now, beginning today. They may be small, great or mind-boggling. Whatever the size, they are yours—and they are on the way today. Open your heart, open your eyes and receive!

We serve the only true God, the God of the Bible, the God of the supernatural. Since God is supernatural, we must not stop short of the goal, the prize captured by those willing to pursue and go beyond. We must not settle for second place or for no place at all. We cannot settle for less and justify our meager accomplishments. Agree with me today that, by the power of the Holy Spirit, we will arise and break into the "new" that God has for all of us.

Notes

1. Author unknown. http://www.christianglobe.com/Illustrations/a-z/b/blessing.html.
2. Paul Borthwick, *Leading the Way* (Colorado Springs, CO: Navpress, 1989), p. 153.
3. Tim Hansel, *Eating Problems for Breakfast* (Dallas, TX: Word Publishing, 1988), p.32.
4. *Reader's Digest*, October 1991, p. 61. http://www.christianglobe.com/Illustrations/az/r/risk.html.
5. Roger F. Campbell, *You Can Win!* http://www.christianglobe.com/Illustrations/a-z/r/risk.html.
6. Gipsy Smith, http://www.christianglobe.com/Illustrations/a-z/b/bible-application-of.html.
7. Max Lucado, *God Came Near* (Sisters, OR: Multnomah Press, 1987), p. 95.

8. http://www.resourcefoundation.org/Community/Schools/Persev-i.shtml.

9. Ed Young, http://www.Sermonnotes.com (Alderson Press Corporation, 2002), 2 January, 2002.

10. "Perfect Pitch," *Context* magazine (Chicago: Diamond Cluster International), http://contextmag.com/archives/200104/FeatureOPerfectPitch.asp.

11. *Today in the Word*, http://www.christianglobe.com/Illustrations/a-z/p/prayer.html.

12. *Our Daily Bread*, http://www.christianglobe.com/Illustrations/a-z/p/prayer-answered.html.

13. Bill Bright, *God: Discover His Character* (Orlando: New Life Publications, 1999), pp. 43-44.

7

Miracles Contended For

ON THE FIRST DAY OF CLASS, a philosophy professor would begin with some forceful questions. "Who here believes in God? Is God all-powerful? Can He do miracles?" Then he would say, "Anyone who does believe in God is a fool. If God existed, He could stop this jar from breaking when I drop it. Such a simple task to prove that He is God, and yet He can't do it." And every year the professor would drop the jar onto the tile floor of the classroom, and it would shatter into a hundred pieces. One year a student spoke up, "I believe in God." Holding the jar with one hand, the professor scoffed, "Then pray to your God and ask Him not to let this break." Very simply the student prayed, "God, honor Your name." Then the professor dropped the jar. As he did, it slipped out of his fingers, down his leg and off his shoe, rolling onto the ground and across the floor, unbroken.

If God exists, miracles are possible!

Dr. Norman Geisler (1932–), Christian apologist, author and president of Southern Evangelical Seminary, says, "If there is a God who can act, then there can be acts of God. The only way to show that miracles

123

are impossible is to disprove the existence of God and that is something that cannot be done."[1] Our basic presupposition is very simple. If God exists, then miracles are possible. We believe He exists, so our faith reaches out to see the supernatural acts of God released today. In *All The Miracles of the Bible*, prolific author and scholar Herbert Lockyer describes a miracle as "a work wrought by a divine power for a divine purpose by means beyond human reach."[2] And because we know that God can and does work beyond our human reach to perform miracles, we must have a right perspective on the supernatural power of God to do so before we can contend for that perspective.

If God exists, miracles are possible!

A Right Perspective on the Supernatural

The Holy Spirit is upon us to enable us to contend for a right perspective on the supernatural. A perspective is a particular way of considering something, to think about something in a wise and reasonable way, the comparing of something to other things so that the comparison can be accurate and fairly judged. Our perspective may be shaped by several different internal and external forces. Here are a few:

- Our Worldview: The culturally structured assumptions, values and commitments underlying a people's perception of reality.
- Our Experiences: All of us are hampered to a greater or lesser extent in our attempts to understand the experiences of others that we ourselves have not had.
- Our Personality: Our predisposition, motivation, degree of openness to new ideas, conservative or liberal view of life, optimistic or pessimistic outlook on life.
- Our Will: The will factor is simply that we will choose to view any given thing either as we have been taught to view it or differently. When confronted with new information or a new

experience that may challenge our present views, we will either reconsider our position or remain unchanged in our opinion.

- Our Christian or Church Background: The experiences, both good and bad, which determine our feelings about church, about how church operates and about how we see the church. We may have some faulty teaching or absent teachings on certain subjects such as prayer, worship, healing, gifts. Thus we choose a certain perspective built on our Christian or church experience. We may ask, "Why is my experience of Christianity so different from what we read about in the New Testament? What is wrong with my brand of Christianity? Is there more?"

- Our Bible Knowledge: We are shaped by what we know and by what we think we know. An individual's knowledge of Scripture will greatly change the way he or she thinks about everything: God, the devil, sin, hell, heaven, church, the Holy Spirit, authority, etc. Our perspective is connected to our understanding of the Word of God. Teaching that says healing, miracles and gifts of the Spirit are not for today can greatly influence a person's perspective.

- Our Spiritual Health: Our spiritual health has a lot to do with our spiritual eyes. The way we see things will be greatly influenced by our level of spiritual maturity—at peace with God, in love with God, great prayer life, positive outlook, living in victory, encouraged by the Holy Spirit, enjoying the things of God, happy, healthy church member, functioning faithfully.

Our challenge, of course, is to nurture a biblical perspective on all things, especially on our case here—miracles, the supernatural, healing, dealing with the unseen world. Romans 12:2 says, "And do not be conformed to this world, but be transformed by the renewing of your mind, that you may prove what is that good and acceptable and perfect will of God." Our job is to submit our minds to the Word of God more than we do to the world's system or to the system of thought that is founded upon human opinions. We must contend for a biblical perspective that sees things clearly. First Corinthians 13:12 explains:

> For now we see in a mirror, dimly, but then face to face. Now I know in part, but then I shall know just as I also am known.

CONTENDING FOR THE SUPERNATURAL

To contend is to exert oneself without distraction to attain a goal. It means self-denial to overcome obstacles, to avoid perils and, if need be, to accept martyrdom for the cause. We are called to contend for the return of miracles and the supernatural in the Church of today. The Greek word for contend is *athleo*, which means to engage in a contest, to strive for the good, to separate oneself from so as to contend wholly, with intensity and with an attitude that will not draw back, give up or let go. Jude 3 talks about contending:

> Beloved, while I was very diligent to write to you concerning our common salvation, I found it necessary to write to you exhorting you to contend earnestly for the faith which was once for all delivered to the saints.

The Message translates it this way:

> I have to write insisting, begging, that you fight with everything you have in you for this faith entrusted to you as a gift to guard and cherish.

And the *J.B. Phillips* says:

> Put up a real right for the faith which has been once for all committed to those who belong to Christ.

Let's look at this verse phrase by phrase.

"Found it necessary"

After only a few decades, the Church had moved from a Holy Spirit empowered force to a people who were drifting from the original foundational doctrines of Christ and the apostles. They were drifting and being pressured by culture and by hell itself to give up or to give over some of the main power truths that had established the Church.

"Have to write...insisting...begging...that you fight with everything in you"

These are the words of a very concerned apostle. They are words expressing a deep burden, words of passion, as he begs the Church to reach way down inside and fight the spirit of resistance within them. He begs them to find a spirit of spiritual fighting and warfare. As the enemy has stormed the walls and is fast approaching, you must—we must—fight with everything within us to win the battle.

"Contend for the faith...a gift to guard and cherish"

This word is one of resolve, resistance, settled determination, a decision to honor and to hold in high esteem those doctrines that belong to the Church. The deity of Christ, the cross of Christ, the doctrine of the Holy Spirit, Holy Spirit baptism, the truth of speaking in tongues, water baptism by immersion, the gifts of the spirit—we must contend for these truths that built the First Church. We must contend for the power of the Holy Spirit as it was in the First Church. We are to guard these truths with a passion, alert to all strategies of the enemy.

The Church has been called upon to be the custodians of the truth, to keep the integrity of the doctrines, which can only be accomplished through unswerving fidelity to the truth, holding fast to it.

"Once delivered"

This faith had once been given to the Church at the beginning through the infallible writers of the New Testament and handed down to us. It had not come in installments. The content of the apostolic faith and truth is fixed, not to be revisited each new era for each new culture.

CONTENDING FOR FULL RESTORATION

Let us contend to believe for the full restoration of the Church as seen in the book of Acts and the Epistles. We contend for the fact that God desires to restore the individual believer to the image of God and to restore the corporate Church to the full power and full truth expression He has promised. When we use the term "restoration," we mean the full recovery and returning to the Church of all that has been stolen. Restoration is causing to return to a former position or condition by renewing or returning that which has been stolen, lost, destroyed or forcibly removed. Isaiah 42:22 words it this way:

> But this is a people robbed and plundered; all of them are snared
> in holes, and they are hidden in prison houses; they are for prey,
> and no one delivers; for plunder, and no one says, "Restore!"

Restoration teaching sees a spiritual restoration of the New Testament Church to fulfill all of God's ultimate purposes. Isaiah 58:12 says, "Those from among you shall build the old waste places; you shall raise up the foundations of many generations; and you shall be called the Repairer of the Breach, the Restorer of Streets to Dwell In." And Haggai 2:7-9 says, "'And I will shake all nations, and they shall come to the Desire of All Nations, and I will fill this temple with glory,' says the Lord of hosts. 'The silver is Mine, and the gold is Mine,' says the Lord of hosts. The glory of this latter temple shall be greater than the former,' says the Lord of hosts. 'And in this place I will give peace,' says the Lord of hosts."

The Church of today is not seeing the restoration of the miracles and the supernatural power of God the same way the First Church experienced God's power. Why? Maybe the answer is less prayer, less Bible, less Holy Spirit and less expectation. It could be that we have accommodated culture in too many ways too many times with shorter services, shallow worship, little commitment, no real fasting or prayer intensity. We do the same thing again and again, and yet we expect different results!

Some say that 95 percent of American Church growth is due to transplant and biological growth and only 5 percent is from true conversion growth. We need a power restoration of all the power gifts, power Word, power prayers, power church services and power breakthrough. The book of Acts displays a power-driven Church with the supernatural being used continually. In *Christianity Today* magazine, Sharon Mumper said, "Healings, exorcisms and other supernatural signs and wonders have accompanied phenomenal growth of the Church in China and in many other surprising parts of the world." Let's read a few of the miracles seen in the book of Acts.

This first miracle added at least 5,000 people to the Church immediately:

Acts 3:1-11: Now Peter and John went up together to the temple at the hour of prayer, the ninth hour. And a certain man lame from his mother's womb was carried, whom they laid daily at the gate of the temple which is called Beautiful, to ask alms from those who entered the temple; who, seeing Peter and John about to go into the temple, asked for alms. And fixing his eyes on him, with John, Peter said, "Look at us." So he gave them his attention, expecting to receive something from them. Then Peter said, "Silver and gold I do not have, but what I do have I give you: In the name of Jesus Christ of Nazareth, rise up and walk." And he took him by the right hand and lifted him up, and immediately his feet and ankle bones received strength. So he, leaping up, stood and walked and entered the temple with them—walking, leaping, and praising God. And all the people saw him walking and praising God. Then they knew that it was he who sat begging alms at the Beautiful Gate of the temple; and they were filled with wonder and amazement at what had happened to him. Now as the lame man who was healed held on to Peter and John, all the people ran together to them in the porch which is called Solomon's, greatly amazed.

Acts 4:4: However, many of those who heard the word believed; and the number of the men came to be about five thousand.

Acts 5:12: And through the hands of the apostles many signs and wonders were done among the people. And they were all with one accord in Solomon's Porch.

This miracle added multitudes to the Church:

Acts 5:14-16: And believers were increasingly added to the Lord, multitudes of both men and women, so that they brought the sick out into the streets and laid them on beds and couches, that at least the shadow of Peter passing by might fall on some of them. Also a multitude gathered from the surrounding cities to Jerusalem, bringing sick people and those who were tormented by unclean spirits, and they were all healed.

Acts 8:6: And the multitudes with one accord heeded the things spoken by Philip, hearing and seeing the miracles which he did.

This miracle caused all who saw the healed man to turn to the Lord and affected two cities:

Acts 9:32-35: Now it came to pass, as Peter went through all parts of the country, that he also came down to the saints who dwelt in Lydda. There he found a certain man named Aeneas, who had been bedridden eight years and was paralyzed. And Peter said to him, "Aeneas, Jesus the Christ heals you. Arise and make your bed." Then he arose immediately. So all who dwelt at Lydda and Sharon saw him and turned to the Lord.

This miracle caused many from the whole city to believe:

Acts 9:36-41: At Joppa there was a certain disciple named Tabitha, which is translated Dorcas. This woman was full of good works and charitable deeds which she did. But it happened in those days that she became sick and died. When they had washed her, they laid her in an upper room. And since Lydda was near Joppa, and the disciples had heard that Peter was there, they sent two men to him, imploring him not to delay in coming to them. Then Peter arose and went with them. When he had come, they brought him to the upper room. And all the widows stood by him weeping, showing the tunics and garments which Dorcas had made while she was with them. But Peter put them all out, and knelt down and prayed. And turning to the body he said, "Tabitha, arise." And she opened her eyes, and when she saw Peter she sat up. Then he gave her his hand and lifted her up; and when he had called the saints and widows, he presented her alive. It became known throughout all Joppa, and many believed on the Lord.

"According to A.T. Pierson (1837-1911), a nonconformist preacher and author, three things needed to take place for the evangelization of the world to be a reality. First, the whole church had to be involved in evangelization. Second, evangelistic zeal was needed in the lives of all believers. And lastly, a baptism of the power of the Holy Spirit was needed. Only then, was the goal realistic and reachable. Others concurred, 'To do this work in twenty years, we must get more Gospel, more vitality.... The church has money, brains, organizations, rivers of prayer and oceans of sermons, but she lacks in power.'"[3]

Dr. Ed Murphy, Vice President of Overseas Crusades, travels around the world. "In India he occasionally works with an evangelist named Patro, a strong proponent of the power encounter. In fact, according to Murphy, Patro and his team will enter a hostile Hindu village, call out the village priest and say loudly, 'The God of Jesus Christ is the only true and living God—a God of power. Bring us the sickest person in your village.' When they do, Patro prays for healing in public, and when the person is healed, hearts are quickly opened to the gospel. Sometimes demonized people are brought out, tied up or locked in a cage, and they are delivered."[4]

"One of the fastest growing metachurches is the Sung Rak Baptist Church of Seoul, Korea, pastored by Ki Dong Kim. Since it traces its ancestry to the U.S. Southern Baptists, it is not included in the usual Pentecostal or charismatic statistics. David Barrett counts it in his category of third wave. In 1987 it passed the 40,000-member mark; a sanctuary seating 20,000 is planned. Pastor Kim testifies to being used to raise 10 people from the dead, casting out thousands of demons and seeing 59 totally crippled people who are now walking."[5]

In Papua, New Guinea, "two young believers from Madang traveled 100 miles up the coast to Bogia. Finding two children in the hospital who had died from malaria, they boldly laid hands on them and prayed in Jesus' name—and they came back to life! 'The power of God came over that entire 60-bed hospital and all the sick were healed.'...'The hospital was literally emptied out!' The missionary, Graham Baker, said people told him, 'I don't believe that story.' To be honest, I questioned it also. But a month later I received a call from the government health department asking me to come over to the government offices so that I could explain this situation to the officials. I asked, 'Explain what situation?' They replied, 'A charge has been made that your workers have been practicing medicine without a license.' That's how we all found out the story was true!"[6]

A New Perspective

Author Max Lucado tells of a friend named Kenny who took his family to Disney World and saw the supernatural power of God from a new perspective:

He and his family were inside Cinderella's castle. It was packed with kids and parents. Suddenly, all the children rushed to one side. Had it been a boat, the castle would have tipped over. Cinderella had entered.

Cinderella. The pristine princess. Kenny said she was perfectly typecast. A gorgeous young girl with each hair in place, flawless skin, and a beaming smile. She stood waist-deep in a garden of kids, each wanting to touch and be touched.

For some reason Kenny turned and looked toward the other side of the castle. It was now vacant except for a boy maybe seven or eight years old. His age was hard to determine because of the disfigurement of his body. Dwarfed in height, face deformed, he stood watching quietly and wistfully, holding the hand of an older brother.

Don't you know what he wanted? He wanted to be with the children. He longed to be in the middle of the kids reaching for Cinderella, calling her name. But can't you feel his fear; fear of yet another rejection? Fear of being taunted again, mocked again?

Don't you wish Cinderella would go to him? Guess what? She did!

She noticed the little boy. She immediately began walking in his direction. Politely but firmly inching through the crowd of children, she finally broke free. She walked quickly across the floor, knelt at eye level with the stunned little boy, and placed a kiss on his face.

"I thought you would appreciate the story," Kenny told me. I did. It reminded me of another one. The names are different, but isn't the story almost the same? Rather than a princess of Disney, it's the Prince of Peace. Rather than a boy in a castle, it's a thief of a cross. In both cases a gift was given. In both cases love was shared. In both cases the lovely one performed a gesture beyond words.

But Jesus did more than Cinderella. Oh, so much more.

Cinderella gave only a kiss. When she stood to leave, she took her beauty with her. The boy was still deformed. What if Cinderella had done what Jesus did? What if she assumed his state? What if she had somehow given him her beauty and taken on his disfigurement?

That's what Jesus did.

"He took our suffering on him and felt our pain for us.... He was wounded for the wrong we did; he was crushed for the evil we did. The punishment, which made us well, was given to him, and we are healed because of his wounds."[7]

Because of what He did, we can and should contend for miracles!

Notes

1. Norman Geisler, "Miracle" (www.John Ankerberg.org). <http://www.ankerberg.com/Articles/theological-dictionary/TD1002W3.htm>. 25, January 2003.
2. Herbert Lockyer, *All the Miracles of the Bible* (Grand Rapids: Zondervan Publishing House, 1961), p.13.
3. Todd M. Johnson, *Countdown to 1900: World Evangelization at the End of the 19th Century.* (http://gem-werc.org/books/c1900/chap05.htm), 11 April 2002.
4. C. Peter Wagner, *How to Have a Healing Ministry in Any Church* (Ventura, CA: Regal Books, 1988), p. 150.
5. Ibid., p. 71.
6. Deborah Anne Perez, "Pioneering Missions in Papua New Guinea," *Christ for the Nations* magazine (January 2002), p. 11.
7. Alice Gray, ed., *More Stories for the Heart*, "Cinderella" by Max Lucado (Sisters, OR: Multnomah, 1997), pp. 245-246.

8

Miracles Through Our Spiritual Gifts

A STORY IS TOLD OF A POOR half-witted fellow whose companion, working beside him, dropped dead. He was found trying to hold up the dead man, trying to make him stand and sit upright. Finding his effort without avail, he was saying to himself, "He needs something inside him." Perhaps that is the reason we live at a poor dying rate. We need a living Spirit within to control and uphold us.[1] And that is what the kingdom of God is all about.

The Kingdom is God the Holy Spirit upholding and controlling us in every circumstance of life. We are called to be people of the Holy Spirit who live in the Spirit, by the Spirit and for the Spirit. We are to be born of the Spirit, filled with the Spirit and walk in the Spirit. We are to grow the fruit of the Spirit and use the gifts of the Spirit. The kingdom of God is a kingdom of spiritual power, and that spiritual power finds its way into every sphere of human life by the believers who become channels of God's great power. The gifts of the Spirit are part of the package that believers receive when they are adopted into the Spirit-filled community called the Church.

The miracles destined to be released in you, around you and through you are connected to your willingness to release the gifts of the Holy Spirit. Jesus manifested all of the gifts of the Spirit during His three-and-one half-year ministry. He is our model. We should prayerfully pursue all gifts of the Spirit so that we may reflect the life of Christ in our day and in our world.

A research statistic reveals a disturbing problem: a remarkable number of born-again Christians who have heard of spiritual gifts do not believe they have any spiritual gifts at all. Unfortunately, this number seems to be growing in the extended Body of Christ. Some people may have no teaching at all about spiritual gifts, or they may have faulty teaching.

You might be a well-taught believer who has already discovered your spiritual gifts, developed them and is functioning in those gifts—or perhaps you are not sure about your gifts, yet you desire to know and to use your spiritual gifts to encourage the manifestations of God's power in a sick and dying world. Whichever category you fit into, it is clear from the following passages of Scripture that you do have gifts:

Romans 12:4-7: Or as we have many members in one body, but all the members do not have the same function, so we, being many, are one body in Christ, and individually members of one another. Having then gifts differing according to the grace that is given to us, let us use them: if prophecy, let us prophesy in proportion to our faith.

1 Corinthians 12:4-8: There are diversities of gifts, but the same Spirit. There are differences of ministries, but the same Lord. And there are diversities of activities, but it is the same God who works all in all. But the manifestation of the Spirit is given to each one for the profit of all.

It Is Right to Use Your God-Given Gifts

When we speak of spiritual gifts, we mean the supernatural enabling of the Holy Spirit that equips a Christian for his or her work of service and ministry. It is right to use your God-given gifts in powerful and useful ministry every day of your life. First Peter 4:10 encourages us that "as each one has received a gift, minister it to one another, as good stewards of the manifold grace of God."

My wife, Sharon, comes from a very musical family—both of her parents sang and played instruments. Sharon's mother even won a state competition in music but chose to marry and pastor with her new husband instead of pursuing her musical career. Her father, on the other hand, was self-taught. He had been abandoned as a child and grew up in a boys' home so he didn't think much about music as a youth. Then, in his early 20s, he taught himself how to play trumpet, trombone, piano and a few more instruments. I think I'll let Sharon tell the story:

My mother's incredible voice somehow seemed to bypass my genes. And even though my father was a self-taught but very gifted songwriter, I never thought anything would happen from that heritage because I didn't have Mom's range or any training in writing music.

For several years, I struggled with the discipline of practicing the piano and eventually started playing for the church youth group. Then, to my amazement at 19 years old, I was offered one of the leading roles in a musical drama. I loved it. After Frank and I married, my devotional times alone with the Lord were often consumed with a chorus running through my mind from a passage of Scripture that I had read. Before long, I found that God was pouring all kinds of music through me, so I started leading worship and writing songs for our church. This gift led to a new ministry involvement, though I call myself a "reluctant leader." Although I consider myself more of a background person, the musical gifting of God has brought me into the forefront and sometimes I've just had to step out in spite of my shaking knees and thunderous heart palpitations. God's gifting in me has kept me reliant upon Him and His power to flow through me. I have no training in songwriting and I don't really know what I'm doing, but I know who the gift comes from and I simply trust Him to write through me. The gift is God's and I am a steward of that gift.

Several years ago while I was at the dentist, I heard a melody and words in my head. I went home and wrote it down and that song has become a favorite in our church. Another time I went home to Australia and started playing on Grandma's piano. There I got the melody and words to "Crown Him King of Kings," a song that was picked up by Integrity Music and has traveled around the world. I've learned that our God gives good gifts to His children, whether or not we have the qualifications for receiving them. If I have a gift, so do you—and I challenge you to open it now.

Spiritual gifts are for today's believer and for today's Church. Dr. B.B. Warfield (1851-1921), the great Princeton theologian, wrote: "We believe in a wonder-working God but not in a wonder-working church."[2] (This is an unbiblical perspective that comes out of a dispensational view that the gifts are no longer needed and that they ceased with the 12 apostles and with the writing of the Scriptures.)

OUR FIRST SPIRITUAL GIFT
IS THE GIFT OF SALVATION

Salvation is the gift we receive when we are truly born again. Romans 5:15 says that "the free gift is not like the offense. For if by the one man's offense many died, much more the grace of God and the gift by the grace of the one Man, Jesus Christ, abounded to many."

Our salvation is a free gift that can be received by all those who ask Christ to forgive their sins and ask Him to enter into their inner man in order to take charge of their lives. Ephesians 2:8 says, "For by grace you have been saved through faith, and that not of yourselves; it is the gift of God."

The Gift of the Baptism of the Holy Spirit

Every believer may also receive the gift of the baptism of the Holy Spirit. In Acts 2:38 all people were called to repentance, the first step toward salvation. Peter also called all those who repented to be baptized in water and then to receive the gift of the Holy Spirit. Luke 11:9-13 says, "So I say to you, ask, and it will be given to you; seek, and you will find; knock, and it will be opened to you. For everyone who asks receives, and he who seeks finds, and to him who knocks it will be opened. If a son asks for bread from any father among you, will he give him a stone? Or if he asks for a fish, will he give him a serpent instead of a fish? Or if he asks for an egg, will he offer him a scorpion? If you then, being evil, know how to give good gifts to your children, how much more will your heavenly Father give the Holy Spirit to those who ask Him!"

We are to believe that our heavenly Father desires to give us the Holy Spirit as a good gift. All we need to do is ask. If you have never been born again, why not pause right now and repeat the following prayer:

Father God, I don't know You, but I want to. I pray that You would forgive me of my sins and cleanse me by the power of Christ's work on the cross. I believe Jesus died for me, rose from the dead and is alive right now receiving my prayer. Thank You, Jesus, for receiving me into Your family. Amen.

If you are born again but have never been baptized in the Holy Spirit, you may wish to stop and pray:

Lord, I need more of Your Spirit today. Overflow me with Your presence, fill me full of Your Spirit. I ask that You give me my own spiritual language as the Holy Spirit fills me.

All believers can also receive spiritual gifts that we will call grace gifts from God through the Holy Spirit. The Greek word for "gift" is *charisma*, which comes from the root word *charis*, meaning grace. A close relationship exists between our spiritual gifts and the grace of God. Romans 12:6 tells us that "having then gifts differing according to the grace that is given to us, let us use them: if prophecy, let us prophesy in proportion to our faith."

> *Spiritual gifts are given to the uneducated and the educated, to the mature and the immature, to people with sinful shortcomings, personal problems and feelings of unworthiness.*

Spiritual gifts are rooted in the grace of God and flow freely through imperfect people. Ephesians 4:7 says that "to each one of us grace was given according to the measure of Christ's gift." Our spiritual gifts are given to us so that we might minister in the power of the Spirit to others, both the saved and the unsaved. First Corinthians 12:7 tells us that "the manifestation of the Spirit is given to each one for the profit of all."

Our spiritual gifts are different from our natural talents. First Corinthians 12:4 explains that "there are diversities of gifts, but the same Spirit." As we see in 1 Corinthians 12:8, spiritual gifts can be discovered and developed by any and all believers:

> For to one is given the word of wisdom through the Spirit, to another the word of knowledge through the same Spirit.
> (See also 1 Pet. 4:10, 1 Cor. 12:31; 14:1,12,13.)

The Word of God commands us to eagerly desire spiritual gifts and to pray for and excel in the gifts that build the Church. This is not an option. Every believer is responsible!

We begin by gaining a right perspective on ourselves for seeing miracles. Romans 12:3 cautions, "For I say, through the grace given to me, to everyone who is among you, not to think of himself more highly than he ought to think, but to think soberly, as God has dealt to each one a measure of faith."

To think soberly is to realistically evaluate ourselves, seeing ourselves as God sees us. It is not allowing ourselves to think more highly of ourselves than we ought to think, making room for pure and proper thoughts about our lives, our ministries and our gifts. We are to recognize that part of our spiritual constitution is a measure of faith that God distributes to every believer.

Spiritual gifts are given to the uneducated and the educated, to the mature and the immature, to people with sinful shortcomings, personal problems and feelings of unworthiness. Nevertheless, we are to accept God's grace and not neglect our spiritual heritage. Paul exhorts Timothy in 1 Timothy 4:14, "Do not neglect the gift that is in you, which was given to you by prophecy with the laying on of the hands of the eldership." And Paul emphasizes the importance of this exhortation by repeating it in 2 Timothy 1:6, "Therefore I remind you to stir up the gift of God which is in you through the laying on of my hands."

THE SPIRITUAL GIFTS

As we understand the gifts, hopefully we will discover and activate our gifts. Let's carefully examine 1 Corinthians 12:4-11, which gives one of the best lists for spiritual gifts:

> There are diversities of gifts, but the same Spirit. There are differences of ministries, but the same Lord. And there are diversities of activities, but it is the same God who works all in all. But the manifestation of the Spirit is given to each one for the profit of all: for to one is given the word of wisdom through the Spirit, to another the word of knowledge through the same Spirit, to another faith by the same Spirit, to another gifts of healings by the same Spirit, to another the working of miracles,

to another prophecy, to another discerning of spirits, to another different kinds of tongues, to another the interpretation of tongues. But one and the same Spirit works all these things, distributing to each one individually as He wills.

Diversities of Gifts

The word "diversities" or "varieties" gives the idea of distribution—and clearly this distribution is done by the choice of the Holy Spirit. In other words, the gift's presence in someone does not necessarily signify great holiness, sanctification or maturity. People may confuse powerful giftings with a person's character or lifestyle, and yet they may not be the same. We should pursue holiness and right living, but the fact is that God uses sinful people who are still changing into mature believers.

Differences of Ministries

The word "ministries" (translated administration in some versions of the Bible) comes from the Greek word *diakonia*, which means service, especially service to or for God. It can refer to a recognized office of ministry, such as the place of apostles, prophets, evangelists and elders in the church. Or, it can also refer to the practice of offering charity to others in the name of Christ. But this is not all. It can also refer to the office of deacon in the church. And we should remember regarding this word "deacon" that in Acts 6 the same Philip who rendered "service" (Greek: *diakoneo*) in the distribution of alms to widows, just two chapters later in Acts 8 preached the gospel in Samaria, performed miraculous signs, banished demons from people and healed cripples, baptized new believers, obeyed the voice of the Lord to go to the dangerous southern road out of Jerusalem, met the Ethiopian official, led him to Christ, taught the Ethiopian how prophetic Scriptures were fulfilled in Jesus, baptized him, and then apparently was supernaturally transported to Azotus. *Diakonia*, in other words, could perform many different kinds of "ministries" (services) for strengthening the Church and serving the Lord.

Diversities of Activities

The word "activities" comes from the Greek word *energema*, and in this context means that which is wrought or accomplished by the Holy Spirit. These activities (sometimes translated workings or operations) reveal both the availability and the effect of divine power. They accompany the varieties of gifts and ministries Paul has already mentioned.

MANIFESTATIONS OF THE SPIRIT

The next verse gives some examples of how the Holy Spirit manifests for the edification and profit of everyone in the Church. We can categorize these manifestations three ways:

1. Discernment gifts, which include the word of wisdom, word of knowledge and discerning of spirits. These gifts "see" things as God sees them. They are God's insights into people's lives, circumstances and, at times, even the secrets of their past, present or future.
2. Power gifts, which include the gift of faith, the gift of healing and the gift of miracles. These gifts are channels of the "supernatural power" of God and God's hand to touch people. They can be seen as the divine power of God is released through the divine energy of God, which accomplishes a particular result in word or work.
3. Speech gifts, which include the gift of prophecy, the gift of tongues and the gift of the interpretation of tongues.

The first group could be considered the eyes of God, the second group the hands of God and this third group the mouth of God. Throughout Scripture we see God as a "speaking God," who desires to communicate with His people. These gifts may be used to minister to people by spiritual means that come by faith, encouragement and insight into people's lives. The spoken Word of God has power to work supernaturally in people's lives every day.

Pertaining to miracles, these manifestation gifts are important. Word gifts help us know how and for what to pray. Power gifts pertain to effective results of our prayers, and language gifts relate specifically to praying in unknown tongues and in discerning what the Spirit desires to do.

The gifts are tools for the believer to use at any given moment—spiritual tools for spiritual situations. The right tool at the right time in the right place used by the right person will have the right results.

You have been singled out to receive just the right gift to accomplish Kingdom works. These gifts have not been put into your hands because of how good you are or how talented you are. They are grace gifts, so in a way, you had nothing to do with it. The Giver of the gifts decided to make a deposit into your life, a free gift, a generous gift, a powerful gift. The gift is yours, but it is not just for your enjoyment. It is for the people around you—the hurting, confused, broken, unsaved, the single, the married, the rich and the poor. It is for those in need of a God-touch. You are their hope. You are their way out of bondage. Your gift is important!

Now, let's take a closer look at the gifts.

The Word of Wisdom

The word of wisdom is a word inspired by the Holy Spirit and revealed to the believer. It is seeing what God sees in a situation and saying it. It is applying God's wisdom to a specific situation. For example, in 1 Kings 3:24-27, King Solomon was given a word of wisdom to evidence the truth when two mothers claimed to be the same baby's biological mother.

> The king said, "Bring me a sword." So they brought a sword before the king. And the king said, "Divide the living child in two, and give half to one, and half to the other." Then the woman whose son was living spoke to the king, for she yearned with compassion for her son; and she said, "O my lord, give her the living child, and by no means kill him!" But the other said, "Let

him be neither mine nor yours, but divide him." So the king answered and said, "Give the first woman the living child, and by no means kill him; she is his mother."

(See also Matt. 22:15-22; 2 Kings 5:8-14.)

The Word of Knowledge

The word of knowledge is a word inspired by the Holy Spirit that reveals facts or pieces of information not seen before, but now is seen in the new light of the Holy Spirit's knowledge. A word of knowledge is a particular word given in a particular instance, thus revealing God's mind toward a specific situation. In Acts 5:1-11, we see the word of knowledge operating through the apostle Peter when he was supernaturally told that Ananias and his wife, Sapphira, were lying about the amount of money they received for a parcel of land. Jesus also operated though a word of knowledge:

> John 4:17: The woman answered and said, "I have no husband."
> Jesus said to her, "You have well said, 'I have no husband.'"
> Matthew 9:4: Jesus, knowing their thoughts, said, "Why do you think evil in your hearts?"
> (See also 1 Sam. 9:20; Matt. 9:2; 5:6.)

The Discerning of Spirits

The discerning of spirits is the spiritual capacity to judge whether the spirit operating has a source that is human, demonic or divine. It is a supernatural perception into the spiritual realm. The apostle Paul provides a good example of the discerning of spirits at work in Acts 16:16-18:

> Now it happened, as we went to prayer, that a certain slave girl possessed with a spirit of divination met us, who brought her masters much profit by fortune-telling. This girl followed Paul and us, and cried out, saying, "These men are the servants of the Most High God, who proclaim to us the way of salvation." And

this she did for many days. But Paul, greatly annoyed, turned and said to the spirit, "I command you in the name of Jesus Christ to come out of her." And he came out that very hour.

First Thessalonians 5:21 says that we are to "test all things; hold fast what is good." We must even test our own motives and words lest we think that only those who are demonically possessed can be used for our enemy's work. Consider the following scenario from Matthew 16:21-23:

> From that time Jesus began to show to His disciples that He must go to Jerusalem, and suffer many things from the elders and chief priests and scribes, and be killed, and be raised the third day. Then Peter took Him aside and began to rebuke Him, saying, "Far be it from you, Lord; this shall not happen to you!" But He turned and said to Peter, "Get behind me, Satan! You are an offense to me, for you are not mindful of the things of God, but the things of men."

The Gift of Faith

The gift of faith is a Holy Spirit-inspired level of expectation that God *can* and *will* move in any and all circumstances. This kind of faith is usually accompanied by a word to stand on. It is both the irresistible knowledge of God's intervention at a certain point and the authority to effect this intervention through the power of the Holy Spirit.

In Genesis 22:1-18 we read the story of Abraham's gift of faith as he ascended Mount Moriah to offer Isaac as a sacrifice to the Lord. Throughout this passage of Scripture we see the gift of faith being expressed (italics added):

> Verse 5: And Abraham said to his young men, "Stay here with the donkey; the lad and I will go yonder and worship, and *we will* come back to you."

Verse 8: And Abraham said, "My son, *God will provide* for Himself the lamb for a burnt offering." So the two of them went together. (See also Matt. 17:20; 21:21,22; 1 Cor. 13:2.)

The Gifts of Healing

The "gifts of healing" is in the plural. Many different kinds of illnesses affect spirit, soul and body, and many different gifts of healing are required to minister to spirit, soul and body. Let's consider the story of Naaman in 2 Kings 5:1-15. In this story we see the gifts of healing working through Elisha to affect first the soul, then the body and finally the spirit of Naaman. Let's read it together:

> Now Naaman, commander of the army of the king of Syria, was a great and honorable man in the eyes of his master, because by him the Lord had given victory to Syria. He was also a mighty man of valor, but a leper. And the Syrians had gone out on raids, and had brought back captive a young girl from the land of Israel. She waited on Naaman's wife. Then she said to her mistress, "If only my master were with the prophet who is in Samaria! For he would heal him of his leprosy." And Naaman went in and told his master, saying, "Thus and thus said the girl who is from the land of Israel." Then the king of Syria said, "Go now, and I will send a letter to the king of Israel." So he departed and.... Then Naaman went with his horses and chariot, and he stood at the door of Elisha's house. And Elisha sent a messenger to him, saying, "Go and wash in the Jordan seven times, and your flesh shall be restored to you, and you shall be clean." But Naaman became furious, and went away and said, "Indeed, I said to myself, 'He will surely come out to me, and stand and call on the name of the Lord his God, and wave his hand over the place, and heal the leprosy.' "Are not the Abanah and the Pharpar, the rivers of Damascus, better than all the waters of Israel? Could I not wash in them and be clean?" So he turned and went away in a rage.

And his servants came near and spoke to him, and said, "My father, if the prophet had told you to do something great, would you not have done it? How much more then, when he says to you, 'Wash, and be clean'?" So he went down and dipped seven times in the Jordan, according to the saying of the man of God; and his flesh was restored like the flesh of a little child, and he was clean. And he returned to the man of God, he and all his aides, and came and stood before him; and he said, "Indeed, now I know that there is no God in all the earth, except in Israel; now therefore, please take a gift from your servant."

Notice that Elisha didn't even go out to Naaman, but sent his messengers to tell him to dip seven times in the Jordan. Perhaps that was to keep Naaman from looking to a prophet rather than the Lord for his healing. Perhaps it was to show Naaman that he was not in control. The point is that Elisha ordered Naaman to do a very humbling thing in order to heal the leprous pride in Naaman's soul before healing the leprosy in his physical body. Eventually Naaman's healing extended to his spirit when he came to confess the God of Israel as the one true God. When the gifts of healing are operating through a believer, he or she will work according to the Holy Spirit's direction, which can require a very different action in each case.

(See also Luke 6:19; 7:7; 8:43; Mark 8:22-26.)

The Gift of Miracles

The gift of miracles is a working of the Holy Spirit in and through a person to see supernatural occurrences and activities. Beyond the healing of the sick, the power of God is released in such a way that miraculous things happen. Acts 5:12 says, "And through the hands of the apostles many signs and wonders were done among the people."

We see the prophet Isaiah operating in the gift of miracles when King Hezekiah asked for a sign that he would be healed:

And Hezekiah said to Isaiah, "What is the sign that the Lord will heal me, and that I shall go up to the house of the Lord the third day?" Then Isaiah said, "This is the sign to you from the Lord, that the Lord will do the thing which He has spoken: shall the shadow go forward ten degrees or go backward ten degrees?" And Hezekiah answered, "It is an easy thing for the shadow to go down ten degrees; no, but let the shadow go backward ten degrees." So Isaiah the prophet cried out to the Lord, and He brought the shadow ten degrees backward, by which it had gone down on the sundial of Ahaz.

(See also Mark 4:35-41; Acts 6:8; 8:16; 19:11,12.)

The Gift of Prophecy

The gift of prophecy is a supernaturally inspired utterance by the Holy Spirit in one's own language. Its purpose is to build up, instruct, comfort and in some cases give hints into the future.

Prophecy in the New Testament Church always assumed and built on the truths of the Old Testament and the foundation of the holy apostles (Eph. 2:20; 3:5), and never contradicted what God had clearly revealed in biblical prophecy and instruction. Paul's early missionary band consisted of "prophets and teachers" (Acts 13:1). Judas and Silas, who were prophets, used their gifting to exhort and strengthen the brethren (Acts 15:32). Prophecy came in dreams and visions, like Paul's vision of the Macedonian calling, "Come over to help us" (Acts 16:9), as well as Agabus's predictions of famine (Acts 11:28) and Paul's imprisonment at the hands of the Gentiles (Acts 21:9,10). People "prophesied" when they were filled with the Holy Spirit (Acts 19:6). The New Testament Church was not to "despise" prophecy (1 Thess. 5:20). Rather, the Church listened with discerning ears to the voice of prophecy. They did not just willy-nilly follow anyone who claimed to be a prophet; prophecies were to be weighed by those experienced in hearing God's voice (1 Cor. 14:32). The New Testament Church was aware of the seductive power of false prophets, and diligently warned against them (2 Pet. 2:1; 1 John 4:1).

I have personally received numerous prophetic words, and I always test them in the light of Scripture. I'll never forget the time Demos Shakarian (1913-1993), founder of the Full Gospel Businessmen's Fellowship, visited our church in Eugene. We were bulging at the seams with no where to park and no place to grow, but I hadn't shared with Demos that we were considering the purchase of a large boat building. Then, Demos began to prophesy and could never have known the details of the word he gave. "The building you are trying to buy is the wrong building." I didn't know what to think. He continued, "The property you are to buy is on the city limits line. It is owned by a farmer or someone like that. It's 15 or 20 acres." He described the whole place with amazing detail. The following Monday, I received a call that the deal on the boat building had fallen through and that we would have to look for another property. I asked our Realtor if he knew of any large pieces of property on the edge of the city limits. Surprisingly, he told me about a contractor who had 10 acres for sale, but the property was landlocked by 5 acres that were owned by an old rabbit farmer and his wife who refused to sell. I decided to visit the farmer and share the prophetic word with him. He and his wife discussed the sale and decided they wanted their property to be used for God. We bought the property and God received the glory, all because one man stepped out in faith with a prophetic gift.

The Gift of Tongues

The gift of tongues is defined as the power to speak by the Holy Spirit in a spiritual language or an unlearned language. We see the gift of tongues clearly at work in Acts 2:1-4:

> Now when the Day of Pentecost had fully come, they were all with one accord in one place. And suddenly there came a sound from heaven, as of a rushing mighty wind, and it filled the whole house where they were sitting. Then there appeared to them

divided tongues, as of fire, and one sat upon each of them. And they were all filled with the Holy Spirit and began to speak with other tongues, as the Spirit gave them utterance.

This event, which happened on the Feast of Pentecost, the fiftieth day after Passover, describes the birthday of the Church. Many churches derive Pentecostal in their names from this great event. Just after this event, the disciples spilled out into the streets, and Jews from the entire Mediterranean region who had come for the Feast of Pentecost heard the gospel in their own languages. It was a miracle of communication from God, from "tongues of fire" to "we hear them speaking in our own tongues the wonderful works of God."

Later, the apostle Paul describes the gift of tongues as a prayer of private edification or devotion that profits the spirit but not the rational understanding: "For he who speaks in a tongue does not speak to men but to God, for no one understands him; however, in the spirit he speaks mysteries" (1 Cor. 14:2). And "if I pray in a tongue, my spirit prays, but my understanding is unfruitful" (1 Cor. 14:14).

Paul says he wishes all spoke in tongues (v. 5) and that he himself speaks in tongues more than any (v. 18), but that better is the gift of interpretation. Paul says the gift of tongues only benefits the Church if it is interpreted, as we shall see in the next subsection. Notice in reading 1 Corinthians 14 that the interpretation of tongues is closely associated with the gift of prophecy.

The Interpretation of Tongues

The interpretation of tongues is to render tongues understandable to the audience, thus producing spiritual profit. The interpretation must always be judged by the Word of God for spiritual quality and scriptural correctness.

There is an extended discussion of the protocol on how to use tongues and the interpretation of tongues/prophecy in public worship in 1 Corinthians 14. Here are some guidelines:

- Tongues should be interpreted. When tongues are interpreted properly, it brings revelation, knowledge, prophecy, instruction and edification (vv. 6,12).

- Tongues uninterpreted bring confusion (vv. 7-12). Those who pray/speak in tongues should pray for interpretation (v. 13). Prayers and singing can be "with the mind" (intelligible language) or "with the Spirit" (tongues), but if we pray and sing "in the Spirit," those around us won't understand what we're saying, so it is relatively unprofitable (vv. 14-17). In public worship, five intelligible words are better than ten thousand unintelligible ones (vv. 18,19).

- Tongues prophetically interpreted in the church are a sign for unbelievers that God is among us. Tongues alone will lead to ridicule (vv. 22-25).

ACTIVATING YOUR SPIRITUAL GIFTS

The giver of varied gifts is the Holy Spirit. Gifts, service and workings are different forms of the same ministry of the triune God whose gifts cannot be superficially separated. There is only one God whose grace is distributed by the Spirit to individuals as He wishes. It is according to His incomparable justice and power, not according to the merits or will of any particular person. The gifts are for the upbuilding of His Church by each believer who receives the Spirit's gift, so that he or she may be useful both to self and others. Every church should create an atmosphere where people know they are valued, respected and trusted to serve.

During the Depression, Mr. Yates struggled to maintain possession of his sheep ranch. Because he couldn't pay his mortgage, he was losing his ranch. He didn't have enough money for clothes and food, so he and his family lived on government subsidy. Every day, he looked out at the sheep on his Texas hills and worried about the bills that were piling up. One day a crew from an oil company came by and asked permission to drill on his land to see if there was oil. At 1,115 feet they struck a huge oil reserve. The first well came in at 80,000 barrels of oil a day, and many wells drilled after that came in twice as large. Even 30 years after the first well had been drilled, they were pumping 125,000 barrels of oil a day from his barren land. The oil had always been there and the rights to it had always been his because he owned the land. He was a multi-millionaire living on government handouts, a rich man living in poverty because he did not know what he had.

BELIEVE YOU HAVE ALREADY RECEIVED
A GIFT OR GIFTS FROM THE HOLY SPIRIT

Ask the Holy Spirit to reveal to you which gift or gifts you have (see 1 Cor. 12:11; 1 Tim. 4:14). Each individual's spiritual passions and disciplines affect every member in the Body. The working of the Body consists of the fact that its many members supply the things that the other parts lack. When a member refuses development, resists spiritual disciplines or is lazy toward his or her gifting, the whole Body is hindered to some measure. Each person receives the gifts, so that by governing his or her life by divine constraints, he or she may be useful to the Body. If this member becomes spiritually alive, filled with the Spirit, ready to serve when needed, and has developed his or her giftings to the highest degree, then the whole Church prospers.

> *When a member refuses development, resists spiritual disciplines or is lazy toward his or her gifting, the whole Body is hindered to some measure.*

Ask yourself four questions:

1. What do I enjoy doing?
2. What service or work has God blessed in my life?
3. When others encourage me, what do they see in me?
4. What has the Holy Spirit been speaking to me about?

Believe that you have a unique and important place in the Body of Christ and that your supply to the Body is absolutely essential for its health and maturity.

Your gift is not for your benefit but for the common good and spiritual growth of the Body (see 1 Cor. 12:15-18; Eph. 4:16). Never think, *I am not important. I don't have anything to offer. I'm not needed. I don't need you.* There is no room for self-centered, self-contained, self-sufficient attitudes in the Body of Christ.

Believe that you can use your spiritual gifts by faith, by obedience and with a servant's heart—then memorize the following verses:

Ecclesiastes 9:10: Whatever your hand finds to do, do it with your might; for there is no work or device or knowledge or wisdom in the grave where you are going.

Mark 10:45: For even the Son of Man did not come to be served, but to serve, and to give His life a ransom for many.

Luke 16:10: He who is faithful in what is least is faithful also in much; and he who is unjust in what is least is unjust also in much.

2 Timothy 1:6: Therefore I remind you to stir up the gift of God which is in you through the laying on of my hands.

2 Timothy 2:2: And the things that you have heard from me among many witnesses, commit these to faithful men who will be able to teach others also.

Step out, get involved, find a need and minister to it. In Carthage, North Africa, during the fourth century, the bubonic plague had brought terror to the heart of the city. As death spread across the city, people retreated into their homes, terrified of helping anyone lest they, too, catch this deadly disease. Because no one would help, the sick lay dying alone with no one to bring them aid, and the dead went unburied. However, a group of people were committed to use their gifts and to serve not only their church, but also their community. They were called the "parabolani," those who put their lives in hazard for others, risk-takers. History records the decisive fact that Carthage was saved from destruction because of these "risk-takers" who used their gifts to serve a need.

What about you...what risks will you take for Jesus' sake?

Notes

1. Walter B. Knight, ed., *Knight's Master Book of Illustrations,* taken from the "Sunday School Times" (Grand Rapids: Wm. B. Eerdmans Publishing Company, 1956), p. 289.
2. B.B. Warfield, *Counterfeit Miracles* (www.ChristianBeliefs.org) http://christianbeliefs.org/books/cm/cm-marvels.html.

9

DURING THE WAR, "TRIAGE" REFERRED to a decision-making policy, indicating what assistance would be given the wounded. It was up to the doctors to "color tag" the wounded, placing them in one of three categories according to the severity of their condition: a red tag represented hopeless, suggesting the patient be left to die; a blue tag indicated that immediate medical care was necessary and should be given to save the patient; a yellow tag meant that the wounded soldier would survive even without treatment. Because medical supplies were limited, only those with blue tags received medical attention.

One day, Lou, a severely wounded soldier who had a leg that was blown apart, lay on a stretcher with a red tag. A nurse passing by noticed that Lou was conscious and began to talk with him. After getting to know Lou as a person, she couldn't just let him die—so she broke the rules and replaced his red tag with a blue one.

Lou was transported to the hospital in the back of a truck and spent the next several months there. You guessed it! Lou lived and went on to marry the nurse. Yes, he was minus one leg, but Lou led a full and happy life because someone broke the rules and changed his tag.[1]

I'm writing this book, my friend, because I want you to remove the red tag from the miracle and healing ministry that has been placed on the Church. I want you to personally take responsibility for bringing life to a world of hurting, hopeless people who have been diagnosed with man's red tag when God, the Great Physician and Healer, has said, "I have come that they may have life, and that they may have it more abundantly" (John 10:10). Permit me to share a little history.

RED-TAGGED THINKING IN THE CHURCH

During the twentieth century, the Church suffered with a faulty "red tagged" theology concerning healing and miracles. Generally speaking, the Church believed that the age of miracles had ceased with the apostolic period and that God no longer healed people. This view is short, limited and erroneous. I lament the fact that today's Church seems to have descended to the level of the natural in preaching, in soul winning, in doing church and specifically in the area of healing. The gifts of the Spirit have been supplanted by the arts of logic and rhetoric when it is God's desire that the miraculous function in His Church. He wants the gifts to be operating fully. He wants a full release of His power through His people.

Today, the subject of divine healing is awakening with unusual interest throughout the world, both within and outside the Church. Even the media has begun to pursue an interest in "supernatural" healings. We as Christians, therefore, must pursue genuine, authentic, biblical and supernatural healings and miracles.

The healing and gift-based ministry is a normal and biblical part of a life of faith in Christ. It is not something to be overlooked, ignored and left in the past—neither is it to be elevated above any other ministry. Rather, it should be kept in proper balance as simply a normal aspect of what it means to live under the reign of God.

Christianity, with its roots of believing the supernatural, has been disempowered and overshadowed by modern liberal theology. An academic community has risen to resist the healing ministry as an unbiblical, erroneous ministry (see Matt. 16:4; Mark 13:22; 1 Cor. 1:22-23). Some modern theologians hold to a "cessationist position," asserting that the New Testament epistles show only slight interest in miracles, and drawing the implication that the nature of the sign gifts—healing, miracles, prophecy, tongues and interpretation of tongues—is only temporary.

Cessation is absolutely not my line of belief, and I personally see in the Epistles much evidence that the apostles did not think the gifts of power were unnecessary after the Day of Pentecost. At least five Epistles devote explicit attention to the gifts of the Spirit: Romans 12:3-8; 1 Corinthians 12-14; Ephesians 4:1-16; 1 Thessalonians 5:19-22; and 1 Peter 4:10,11. The New Testament writers did not deal with the gifts, including healing and miracles as temporary, but as permanent. The Scriptures are clear that the gifts of the Spirit, the ministry of miracles and the releasing of the supernatural are intended to be operational throughout the Church Age and that they are vital to the ministry God wants to grant us because we *all* need them.

> *The Church is afraid to expect much from God because it has been disappointed so many times, but this thinking is a stronghold of "no expectation" that needs to be confronted and challenged.*

Some "red taggers" hold to the tenets of modern science, which says that nothing can be true unless proved by scientific method. They say that if the supernatural cannot be understood scientifically, it must not be real. Is belief in the supernatural moving toward extinction because it cannot be scientifically explained? Heaven forbid!

Extremists, frauds and charlatans have caused a reproach upon the healing ministry, and some extreme practices within Pentecostal groups have caused reaction, question and denial of the healing ministry—but we don't throw out God's work just because of a few sick workers.

Churches today need strong, biblical, theological preaching on the subject of healing and miracles from the pulpit, creating a spirit of faith and an expectation for healing and miracles to operate. There has been and still seems to be a suppressed attitude toward expectation. The Church is afraid to expect much from God because it has been disappointed so many times, but this fear-based thinking is a stronghold of "no expectation" that has and always will need to be confronted and challenged.

In the years approaching the Civil War in America, Horace Bushnell was a leading theologian who observed that:

Christian souls were falling into "a stupor of intellectual fatality.... Prayer becomes a kind of dumb-bell exercise, good as exercise, but never to be answered. The word is good to be exegetically handled, but there is no light of interpretation in souls, more immediate; all truth is to be secondhand truth, never a vital beam of God's own light.... Expectation is gone—God is too far off, too much imprisoned by laws, to allow expectation from Him. The Christian world has been gravitating, visibly, more and more, toward this vanishing point of faith, for whole centuries, and especially since the modern era began to shape the thoughts of men by only scientific methods. Religion has fallen into the domain of the mere understanding, and so it has become a kind of wisdom to not believe much, therefore to expect as little."

Let Him [God] now break forth in miracle and holy gifts, let it be seen that He is still the living God, in the midst of His dead people, and they will be quickened to a resurrection by the sight. Now they see that God can do something still, and has His liberty. He can hear prayers, He can help them triumph in dark hours, their darkest sins He can help them master, all His promises in the Scripture He can fulfill, and they go to Him with great expectations. They see, in these gifts, that the Scripture stands, that the graces and works, and holy fruits of the Apostolic ages, are also for them. It is as if they had now a proof experimental of the resources embodied in the Christian plan. The living God, immediately revealed, and not historically only, begets a feeling of present life and power, and religion is no more a tradition, a secondhand light, but a grace of God unto salvation, operative now.[2]

A spiritual war existed then and remains today. It is a war fought within the contexts of natural man, a war that fights against God's will, God's best and God's plan for humanity—body, soul and spirit (see Matt. 8:15; Acts 9:36; Phil. 2:25-30). Spiritual resistance to healing, signs and wonders is strong because, throughout Scripture and history, they were gateways to the harvest of souls (see Matt. 9:8; 14:14; John 9:3; Acts 8:6-8).

HENRIETTA MEARS, A LIFE CHANGED THROUGH HEALING

One young soul whose life was changed through healing was Henrietta Mears. In 1906, a 16-year-old Henrietta (later known as Dr. Henrietta Mears, who in 1933 launched Gospel Light Publications and in the 1950s wrote the best-selling Christian book *What the Bible Is All About*) had a painful accident. She was jabbed in the pupil of her eye with a hat pin. Doctors could do nothing for the condition and predicted possible blindness for her. Though Henrietta's family attended the First Baptist Church of Minneapolis, they asked close friend Mr. Ingersoll, an elder in the local Presbyterian church, to come and pray for Henrietta's damaged eye in accordance with James 5:14-16, "Is anyone among you sick? Let him call for the elders of the church, and let them pray over him, anointing him with oil in the name of the Lord. And the prayer of faith will save the sick, and the Lord will raise him up. And if he has committed sins, he will be forgiven. Confess your trespasses to one another, and pray for one another, that you may be healed. The effective, fervent prayer of a righteous man avails much."

Henrietta had no doubt that the God who had made her could also heal her eye—and He did. Specialists who later examined the eye, agreed that there was indeed a hole in the pupil and shook their heads in amazement that she could see anything out of it. That she was, in fact, seeing could not be explained except that God had stretched forth His hand and healed her eye, even though the hole remained! Henrietta learned from this experience and from her mother to accept all Scripture at face value. For God to touch her body simply meant taking Him at His Word.

IT IS RIGHT TO BELIEVE IN MIRACLES

If God exists, miracles are possible! It is right to pray for the sick, believing they will improve and be healed. Luke 4:40, for example, tells us that "when the sun was setting, all those who had any that were sick with various diseases brought them to Him; and He laid His hands on every one of them and healed them." And Acts 5:16 allows us a glimpse into the healing ministry of the Church in the first century. Read it with me:

> Also a multitude gathered from the surrounding cities to Jerusalem, bringing sick people and those who were tormented by unclean spirits, and they were all healed.

First Peter 2:24 was a foundational doctrine for the Early Church. In this Scripture, the apostle Peter exhorted the Church with, "Who Himself bore our sins in His own body on the tree, that we, having died to sins, might live for righteousness—by whose stripes you were healed." We are to believe the words of Peter today as well as the words of Mark 16:17,18:

> And these signs will follow those who believe: In My name they will cast out demons; they will speak with new tongues; they will take up serpents; and if they drink anything deadly, it will by no means hurt them; they will lay hands on the sick, and they will recover.

I believe in the God of the Bible, and He is and always has been a healing God. Exodus 15:26 says, "If you diligently heed the voice of the Lord your God and do what is right in His sight, give ear to His commandments and keep all His statutes, I will put none of the diseases on you which I have brought on the Egyptians. For I am the Lord who heals you." We at City Bible Church sing a beautiful little chorus written from this verse, the words are simple yet powerful and faith building:

I am the Lord that healeth thee,
I am the Lord, your Healer.
I sent My Word
And healed your diseases.
I am the Lord, your Healer[3]

Scripture confirms that our God is and always has been a healing God. The Hebrew word for "heal" is *rapha*, which is used to refer to restoring a wrong, restoring the sick to wholeness, restoring the broken bone or the deficient condition to its original working order or proper state, to make whole. "Sickness" means to be weak, debilitated. To be sick is to suffer, to be in pain, to degenerate to a lesser level. The Bible teaches us that God is a healing God, a restoring God, a repairing God. Let's ponder the healing attributes of God as we read the following Scriptures (italics added):

• **The God who is able to heal:**

Deuteronomy 32:39: Now see that I, even I, am He, and there is no God besides Me; I kill and I make alive; I wound and I *heal*; nor is there any who can deliver from My hand.

• **The God who heals our wounds:**

Jeremiah 30:17: "For I will *restore health* to you and *heal* you of your wounds," says the Lord, "because they called you an outcast saying: 'This is Zion; no one seeks her.'"

- **The God who restores our health:**

Jeremiah 33:6: "Behold, I will bring it *health* and *healing*; I will *heal* them and reveal to them the abundance of peace and truth."

- **The God who honors repentance with healing:**

Hosea 6:1: Come, and let us return to the Lord; for He has torn, but He will *heal* us; He has stricken, but He will bind us up.

- **The God who covers us with His healings:**

Malachi 4:2: "But to you who fear My name, the Son of Righteousness shall arise with *healing in His wings*; and you shall go out and grow fat like stall-fed calves."

- **The God who heals the nations:**

Revelation 22:2: "In the middle of its street, and on either side of the river, was the tree of life, which bore twelve fruits, each tree yielding its fruit every month. The leaves of the tree were for the *healing* of the nations."

- **The God who sends His Word to heal:**

Psalm 107:20: He sent His word and *healed* them, and delivered them from their destructions.

- **The God who heals through the cross of Christ:**

Isaiah 53:5: But He was wounded for our transgressions, He was bruised for our iniquities; the chastisement for our peace was upon Him, and by His stripes we are *healed*.

- **The God who brings life and healing:**

Ezekiel 47:9: "And it shall be that every living thing that moves, wherever the rivers go, will live. There will be a very great multitude of fish, because these waters go there; for they will be *healed*, and everything will live wherever the river goes."

Our God is an awesome God who has power to heal and to make whole again. Nothing is too hard for God. He created humankind, and because He created us, He knows how to heal us (see Gen. 1:28). Our God is a God of creative power, and He is able to do things outside of our human thinking and believing, to do things outside the box. Scripture talks about God's power in Exodus 15:6 when it says, "Your right hand, O Lord, has become glorious in power; Your right hand, O Lord, has dashed the enemy in pieces." The psalmist said that he looked for God's power in the sanctuary, to see His power and glory manifested (see Ps. 63:2). God's power has not changed.

Let us believe that what happened in the Gospel of Luke will happen again today in every gathering of God's people:

Luke 5:17: Now it happened on a certain day, as He was teaching, that there were Pharisees and teachers of the law sitting by, who had come out of every town of Galilee, Judea, and Jerusalem. And the power of the Lord was present to heal them.

Luke 6:19: And the whole multitude sought to touch Him, for power went out from Him and healed them all.

God has proven Himself to be a healing God!

PEOPLE GOD HEALED IN SCRIPTURE

Now that we have established that God is a healing God, let's examine some biblical examples of people who were healed.

Abimelech - Genesis 20:17,18: So Abraham prayed to God; and God healed Abimelech, his wife, and his female servants. Then they bore children; for the Lord had closed up all the wombs of the house of Abimelech because of Sarah, Abraham's wife.

Hezekiah - 2 Kings 20:5-8: Return and tell Hezekiah the leader of My people, "Thus says the Lord, the God of David your father: I have heard your prayer, I have seen your tears; surely I will heal you. On the third day you shall go up to the house of the Lord. And I will add to your days fifteen years. I will deliver you and this city from the hand of the king of Assyria; and I will defend this city for My own sake, and for the sake of My servant David." Then Isaiah said, "Take a lump of figs." So they took and laid it on the boil, and he recovered.

Miriam - Numbers 12:12,13: "Please do not let her be as one dead, whose flesh is half consumed when he comes out of his mother's womb!" So Moses cried out to the Lord, saying, "Please heal her, O God, I pray!"

Namaan - 2 Kings 5:3-7,11,13,14: Then she said to her mistress, "If only my master were with the prophet who is in Samaria! For he would heal him of his leprosy." And Naaman went in and told his master, saying, "Thus and thus said the girl who is from the land of Israel." Then the king of Syria said, "Go now, and I will send a letter to the king of Israel." So he departed and took with him ten talents of silver, six thousand shekels of gold, and ten changes of clothing. Then he brought the letter to the king of Israel, which said, "Now be advised, when this letter comes to you, that I have sent Naaman my servant to you, that you may heal him of his leprosy." And it happened, when the king of Israel read the letter, that he tore his clothes and said, "Am I God, to kill and make alive, that this man sends a man to me to heal him of his leprosy? Therefore please consider, and see how he seeks a quarrel with me."..."But Naaman became furious, and went away and said, "Indeed, I said to myself, 'He will surely come out to me, and stand and call on the name of the Lord his God, and wave his hand over the place, and heal the leprosy.'"...And his servants came near and spoke to him, and said, "My father, if the prophet had told you to do something great, would you not have done it? How much more then, when he says to you, 'Wash, and be clean'?" So he went down and dipped seven times in the Jordan, according to the saying of the man of God; and his flesh was restored like the flesh of a little child, and he was clean.

During his healing ministry, Oral Roberts used what he called the "point of contact," which is something you do to release your faith to God in order to create an expectation to receive your miracle. Here in Namaan's situation, the point of contact was the action of dipping seven times in the Jordan River.

GOD HEALS TODAY

As we have previously established, Hebrews 13:8 is our foundational Scripture for believing in a healing Jesus today:

Jesus Christ is the same yesterday, today, and forever.

Christ was sent from heaven to earth on a mission that involved the redemption of humankind—body, soul and spirit. Christ's mission involved healing and miracles. In Isaiah 61:1 it is said of Jesus that "the Spirit of the Lord God is upon Me, because the Lord has anointed Me to preach good tidings to the poor; He has sent Me to heal the broken-hearted, to proclaim liberty to the captives, and the opening of the prison to those who are bound." Jesus quoted Isaiah as He opened His miracle ministry in Luke 4:18.

Jesus performed many miracles and healed every kind of sickness and disease. The people mocked Him, resisted Him, persecuted Him and turned away from His power. In Luke 4:23 He said to them, "You will surely say this proverb to Me, 'Physician, heal yourself! Whatever we have heard done in Capernaum, do also here in Your country.'"

According to Acts 10:38, Jesus was clearly anointed by God to work miracles:

God anointed Jesus of Nazareth with the Holy Spirit and with power, who went about doing good and healing all who were oppressed by the devil, for God was with Him.

Wherever He went, great multitudes followed Him because of the miracle power. Matthew 12:15 says that "great multitudes followed Him, and He healed them all." And Matthew 14:14 tells us that "when Jesus went out He saw a great multitude; and He was moved with compassion for them, and healed their sick."

Today the Church around the world grows rapidly when the supernatural is released with miracles, signs, wonders and healings. If the devil wanted (and he does) to stop the Church from growing with new conversion growth, where do you think he would work overtime to steal from the Church? Of course! The power ministry that God has given the Church. The power ministry promised to the Church is in the releasing of miracles and healings. We must contend for the miracles and healings because this ministry will not come easily or quickly. Rise in faith and pursue the rights to operate in the realm of the supernatural.

GOSPEL HEALINGS OF JESUS

Let the following list of healings seen in the life of Christ inspire you to lift your vision and to release your faith in your own world.

The centurion's servant - Matthew 8:5-7: Now when Jesus had entered Capernaum, a centurion came to Him, pleading with Him, saying, "Lord, my servant is lying at home paralyzed, dreadfully tormented." And Jesus said to him, "I will come and heal him."

The man with the withered hand - Matthew 12:10,13: And behold, there was a man who had a withered hand. And they asked Him, saying, "Is it lawful to heal on the Sabbath?"—that they might accuse Him.... Then He said to the man, "Stretch out your hand." And he stretched it out, and it was restored as whole as the other.

The paralyzed man - Luke 5:17,18: Now it happened on a certain day, as He was teaching, that there were Pharisees and teachers of the law sitting by, who had come out of every town of Galilee, Judea, and Jerusalem. And the power of the Lord was present to heal them. Then behold, men brought on a bed a man who was paralyzed, whom they sought to bring in and lay before Him.

All kinds of sicknesses and diseases - Matthew 4:23: And Jesus went about all Galilee, teaching in their synagogues, preaching the gospel of the kingdom, and healing all kinds of sickness and all kinds of disease among the people.

Epileptics - Matthew 4:24: Then His fame went throughout all Syria; and they brought to Him all sick people who were afflicted with various diseases and torments, and those who were demon-possessed, epileptics, and paralytics; and He healed them.

Demon possessed - Matthew 8:16: When evening had come, they brought to Him many who were demon-possessed. And He cast out the spirits with a word, and healed all who were sick.

The blind and deaf mute - Matthew 12:22: Then one was brought to Him who was demon-possessed, blind and mute; and He healed him, so that the blind and mute man both spoke and saw.

The Canaanite woman's daughter - Matthew 15:22,28: And behold, a woman of Canaan came from that region and cried out to Him, saying, "Have mercy on me, O Lord, Son of David! My daughter is severely demon-possessed."... Then Jesus answered and said to her, "O woman, great is your faith! Let it be to you as you desire." And her daughter was healed from that very hour.

The lame, blind, mute and maimed - Matthew 15:30: Then great multitudes came to Him, having with them the lame, blind, mute, maimed, and many others; and they laid them down at Jesus' feet, and He healed them.

The blind and lame in the Temple - Matthew 21:14: Then the blind and the lame came to Him in the temple, and He healed them.

Jairus's daughter - Mark 5:22,23: And behold, one of the rulers of the synagogue came, Jairus by name. And when he saw Him, he fell at His feet and begged Him earnestly, saying, "My little daughter lies at the point of death. Come and lay Your hands on her, that she may be healed, and she will live."

The woman with the 12-year blood problem - Mark 5:25-29: Now a certain woman had a flow of blood for twelve years, and had suffered many things from many physicians. She had spent all that she had and was no better, but rather grew worse. When she heard about Jesus, she came behind Him in the crowd and touched His garment; for she said, "If only I may touch His clothes, I shall be made well." Immediately the fountain of her blood was dried up, and she felt in her body that she was healed of the affliction.

Multitudes healed - Luke 4:40: When the sun was setting, all those who had any that were sick with various diseases brought them to Him; and He laid His hands on every one of them and healed them.

The Scriptures show that one function of signs, wonders and miracles in the ministry of Jesus and the Early Church was to awaken and encourage faith in the gospel that was being preached. Usually signs, wonders and miracles done by Christ were followed by a clear explanation of the power of God as well as a gospel message that turned people to Him. The Gospel of John in particular stresses the miraculous signs as a means of arousing faith (see John 2:11; 4:53; 6:14; 7:31; 9:30-39; 11:15; 11:42; 11:45; 12:11; 12:17-19; 20:30,31).

WE HAVE RECEIVED
CHRIST'S MINISTRY OF HEALING AND MIRACLES

Let's now consider biblical examples of those who received Christ's ministry of healing and miracles.

The Disciples Received Christ's Ministry of Healing and Miracles

The first disciples received this ministry as stated in Matthew 10:1, which says that "when He had called His twelve disciples to Him, He gave them power over unclean spirits, to cast them out, and to heal all kinds of sickness and all kinds of disease." And in Matthew 10:8 Jesus tells the disciples to "heal the sick, cleanse the lepers, raise the dead, cast out demons. Freely you have received, freely give." (See also Mark 3:15, Luke 9:2; 10:9.) These first disciples were ordinary people like you and me. They had their shortcomings, character flaws, unbeliefs, wrong attitudes and carnal ambitions, and yet they—with all their weaknesses—were used mightily of God to see miracles and to touch needy people.

The Early Church Received Christ's Ministry of Healing and Miracles

The First Church, the Church in the book of Acts, received this miracle ministry. Acts 3:11,12 says that "as the lame man who was healed held on to Peter and John, all the people ran together to them in the porch which is called Solomon's, greatly amazed. So when Peter saw it, he responded to the people: 'Men of Israel, why do you marvel at this? Or why look so intently at us, as though by our own power or godliness we had made this man walk?'" The response to this miracle is seen in Acts 4:14,15 when "seeing the man who had been healed standing with them, they could say nothing against it."

This miracle was not a one-time event. Acts 5:16 tells us that "a multitude gathered from the surrounding cities to Jerusalem, bringing sick people and those who were tormented by unclean spirits, and they were all healed."

The First Church believed and functioned in the gifts of miracles and healings, including deliverance as seen in Acts 8:7, which tells us that "unclean spirits, crying with a loud voice, came out of many who were possessed; and many who were paralyzed and lame were healed." These people were delivered and also healed. The two experiences were connected.

Paul Had a Ministry of Teaching, Healing and Miracles

In Acts 28:8 we read that "it happened that the father of Publius lay sick of a fever and dysentery. Paul went in to him and prayed, and he laid his hands on him and healed him."

We Have This Same Ministry of Healing in the Church Today

We have the same Jesus, the same Holy Spirit, the same Scriptures to preach, teach and believe. If we have the same God, the same Jesus, the same Holy Spirit, the same Bible, why don't we have the same results?

The answer is easy: we are having the same results, but we want more in both quantity and quality of miracles.

Some people may have a worldview that doesn't allow the flow of the supernatural in the realm of the miraculous. Some may have a theological problem with miracles, especially in the teaching of the gifts of healing, gift of miracles, gift of faith; they believe these have all passed away and that the Church doesn't need them anymore. Obviously, I have already concluded that the gifts are needed today and that miracles never ceased. We need miracles more than ever, and we need a faith that expects miracles to happen.

People in your present sphere of influence are in need of miracles. Some may need a miracle in their physical bodies, others in their domestic worlds. Jeremiah 33:6 says, "Behold, I will bring it health and healing; I will heal them and reveal to them the abundance of peace and truth." People are crying out for something more; they are crying out for healings and for miracles. Can you hear them?

Psalm 6:2: "Have mercy on me, O Lord, for I am weak; O Lord, heal me, for my bones are troubled."

Psalm 30:2: "O Lord my God, I cried out to You, and You healed me."

Jeremiah 17:14: "Heal me, O Lord, and I shall be healed; save me, and I shall be saved, for You are my praise."

How will people receive healings and miracles? Through your faith and prayers! You are a channel for God's power and God's love. You are God's feet and God's hands. God needs you to cooperate with His Holy Spirit. You are essential.

We can believe in healing and miracles, but having the faith to pray for results is something else.

James 5:14,15 asks, "Is anyone among you sick? Let him call for the elders of the church, and let them pray over him, anointing him with oil in the name of the Lord. And the prayer of faith will save the sick, and the Lord will raise him up. And if he has committed sins, he will be forgiven. Confess your trespasses to one another, and pray for one another, that you may be healed. The effective, fervent prayer of a righteous man avails much. Elijah was a man with a nature like ours, and he prayed earnestly that it would not rain; and it did not rain on the land for three years and six months."

These verses from James underline what I am expounding to you. If you are sick, call for the elders. This passage does not say to call for God or for angels. It says to call for a person, a person who will pray for you, touch you with his or her hands, anoint you with oil, and then the Lord will raise you up.

PEOPLE MAY BE HEALED IN DIFFERENT WAYS

God cannot be put into a box. He heals in different ways, in different time frames, through different channels and with different points of contact—but God heals. Let's consider some of the different healings mentioned in Scripture.

Healing Miracles That Are Miracles of Creation

These are instantaneous miracles, that is "instantaneous healings." Remember the man at the pool of Bethsaida who was instantly and completely healed, or the man born without eyesight who suddenly received perfect eyes? These are creative miracles that require God's creative power.

Healing Miracles That Intervene in the Operation of Natural Processes

Miracles of healing can occur with God working through doctors, medicine and hospitals. He works providentially over time to bring about a desired healing within the framework of His natural laws.

Healing Miracles That Happen Slowly, but Are Outside of Natural Laws

Sometimes when healing occurs, the sickness is not treated by medicine, but the person continues to recover, receiving healing by prayer and faith. In these instances the miracle is a slow-moving work of healing, but it is supernatural because it is outside of natural laws.

WE CAN IMPROVE OUR
PRAYING FOR MIRACLES AND HEALING

We must move out of simply "head knowledge" into habitual action, move from intellectual knowledge to observational knowledge—and then to experiential knowledge. We need to practice, practice, practice. There is a difference between faith and belief. We can believe in healing and miracles, but having the faith to pray for results is something else.

Praying for healing is often a process that requires time, faith and patience. We can and will pray for healing over the same person as may times as it takes. The answer may happen in an instant or it may take time. When praying for healing, we can pray for several things:

- Pray for the pain to stop. This can be a beginning of a healing or a sign that a healing is occurring. When the pain stops, however, that doesn't necessarily mean the healing is complete.
- Pray for the medical treatments to bring healing without any harmful side effects. Pray for protection. Pray for the medicine to be expanded and to work beyond its normal power.
- Pray for the sickness or disease to stop in its tracks and go no further. Arresting a disease can be the beginning of a healing.
- Pray for total and complete healing, recognizing the levels or degrees of healing.

John G. Lake (1870-1935), founder of a strong teaching and healing ministry, gave instruction on praying for people when healing is not instantaneous:

In one of the letters received from readers, this question is asked, "Why are not all persons healed instantly as Jesus healed?" The writer of this letter is mistaken in thinking that Jesus always healed instantly. A case in point is the healing of the 10 lepers. As they went, they were cleansed. The healing virtue was administered. The healing process became evident later. Again, Jesus laid hands on a blind man, then inquired, "What do you see?" The man replied, "I see men as trees walking." His sight was still imperfect. Then Jesus laid His hands on him the second time, "And he saw clearly." Healing is by degree, based on two conditions: first the degree of healing virtue administered; second, the degree of faith that gives action and power to the virtue administered."[4]

FAITH HOLDS ON FOR RESULTS

A huge degree of faith believes until the answer comes—no matter what obstacles it meets along the way and no matter how long it takes to see results.

On a commuter flight from Portland, Maine, to Boston, Henry Dempsey, the pilot, heard an unusual noise near the rear of the small aircraft. He turned the controls over to his co-pilot and went back to check it out.

As he reached the tail section, the plane hit an air pocket, and Dempsey was tossed against the rear door. He quickly discovered the source of the mysterious noise. The rear door had not been properly latched prior to takeoff, and it flew open. He was instantly sucked out of the jet.

The co-pilot, seeing the red light that indicated an open door, radioed the nearest airport, requesting permission to make an emergency landing. He reported that the pilot had fallen out of the plane, and he requested a helicopter search of that area of the ocean.

After the plane landed, they found Henry Dempsey—holding

onto the outdoor ladder of the aircraft. Somehow he flew 200 mph at an altitude of 4,000 feet, and then, at landing, kept his head from hitting the runway, which was a mere twelve inches away. It took airport personnel several minutes to pry Dempsey's fingers from the ladder.

Things in life may be turbulent, but if we wrap our faith securely around Jesus, He will work outside of the laws of nature when necessary to bring about His perfect plan for our lives.[5]

No matter how long it takes, hold on to your expectation that Jesus can and will heal you.

Notes

1. *Fresh Ideas* (Ventura, CA: Gospel Light, 1997), p. 111.
2. The author apologizes for not being able to locate the Bushnell quote.
3. Don Moen, "I Am The God That Healeth Thee" (Integrity's Hosanna! Music, 1986).
4. Roberts Liardon, comp., *John G. Lake: The Complete Collections of His Life Teachings* (Tulsa, OK: Albury Publications, 1999).
5. Craig Brian Larson, ed., *Illustrations for Preaching and Teaching* (Grand Rapids: Baker Books, 1993), p. 103, adapted.

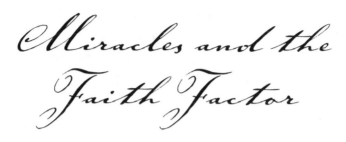

10

Miracles and the Faith Factor

NINE-YEAR-OLD JOEY WAS ASKED by his mother what he had learned in Sunday School. "Well, Mom, our teacher told us how God sent Moses behind enemy lines on a rescue mission to lead the Israelites out of Egypt. When he got to the Red Sea, he had his engineers build a pontoon bridge, and all the people walked across safely. He used his walkie-talkie to radio headquarters and call in an air strike. They sent in bombers to blow up the bridge and all the Israelites were saved."

"Now, Joey, is that REALLY what your teacher taught you?" his mother asked.

"Well, no, Mom, but if I told it the way the teacher did, you'd never believe it!"[1]

Like little Joey, I have often struggled with the gap between my faith and the faith that I see in the Scriptures—the faith of Moses to open the Red Sea, the faith of Joshua to command the sun to stand still, the faith of Israel to march around Jericho and shout the shout of faith as the walls crumbled. Jesus modeled the kind of faith I would like to have in every situation. He spoke the Word and what He spoke happened every time.

When He prayed for healings or miracles, resistance may have occurred, but His faith triumphed over every obstacle of the enemy.

My faith doesn't quite match up to His biblical example. How about yours? I pray and fast, memorize Scripture and speak with authority over every situation. When faced with sickness, diseases or demonic manifestation, I move ahead with faith and confidence, but my results are varied. Sometimes there's a spontaneous miracle of healing. Other times I wait and wait and wait. Sometimes the answer is delayed with no miracle and no healing. Other times, the healing is progressive and healing comes slowly. Faith is a mysterious operation, and until we understand this fact, we can become very frustrated.

Encountering a Culture of Unbelief

Our culture is not one of faith in God or faith in the Bible. World culture has shifted toward unbelief and cynicism and away from faith and believing. It does not believe in one God, but in many lesser non-gods. Our culture does not believe in the supernatural as taught in Scripture, a supernatural experienced and manifested through the cross of Christ and the ministry of the Holy Spirit. Doubt reigns supreme today in the minds of many—doubting the existence of God, doubting the inerrancy of Scripture, doubting that miracles are real today, doubting that God still heals. Sadly, doubt even has a foothold in the Church.

Unbelievers, Believers and Unbelieving Believers

Three types of people represent the Church. We all recognize the first two: first, the unbeliever who does not know God and has no faith; second, the believer who has been born again, has a spiritual life and has faith in God and in the Scripture. The third category includes the unbelieving believer—the one who has faith in God for salvation and perhaps for a few other things, but he or she does not have faith in God for the miracles and healings promised in Scripture. This person is a church-going, Bible-carrying, tithe-giving believer, but one who does not have faith in the supernatural.

In Scripture, a believer is not a person who holds to a certain set of beliefs about God as if it were merely theoretical conviction. A true believer has responded to the gospel message by trusting in Jesus with all of his or her heart, soul and mind, trusting in God's Word and in His work on Calvary. A true believer joins the company of believers in living out the life of believing in the invisible and the unexplainable and of doing the impossible.

Oral Roberts makes an interesting statement in his book *Expect a Miracle*:

> My best work was done when I worked with believing believers. I concentrated on doing my work with believing believers. I mean by that, if people believe God through my calling and my efforts, they are believers in what God called me to do, not ones who have chosen to live in unbelief, regardless of the faith results God gives me.[2]

OUR CHOICE: FAITH OR UNBELIEF

Oral Roberts' statement is a significant truth and a very important principle in developing a miracle atmosphere around your life, your home, your business or your church. God created humans with a free will, giving them the power of choice—to believe God or not to believe God. I choose to believe Him, I choose to work with people who believe God and I choose to pastor a church that believes Him. I choose the atmosphere of my mind and the confession of my mouth. I choose to believe. I choose to have faith. I choose to contend for miracles, even if I don't see all the desired miracles come to pass. I choose to leave the results with God. My job is to believe that God will do what He desires with my faith.

SCRIPTURES ON BELIEVING

Permit me once again to list some Scriptures on believing. I am writing out these passages because they are God's words, and God has told us in Romans 10:17 that "faith comes by hearing, and hearing by the word of God." Please don't skip over these verses, but read them slowly and prayerfully, allowing God to speak to you through them.

- **Miracles according to your faith:**

Matthew 9:28-30: And when He had come into the house, the blind men came to Him. And Jesus said to them, "Do you believe that I am able to do this?" They said to Him, "Yes, Lord." Then He touched their eyes, saying, "According to your faith let it be to you." And their eyes were opened.

> *On your journey to see miracles, you will pass over the mountains of persuasion and across the plains of being convinced to settle in the country called "conviction."*

- **Miracles that cause great amazement:**

Mark 5:36,41,42: As soon as Jesus heard the word that was spoken, He said to the ruler of the synagogue, "Do not be afraid; only believe." Then He took the child by the hand, and said to her, "Talitha, cumi," which is translated, "Little girl, I say to you, arise." Immediately the girl arose and walked, for she was twelve years of age. And they were overcome with great amazement.

- **Miracles believed in the face of impossibility:**

Mark 9:23-26: Jesus said to him, "If you can believe, all things are possible to him who believes." Immediately the father of the child cried out and said with tears, "Lord, I believe; help my unbelief!" When Jesus saw that the people came running together, He rebuked the unclean spirit, saying to it, "Deaf and dumb spirit, I command you, come out of him and enter him no more!" Then the spirit cried out, convulsed him greatly, and came out of him.

• **Miracles are waiting to be received:**

Mark 11:24: "Therefore I say to you, whatever things you ask when you pray, believe that you receive them, and you will have them."

• **Miracles are following your path of life:**

Mark 16:17,18: "And these signs will follow those who believe: In My name they will cast out demons; they will speak with new tongues; they will take up serpents; and if they drink anything deadly, it will by no means hurt them; they will lay hands on the sick, and they will recover."

• **Miracles replace fear by faith:**

Luke 8:50: But when Jesus heard it, He answered him, saying, "Do not be afraid; only believe, and she will be made well."

• **Miracles are the result of believing Christ's Word:**

John 4:48-50: Then Jesus said to him, "Unless you people see signs and wonders, you will by no means believe." The nobleman said to Him, "Sir, come down before my child dies!" Jesus said to him, "Go your way; your son lives." So the man believed the word that Jesus spoke to him, and he went his way.

• **Miracles cannot be rushed, but have their own timing:**

John 11:40-44: Jesus said to her, "Did I not say to you that if you would believe you would see the glory of God?" Then they took away the stone from the place where the dead man was lying.

And Jesus lifted up His eyes and said, "Father, I thank You that You have heard Me. And I know that You always hear Me, but because of the people who are standing by I said this, that they may believe that You sent Me." Now when He had said these things, He cried with a loud voice, "Lazarus, come forth!" And he who had died came out bound hand and foot with grave clothes, and his face was wrapped with a cloth.

- **Miracles are the result of God's exceeding great power:**

Ephesians 1:19,20: And what is the exceeding greatness of His power toward us who believe, according to the working of His mighty power which He worked in Christ when He raised Him from the dead and seated Him at His right hand in the heavenly places.

FROM DESIRE TO KNOWLEDGE TO FAITH

When we embark on the journey of developing our faith to trust and believe like Jesus and the apostles, we start with desire and knowledge. We read Scriptures, seeing in them the great works of God, and we begin to know that God can and that God does mighty and marvelous works. Our desire begins to grow, and we begin to pray for these mighty works to happen in our day and in our world. Slowly, a seed of faith grows into a tree of faith. In our minds and hearts we see that God is a God who works miracles. We have been persuaded when we adopt a new attitude.

From a Right Attitude to a Full Persuasion of Conviction

We move from persuasion to conviction when no further proof is needed, when we have examined and weighed the facts, ending with an unshakable determination. Certainty has been attained. We have been convinced. No feelings are needed. Nothing moves us away from our conviction.

Conviction is your rule of life, your place to stand and defend your ground. On your journey to see miracles, you will pass over the mountains of persuasion and across the plains of being convinced to settle in the country called "conviction." Don't stop short. Don't allow discouragement, frustration, failures or delays to stop you on this important journey.

The word "believe" in the Hebrew is *aman*. The root to this word indicates firmness and certainty, belief and assurance. This powerful Old Testament word captures the biblical meaning of conviction, a conviction that is based on the reliability of what is believed—God's Word! The Greek word *pisteuo* means to be persuaded into a place of conviction, confidence and firm belief.

Our Faith Foundation

Our faith rests in the work of Christ on Calvary and on His resurrection from the dead. Our faith is in the holy Word of God, written and inspired by the Holy Spirit. We have a trust. We have a place to take refuge. When a person is helpless and in danger, he or she rushes to find a secure hiding place. Our trust is placed in a person and is a reliance on someone, not on something (see Pss. 14:6; 46:1; 62:8; 71:7; 91:9).

It is not the work of life, but the worry of life that robs us of our strength and breaks down our faith.

Our faith is our firm foundation. It is what supports us in bad times and in good times, when we have great results from our prayers and when we have no apparent results. Faith is in the faithfulness of God to fulfill His promises. Faith in God is to have complete, unquestionable acceptance of something, even in the absence of proof, especially something not supported by reason. Faith fastens on God as the One who, by His nature, is the sole certain and sure reality. God is faithful and unchanging. He is established in eternity and, because He is who He is, we can commit ourselves to Him. Our faith has validity because God Himself is utterly faithful and trustworthy.

The Trust of True Faith

Believing is the very heart and life of our Christian walk. The Greek adjective for belief is *pistos*, which is used to describe the act of believing and trusting, moving from the passive knowledge of belief to the action of believing. True faith is trusting in and relying upon God and His Word with confidence in spite of the atmosphere, circumstance or crisis. Faith is trusting in our blood-bound covenant in Christ with complete trust in the reliability of the other party—God. Faith confidently trusts at all times in the character and motives of God as He fulfills His promises. Someone put it this way, "God is too kind to do anything cruel, too wise to make a mistake, too deep to explain Himself."

I trust that I can totally surrender my life into the hands of another and that He, God, will keep me in a safe place in spite of storms, attacks and non-explainable events that transpire. I choose to trust and to believe in the real, the dependable, the guarantee that creates the possibility of living as a believing believer. I choose to trust and believe in the logic of God, even when His logic seems a little strange at times and baffles my human logic. I like the way the psalmist says it in Psalm 56:11, "In God I have put my trust; I will not be afraid. What can man do to me?" And then in Psalm 62:8, "Trust in Him at all times, you people; pour out your heart before Him; God is a refuge for us."

Trust and Logic—A Natural Tension

Trust and logic don't always flow together. Logic is the science of correct reasoning—what should be expected based on a system of cause and effect. Expectation is based on what has happened before. Life, however, is not logical. Tragedy is not logical. Disease and untimely death are not logical. So we can't trust our logic to show us the way of life.

In fact, two Wycliffe missionaries in South America were translating the Bible into the language of an unreached people group when a mud slide engulfed their house, killing both of them as well as their children. Why them? Why in that way? It wasn't logical. They were serving God. They were spreading the gospel to people who otherwise would never have heard about Jesus Christ. They were in the will of God. So why did such an awful tragedy happen? Logic will not answer this question. Trusting God will. We must trust God in the light and in the darkness.

Hebrews 11:33-40 is a great passage that speaks about the heroes of faith. In the middle of this great, inspiring list of faith heroes and faith accomplishments are two simple words "and others"—others who were tortured, scourged, imprisoned, stoned; others who had faith:

> Who through faith subdued kingdoms, worked righteousness, obtained promises, stopped the mouths of lions, quenched the violence of fire, escaped the edge of the sword, out of weakness were made strong, became valiant in battle, turned to flight the armies of the aliens. Women received their dead raised to life again. *And others* were tortured, not accepting deliverance, that they might obtain a better resurrection. Still others had trials of mockings and scourgings, yes, and of chains and imprisonment. They were stoned, they were sawn in two, were tempted, were slain with the sword. They wandered about in sheepskins and goatskins, being destitute, afflicted, tormented—of whom the world was not worthy. They wandered in deserts and mountains, in dens and caves of the earth. And all these, having obtained a good testimony through faith, did not receive the promise (italics added).

An unknown prisoner scratched his faith onto the wall of a German prisoner-of-war camp during World War II. "I believe in the sun, even when it is not shining. I believe in love, even when I feel it not. I believe in God, even when He is silent." He had a choice and he chose belief rather than unbelief.

UNBELIEVING UNBELIEVERS

Unbelief means to be without a way or to be double-minded. Unbelief is to be without resources. It represents a mind ruled by reason and logic yet overcome with questions and hesitation. Unbelief misses out on much of life and can be the mind-set of a person who shuts out Christ and the message of the gospel. Luke 12:46 says that "the master of that servant will come on a day when he is not looking for him, and at an hour when he is not aware, and will cut him in two and appoint him his portion with the unbelievers." But Romans 10:9-11 tell us "that if you confess with your mouth the Lord Jesus and believe in your heart that God has raised Him from the dead, you will be saved. For with the heart one believes unto righteousness, and with the mouth confession is made unto salvation. For the Scripture says, 'Whoever believes on Him will not be put to shame.'" Unbelieving people resist and reject the cross of Christ and His redemptive work and refuse to put faith in something they cannot see.

UNBELIEVING BELIEVERS

Obviously, unbelief is costly for the unbeliever who never believes in Christ. But unbelief is also costly for the believer who does believe in Christ and yet lives an unbelieving Christian life. Now let's look at some Scriptures that document this fact. (Italics added.)

- Matthew 13:58: Now He did not do many mighty works there because of their *unbelief*.
- Matthew 17:20: So Jesus said to them, "Because of your *unbelief*; for assuredly, I say to you, if you have faith as a mustard seed, you will say to this mountain, 'Move from here to there,' and it will move; and nothing will be impossible for you."
- Mark 9:24: Immediately the father of the child cried out and said with tears, "Lord, I believe; *help my unbelief!*"
- Romans 4:20: He did not waver at the promise of God through *unbelief*, but was strengthened in faith, giving glory to God.
- Hebrews 3:12: Beware, brethren, lest there be in any of you an evil *heart of unbelief* in departing from the living God.
- Hebrews 3:19: So we see that they could not enter in because of *unbelief*.

The Battle of Doubt and Human Reasoning

Unbelief should not be part of a believer's life. Unfortunately, however, we all deal with doubt, worry and reasoning. It is not the work of life, but the worry of life that robs us of our strength and breaks down our faith. Worry and doubt create mental pictures of what we do not want to happen. Faith creates mental pictures of what can happen with God and His Word. Faith is stepping across the line, getting out of the box and jumping out of the boat. Conversely, doubt and worry cause us to seek security, keeping us from our mission and from living a faith-empowered life.

In Matthew 21:21 Jesus answered and said to them, "Assuredly, I say to you, if you have faith and do not doubt, you will not only do what was done to the fig tree, but also if you say to this mountain, 'Be removed and be cast into the sea,' it will be done." Clearly, faith is key to answered prayer. First Timothy 2:8 says that God desires "that the men pray everywhere, lifting up holy hands, without wrath and doubting."

Levels of Unbelief in Unbelieving Believers

Unbelief is an insidious problem that can deepen and lead from one level of unbelief to another.

Mental unbelief, for example, is a wavering doubt influenced by outward circumstances. It relies on feelings, emotions and moods and is based on what can be seen and understood. It is logic-driven and is controlled by the senses. The following are examples of mental unbelief:

> Mark 9:24: Immediately the father of the child cried out and said with tears, "Lord, I believe; help my unbelief!"
> Matthew 14:29-31: So He said, "Come." And when Peter had come down out of the boat, he walked on the water to go to Jesus. But when he saw that the wind was boisterous, he was

afraid; and beginning to sink he cried out, saying, "Lord, save me!" And immediately Jesus stretched out His hand and caught him, and said to him, "O you of little faith, why did you doubt?"

Emotional unbelief, on the other hand, is a religious, mental rejection of things not seen, understood or experienced. It is the result of a habit of negative responses—a "knowledge" faith only. Here is an example:

Mark 16:14: Later He appeared to the eleven as they sat at the table; and He rebuked their unbelief and hardness of heart, because they did not believe those who had seen Him after He had risen.

Hardened unbelief, however, is a processed, deep-seated unbelief that has experienced failures and disappointments and has wrongly responded to God in the midst of them. It allows doubt, questions and blame, and ultimately rejects God. Hebrews 3:12,13 cautions us to "beware, brethren, lest there be in any of you an evil heart of unbelief in departing from the living God; but exhort one another daily, while it is called 'Today,' lest any of you be hardened through the deceitfulness of sin." The following are other verses that deal with hardened unbelief.

Hebrews 3:15: While it is said: "Today, if you will hear His voice, do not harden your hearts as in the rebellion."
Hebrews 3:18,19: And to whom did He swear that they would not enter His rest, but to those who did not obey? So we see that they could not enter in because of unbelief.

CULTIVATING A BELIEVER'S BELIEVING HEART

Let me illustrate the wrong and the right approach in cultivating a believing heart.

To cultivate a living faith that reaches out and pulls miracles into your world, start with your spirit and not with your emotions:

- **Faith begins in your *spirit*.** Faith is an attribute of the Holy Spirit and, therefore, must be birthed into the believer by a spiritual process and spiritual connection.
- **Faith then moves to your *mind*.** Faith is nurtured by the proper functioning of the mind. The spirit of faith is assimilated into the mind and merged with the Word of God resident in the mind, creating a chemistry of growing faith.
- **Faith involves your *will*.** Faith is transformed into action through the will. Your will is the discipline part of faith, your ability to continue forward in spite of opposition.
- **Faith affects your *emotions*.** Faith is felt and expressed through a variety of emotions, but it is not sustained by emotions.

The miracles God desires to work in your life and world are already paid for by the cross of Christ and are to be received by the prayer of faith. As I have already noted, "faith comes by hearing and hearing by the word of God" (Rom. 10:17). Faith is nurtured as we feed on the Word of God daily, with deep devotion as true disciples. When the prayer of faith is offered and the disease or sickness is rebuked, the case is then in the hands of the Lord. He does the healing, whether it is done instantly, done gradually, or not fully grasped until we enter our eternal home. Either way, our faith in God stands strong.

Matthew 4:4 tells us that "it is written, man shall not live by bread alone but by every word that proceedeth out of the mouth of God." Let me get personal by asking you a question: If you were to feed your physical body as meagerly and infrequently as you feed your soul on God's Word, how long would it be until we attended your funeral?

"Faith cometh." You can keep faith coming by feeding on the living Word of God. Faith does not come by sitting around wishing and hoping. Right now, begin to feed your spirit, mind, will and emotions with the Word of God. Then, you will have the faith to hop out of the box, climb out of the boat or take a risk that could change your world. As someone has said, "Faith is not belief without proof, but trust without reservations." Will you trust Him? Will you become a believing believer today?

Notes
1. http://www.butlerwebs.com/jokes/religious-kids.htm.
2. Oral Roberts, *Expect a Miracle: My Life and Ministry* (Nashville: Thomas Nelson Publishers, 1998), p. 358.

11

Miracles and the Mystery of Suffering

"WHAT ABOUT THE PEOPLE WHO aren't healed? What about those who seek healing without success and mysteriously continue to suffer?"

As a pastor with a deep love for people, these words hit me in the heart with a dagger of pain, and I know that you are probably asking the same questions. For me, they represent the bewilderment of many people. Right now I'm thinking of the mother of a 19-year-old boy who was dying of leukemia. This mother's words were not from a textbook, a magazine article or a sermon I had preached. They were the words of a broken-hearted mother, a desperate, almost angry, seeker of God's miracle-working power in her son's life. My answer was feeble in light of her emotional nightmare, "God can and does heal. I don't know why He hasn't healed your son, but I will continue to pray for his healing, a healing that may take place on earth or in heaven." She was not happy with my answer; I can't say that I was very happy with it either. It was all I had. I walked away with my faith challenged again about why some are healed and some are not. Why do some righteous, wonderful, God-fearing people suffer so much and for so long? Why doesn't God heal everyone?

Anyone seeking to bring healing into a broken and sick world will encounter the agony of the "why." Why doesn't God heal more suffering people? Why is there so much suffering in the world, especially if God is a good and loving God? If we, the Christian community, are chosen to bring healing to broken and sick people, it is our responsibility to understand the mystery of suffering—yes, even the value of suffering. This world is a valley of tears that our technological genius has not been able to dry. The world is full of tragedy, suffering and surprises that leave people with mixed responses to God and the Church. Some people get bitter, some go into their own self-made protective cocoons, some throw up their hands and simply check out of life and all of its problems through isolation, addictions or suicide. Others may break down emotionally or mentally. No matter how we look at it, suffering, tragedy, diseases, accidents and misfortunes happen. We cannot ignore it.

What do we say when we weep with the mother of a little boy dying of cancer, the wife of a police officer killed while on duty, the parents of a teenager who fell while rock climbing, or the family of a little girl who was raped and murdered? What do we say to the agonizing parents of a son or daughter who has been incarcerated? In these situations and more, we all struggle to find the answer. But one thing we do know: Pain and suffering are not measured by human hands. We must believe in the God of the Scriptures and trust that He is just and good—all of the time.

THE SOLDIER'S PRAYER

Amy Carmichael, a missionary to India who directed Dohnavur Fellowship from an invalid's bed for many years, articulated her philosophy on faith in handling suffering without a miracle or healing this side of heaven. Her Soldier's Prayer is worth reading, copying and placing somewhere so you can refer to it when you are facing a tragedy, a season of suffering without a miracle breakthrough:

From prayer that asks that I may be
Sheltered from winds that beat on Thee,
From fearing when I should aspire,
From faltering when I should climb higher,
From silken self, O Captain free,
Thy soldier who would follow Thee.

From subtle love of softening things,
From easy choices, weakenings,
(Not this way are spirits fortified,
Not this way went the Crucified)
From all that dims Thy Calvary,
O Lamb of God, deliver me.

Give me the love that leads the way,
The faith that nothing can dismay,
The hope no disappointments tire
The passion that will burn like fire,
Let me not sink to be a clod:
Make me Thy fuel, Flame of God.[1]

We don't know why each individual tragedy, each accident, each
mind-boggling twist to fairness takes place. But we do know that,
although we're in an ongoing fierce battle with heavy casualties, the victory is sure and absolute. Death will be swallowed up in victory!

THE FALL, THE SOURCE OF SUFFERING

Where does suffering, sickness and tragedy come from? God? The devil?
My own bad decisions or sinful actions? Actually all of these are right.
Suffering originates with the fall of Adam from grace into sin. Before
Adam fell, there was no sin, no suffering, no death. But Adam, the father
of all humankind, did fall, introducing sin and suffering into our universe

and into the nature of every human being born into this world. Now let's zoom in on what Scripture has to say about our suffering and the Fall.

All sickness is the result of original sin.

Romans 5:12 tells us that "through one man sin entered the world, and death through sin, and thus death spread to all men, because all sinned." And Job 5:7 explains that "man is born to trouble, as the sparks fly upward."

All people have been infected by sin's power.

We have all been infected by the fall of Adam and our whole world suffers. All are under the tyrant of sin, a destroyer, a "taker" that is never fair and never merciful. Sin is hateful and cruel and moves over the entire world with its destruction. Matthew 5:45 says, "that you may be sons of your Father in heaven; for He makes His sun rise on the evil and on the good, and sends rain on the just and on the unjust." Both the just and the unjust suffer because of the fall of Adam.

Christ suffered vicariously to redeem what was lost in the Fall.

By one man, Adam, sin and suffering entered this world, and by one man, Christ, sin and suffering were conquered on the Cross. The vicarious suffering of Christ is seen in His full embrace of sin and suffering on the Cross. Isaiah 53:4,5 explains that "surely He has borne our griefs and carried our sorrows; yet we esteemed Him stricken, smitten by God, and afflicted. But He was wounded for our transgressions, He was bruised for our iniquities; the chastisement for our peace was upon Him, and by His stripes we are healed."

Christ could not make a full atonement for sin without absorbing its full consequences in His own person and being. No human can ever suffer the way Christ did. He bore the pain, sickness and sorrow of the whole world—the whole fallen human race. He suffered as perfect man and holy God. He took sin and suffering upon Himself for us. There is no atonement without suffering. There is no Cross without suffering (see Lev. 16:27; Heb. 13:11-13). Christ suffered during His ministry time on earth, and He suffered on the Cross at the end of His ministry (see Acts 1:3; Jude 7). He was the suffering servant, having been tested by suffering—and He becomes our pattern and example (see Mark 8:31; 9:12; Luke 9:22; 22:15).

Suffering Is the Believer's Fellowship

His suffering requires us to follow a similar path (see Rom. 8:17; 2 Cor. 1:7; Gal. 3:4; Phil. 3:10; 1 Thess. 2:2; 2 Thess. 1:5; 2 Tim. 2:12; 3:12; Jas. 5:10, 1 Pet. 2:20). This fellowship in suffering unites us with the saints of God in all times as we see in James 5:10: "My brethren, take the prophets, who spoke in the name of the Lord, as an example of suffering and patience." It is a fellowship with the Lord Himself. Philippians 3:10 says the reason for suffering is "that I may know Him and the power of His resurrection, and the fellowship of His sufferings, being conformed to His death." The Scriptures are clear that God uses this mysterious form of discipline called "suffering" to mold us more and more into His character and likeness (see Heb. 2:18, 4:15, 5:8).

Suffering Defined

The word "suffering" or "suffer" is used at least 53 times in the Bible and is translated from a variety of Hebrew and Greek expressions. The most obvious meaning of the word is to experience, go through, endure, bear, take upon oneself, to be oppressed, to suffer under something, to suffer hardship (see Ps. 34:10; Prov. 19:15; Matt. 11:12; Acts 7:24; 2 Cor. 11:25; 1 Thess. 3:4; 2 Tim. 2:9; Heb. 11:25). The word used in both the Old Testament and New Testament suggests putting up with or tolerating something unpleasant as in undergoing some form of punishment or loss (see Luke 13:2; 1 Cor. 3:15; 2 Cor. 11:9; Phil. 3:8). Suffering can include both emotional and physical pain.

Great writers and thinkers have addressed the subject of suffering. The following are some insights from a few of them.

- Norman Grubb (1895-1993), a missionary to the Congo and author of many books: "The Holy Spirit in the life of the believer will drive him to a life of suffering sacrifice just as He did in the life of Christ."[2]
- Paul Billheimer, American author and pastor for more than 60 years: "God has designed that suffering, which is a consequence of the Fall, shall produce the character and disposition, the compassionate spirit which will be required for rulership in a government where the law of love is supreme."[3]
- Henry Ward Beecher (1813-1887), Presbyterian minister: "Do not be afraid to suffer. Do not be afraid to be overthrown. It is by being cast down and not destroyed; it is by being shaken to pieces and the pieces torn to shreds that men become men of might!"[4]
- Charles Swindoll (1934-), chancellor of Dallas Theological Seminary and pastor of Stonebriar Church in Frisco, Texas: "God's mysteries, especially suffering, defy human explanation because they go beyond human intellect and wisdom. We lack eternal perspective. We can't grasp God's plan, but we can say with Job, 'Although I am without answers, yet I will believe in Him.'"[5]
- Bill Gothard (1934-), founder of the Institute in Basic Life Principles: "Suffering is the fertile soil into which God transplants every growing Christian. Suffering is the motivation to take your eyes off temporal things so that you can see eternal realities. Suffering is the confirmation that you have been chosen for special leadership with Christ in His kingdom."[6]

✷ Blessings follow suffering for the sake of righteousness.

LIVING IN THE REAL—AND PAINFUL—WORLD

These unmerited blows of fate that cause you and me to suffer misfortune are real and usually unexpected. God works His work of grace in us and around us, but He doesn't always remove the thorn or heal the sickness. Life's varied suffering experiences can overtake a person without warning and leave without any explanation. Experiences that are painful, disagreeable or distressing to both body and mind are part of the reality of living in this fallen world. God does deliver us, protect us and send awesome miracles into our storms, but not every time.

Not one man or woman who has ever lived has done so without enduring some measure of adversity, affliction, pain, suffering, sickness, infirmity or tragedy. At this very moment, there are people who are suffering by being deprived of the most elementary things in life: food, shelter, basic medicines for basic sicknesses. People are suffering from a lack of financial security or employment. Countless refugees have lost their homeland. The sick are deprived of health, the infirmed are deprived of hearing or sight, the frail are deprived of mobility and the independence it confers. All are living with some form of suffering.

In *Confessions*, St. Augustine wrote about the death of his friend and how the joy went out of his life:

My heart was utterly darkened by this sorrow and everywhere I looked I saw death.[7]

Perhaps you have lost a loved one and you can identify.

All people from all generations have experienced the mystery of pain, affliction and suffering. An old, wise man in a Nazi concentration camp wrote, "If life as a whole has meaning, then suffering has meaning, for suffering is an inherent part of life. If life is meaningless then suffering is meaningless."

SUFFERINGS AND AFFLICTIONS ARE TOO HEAVY TO CARRY ALONE

Scripture teaches that there will be afflictions, trials, chastisements, sorrow, pain, sickness, suffering and death. God desires that our faith remain strong when faced with any level of suffering, especially unexplainable, tragic suffering. We all have questions at times: Where is the miracle for me? Why did God not stop this tragedy? Can I keep believing, even when I'm hurting and doubt is knocking at my door?"

Listen to the following letter written by a distraught nurse in Chicago:

> Who said time heals all wounds? Who says God comforts? God is everywhere? Does He walk with me to the cemetery to visit the grave of my 6-year-old son who died of leukemia 12 years ago, or the grave of my 18-year-old daughter who died of lymphoma two years ago?
>
> Does He cry with me? What could He possibly do to ease the pain? Christ died for me? Who did they die for? Does He know how it hurts to pray, pray to a God who is merciful? Loving? Understanding? And on Judgment Day, who is going to question whom? I'll speak for all the bereaved. I work in a hospital. Does He walk through the corridors to visit the sick and the dying? Is He there to ease the pain, to wipe the tear? No! No! No![8]

"When you hurt with hurting people, you are dancing to the rhythm of God."
Let's dance.

THE MIRACLE OF GRACE

The letter you just read is the outcry of a broken and bitter heart. The burden of suffering is too great for us unless the Burden-Bearer comes to our rescue. Life is too heavy to carry by ourselves. It is too mysterious to answer by ourselves. Perhaps the miracle for many of us is the miracle that we can laugh and cry without bitterness. Maybe the miracle we don't see is the miracle of grace wrapped around our broken hearts, giving us the strength to go on, to still believe—and maybe even to believe more deeply than before the suffering entered our lives.

Samuel Rutherford (1600-1661), a Puritan pastor in Scotland, wrote:

I can let Christ grip me; but I cannot grip Him. I love to sit on Christ's knee; but I cannot set my feet to the ground, for afflictions bring the cramp upon my faith. All I now do, is to hold out a lame faith to Christ, like a beggar holding out a stump, instead of an arm or leg; and cry, "Lord Jesus, work a miracle."[9]

The pain we experience in life can feel as though it goes beyond what is bearable. We become weary, and fear floods our souls—but then a miracle happens. Strength and courage take over our souls. New life pushes back the old. It's a miracle! We not only go through the valley, we also go through with the miracle strength of God.

OUR ANCHOR IN SUFFERING: GOD'S UNFAILING LOVE

The anchor to our miracle is God's love, not our subjective, changing feelings. In times of suffering, our emotions swing to the extremes of the pendulum, but our confidence does not lie in our emotions. Our assurance and unwavering confidence lies in the miracle that the God of creation is personally involved in our lives. It is a miracle that God loves me all the time and that He will always work all things out for my good and His plan. It is a miracle that I can trust Him. I can let go, and I can go on. I can echo Paul's words in Romans 8:38:

> I stand absolutely convinced beyond the shadow of a doubt that no sickness, no suffering, no pain, no disease, no loss, not a single thing that happens in my life can separate me from the One who loves me without limits.

DELAYS AND GOD'S TIMING

Even when the wait for a miracle of grace or a miracle of healing is long and painful, God has not abandoned us. Never! He is at work, and our lives are in His hands. Even when we cannot see or feel God, He is there. And He is always intimately and passionately concerned with every circumstance that confronts us.

Suffering helps us to live, not for ourselves any longer, but for God and others. Someone once said, "When you hurt with hurting people, you are dancing to the rhythm of God." Let's dance.

Would it be all right with you if I list a few more Scriptures for you to read, meditate upon and accept? As believers, you and I will endure seasons of suffering. And there will also be seasons when miracles come in different-sized packages, wrapped with materials that hide what is within. They may be miracles that we might not call miracles, but they are present with us: the miracle of grace, the miracle of laughter, the miracle of crying, the miracle of strength. Miracles are all around us when we go through the sufferings and trials of life.

Here are the verses on suffering that I want to share with you because even if you don't need them now, someday you will:

The cross of suffering - Luke 9:23: Then He said to them all, "If anyone desires to come after Me, let him deny himself, and take up his cross daily, and follow Me."

The hardships of suffering - 2 Timothy 2:3: You therefore must endure hardship as a good soldier of Jesus Christ.

The many-sided pressures of suffering - 2 Corinthians 4:7,8: But we have this treasure in earthen vessels, that the excellence of the power may be of God and not of us. We are hard pressed on every side, yet not crushed; we are perplexed, but not in despair.

The sufferings of this present time - Romans 8:18: For I consider that the sufferings of this present time are not worthy to be compared with the glory which shall be revealed in us.

The suffering that builds character - Romans 5:3-5: And not only that, but we also glory in tribulations, knowing that tribulation produces perseverance; and perseverance, character; and character, hope. Now hope does not disappoint, because the love of God has been poured out in our hearts by the Holy Spirit who was given to us.

The sufferings appointed by God - 1 Thessalonians 3:3,4: That no one should be shaken by these afflictions; for you yourselves know that we are appointed to this. For, in fact, we told you before when we were with you that we would suffer tribulation, just as it happened, and you know.

The sufferings that nurture intimacy with God - Philippians 3:10: That I may know Him and the power of His resurrection, and the fellowship of His sufferings, being conformed to His death.

The sufferings that promise soon-coming consolation - 2 Corinthians 1:5-7: For as the sufferings of Christ abound in us, so our consolation also abounds through Christ. Now if we are afflicted, it is for your consolation and salvation, which is effective for enduring the same sufferings which we also suffer. Or if we are comforted, it is for your consolation and salvation. And our hope for you is steadfast, because we know that as you are partakers of the sufferings, so also you will partake of the consolation.

INSIGHTS FROM THE SCHOOL OF SUFFERING

The apostle Peter addresses suffering more than any other writer in Scripture. Peter was familiar with both Christ's sufferings and the suffering of His fellow disciples, most of whom died a martyr's death. Peter encountered the great mystery of suffering and was able, by the power of the Holy Spirit, to give inspired God-thoughts on the subject. Many passages from 1 and 2 Peter provide insight about the suffering of the righteous. Within our sufferings, hidden miracles happen that we usually overlook and Peter is quick to get us back in focus.

The reward from suffering is usually hidden during suffering.

First Peter 1:11 tells us that the prophets were "searching what, or what manner of time, the Spirit of Christ who was in them was indicating when He testified beforehand the sufferings of Christ and the glories that would follow."

We can never become all that God has planned for us to be without a periodic dose of suffering. Suffering actually becomes the pathway to glory and a fresh visitation of God's manifested presence. Christ's sufferings were matched with a reward that followed, a reward that was not to be given at the time of suffering but afterward. Let me illustrate this.

SUFFERINGS (many)	GLORIES (many)
Hated by His own people, prosecuted and killed	Resurrection reward
Betrayed by His own close friends and disciples	Enthronement reward
A shepherd forsaken by His flock	Ascension reward
A lamb sacrificed by His own	High priestly position reward

Peter teaches us the suffering principle with an expectation of eternal gains and eternal rewards. In his book *Don't Waste Your Sorrows*, Paul Billheimer says, "It is possible for the great majority who remain financially limited or physically afflicted to make as great a contribution to the Kingdom and bring as much joy to the heart of God and win as great an eternal reward as those who are favorited with supernatural deliverance."[10]

Hardships press us up against God, a very worthy reward for all. We will know God better after our afflictions, and we will draw closer to God through our trials. Our rewards are eternal, invisible and spiritual. Usually they come after the trial. And the equity of suffering will be found in the next life (see Ps. 58:10,11).

There is a suffering that is commendable by God.

First Peter 2:18-20 instructs God's servants to "be submissive to your masters with all fear, not only to the good and gentle, but also to the harsh. For this is commendable, if because of conscience toward God one endures grief, suffering wrongfully. For what credit is it if, when you are beaten for your faults, you take it patiently? But when you do good and suffer, if you take it patiently, this is commendable before God."

The believer must believe that nothing falls on him or her by fate or by accident. All things are in the sovereign hand of God, who is the sovereign ruler of life. When we do wrong and suffer for our bad decisions or are beaten for our own faults, Peter says we have no credit. It's not commendable to God. The word "commendable" that Peter uses means acceptable, pleasing to God and praised by God. Suffering is not a blessing in and of itself, but if one's duty to God is involved, then he or she can meet it with gladness of heart.

No posing as a martyr here, Christians do sometimes deserve persecution and suffering (see Matt. 5:10-12). Only those who suffer for righteous deeds are commended by God. Suffering for the mishandling of our lives or because of our shortcomings, trespasses, sins or offenses is not commendable. These sin-induced sufferings need to be repented for so that God can bless our lives and commend us by His grace (see 2 Cor. 4:17,18; 11:23-33).

First Peter 3:14-17 consoles the believer by saying that "even if you should suffer for righteousness' sake, you are blessed. And do not be afraid of their threats, nor be troubled. But sanctify the Lord God in your hearts, and always be ready to give a defense to everyone who asks you a reason for the hope that is in you, with meekness and fear; having a good conscience, that when they defame you as evildoers, those who revile your good conduct in Christ may be ashamed. For it is better, if it is the will of God, to suffer for doing good than for doing evil."

The suffering servant, our Lord Jesus Christ, is our example. He was without sin, yet He accepted insults and suffering with serene love, bearing them for the sins of humanity. Jesus gave us a pattern to follow. If we suffer insult, injury and injustice and do so with a right attitude, if we have pain and sorrow without complaining, and if we have steadfastness and unfailing love, it will lead others to Christ.

Unexplainable suffering must be committed to Him who judges righteously.

First Peter 2:23 describes Christ as one "who, when He was reviled, did not revile in return; when He suffered, He did not threaten, but committed Himself to Him who judges righteously." And 1 Peter 4:19 exhorts us to "let those who suffer according to the will of God commit their souls to Him in doing good, as to a faithful Creator."

> The miracle is in God's ability to fix us by putting us into "a fix" and using our failures to fix something in us.

Knowing and trusting the name of God is essential if we are to suffer with a godly attitude and receive maximum benefit from the school of suffering. God's justice toward us is motivated by His love, grace and mercy. God is just. To be just describes one who proportions with exactness, who observes divine laws without breaking the law, who is such as He ought to be, who is upright, who is faultless and always fair, who renders to each his due portion, and who passes just judgment on others. God's dealings with us are just. He makes things right with equity; He is impartial in His distribution of justice.

Edith Schaeffer, author and cofounder of L'Abri Fellowship and wife of the famous apologist, Francis Shaeffer, tells a story about God's fairness that opens the eyes of all who say "unfair, not right, this shouldn't happen to me."

The utter fairness of all this is that one day we will have more understanding of where the greatest battles were won, where the greatest miracles of victory took place. No one is shut out of having an outstanding moment in his or her life which can be recorded as a victory in that imaginary museum I picture, or in whatever way God records these proofs that the death of Christ was sufficient for every kind of affliction.

In 1950 Professor Wong came to study at Cambridge University before going back to continue teaching in his native China. It was the year Communists were to take over and, although he did not realize, he was not only never going to return to China in his lifetime, but he would never see his wife and daughter again this side of heaven. It was a sudden shock when Professor Wong found he could not go back, and it was a terrible piece of news when Professor Wong was told that his wife and daughter had been captured and were in prison for being Christians.

A lifetime cannot be lived in a moment or an hour or a day. Professor Wong was to become Pastor Wong and start in London a tiny gathering of Chinese which was going to grow into a really strong church in that city. Here many Chinese were to be given the truth of what is the real meaning of life, that there is a personal and infinite God. They were to be born again, these Chinese who might never have heard the gospel but for Pastor Wong. Out of that there was to flow forth a ministry among the Chinese in Paris and other European countries.

One time when I was talking to Pastor Wong, he said it had been 20 years since he had seen his wife. She was still in prison and at very infrequent intervals he had some bits of news from her with a lapse of years in between. She was still trusting God, loving Him and asking for His strength to go on hour by hour. She could not be hindered from praying, nor could prison bars shut out the sufficient grace of God, sufficient for her in her physical pain and discomfort, her lack of enough food, her frustration at being shut away from life. The prison bars could not shut her away from repeated victories in the heavenly battle. Only God knows how many times she had a victory which counted and which defeated Satan and brought joy and glory to the Lord. I hope we will see an exhibit of Mrs. Wong's victories in the museum in heaven. Who can know what a force she was in praying for her husband and in all that he was doing? Who could know, except God, which was the greatest demonstration of faith?

The exciting thing about God's fairness is that the Mrs. Wongs of history shut away to oblivion in a tiny cell can have a shining array of battle trophies and a long list of results from their prayer lives, results taking place thousands of miles away in the lives of people whom the Mrs. Wongs won't meet until they are introduced in heaven. It is so fair that the just God gives opportunities for important service for everyone of His children in a strategic place and time. Who is given the greatest opportunity in that particular 20 years? Pastor Wong who was suffering loneliness, sorrow and frustration at being exiled and yet who went on and did day by day what God gave him strength to do there in London? Or Mrs. Wong who lived that same 20 years in prison, praying and perhaps even helping other prisoners, certainly winning victories by just loving and trusting God. No one of us can judge.[11]

When we encounter afflictions, crises, tragedies and seemingly unfair sufferings, we must know how to commit ourselves to the righteous fairness of God. He desires the best for His redeemed people; He wants us to rule and reign in life. According to Romans 5:3-5, suffering builds character, and character is a prerequisite to rulership. Because there is little or no character development without the testing of the Lord and without the school of suffering, we, by God's design, at times go through seasons of fiery trials.

The miracle is in God's ability to fix us by putting us into "a fix" and using our failures to fix something in us. God is always just, fair and knows what He is doing. We, however, usually don't know what He is doing, so how do we respond? Do we respond with obedience, submission, yielding and humbling ourselves? Or do we rise up with questions and even hurl some insults at God and His ways (see Ps. 119:67,71; Heb. 2:10; 12:5-8, 10,11)?

Job 19:25,26 shows that Job presented a great attitude and a great perspective at the end of his suffering:

> For I know that my Redeemer lives, and He shall stand at last on the earth; and after my skin is destroyed, this I know, that in my flesh I shall see God.

Joni Eareckson Tada, who has spent most of her life confined to a wheelchair because of a diving accident in her youth, put it this way:

> God may not initiate all our trials, but by the time they reach us, they are His will for us. When Satan, other people, or just plain accidents bring us sorrow, we can answer like Joseph to his brothers who sold him into slavery, "As for you, you meant evil against me, but God meant it for good" (Gen. 50:20).[12]

Suffering can break the sin patterns in our lives.

First Peter 4:1 tells us that "since Christ suffered for us in the flesh, arm yourselves also with the same mind, for he who has suffered in the flesh has ceased from sin." In Psalm 119:66, 67 and 71, the psalmist asks the Lord to "teach me good judgment and knowledge, for I believe Your commandments. Before I was afflicted I went astray, but now I keep Your word. It is good for me that I have been afflicted, that I may learn Your statutes." (See also Heb. 12:4-13.)

The believer who identifies with Christ must be prepared to endure suffering in body, soul and spirit. Peter and the rest of the New Testament writers saw an inseparable link between Christ and His followers in respect to suffering (see 1 Pet. 4:1,13,16; Rom. 8:17; 1 Cor. 11:23-29; Phil. 3:10; Heb. 10:32-34; Rev. 2:10). In the light of how Christ suffered "for us," Peter said to "arm yourselves" with the same mind, same intentional thinking as Christ, who endured the suffering of the cross, despising the shame for the joy set before Him.

This same attitude of sacrificing self, enduring patiently and rejoicing in tribulation will equip us to face false accusations and to resist sinful temptations. The suffering a believer encounters will equip him or her to "break from sin," to be disciplined by the pain of suffering and then to be set free from the sin that caused the suffering. Suffering is a stern teacher but a good one. God wants to bring us face to face with our sinful nature and those sinful habits that we ignore. C.S. Lewis remarked, "I have found, to my regret, that the degrees of shame and disgust which I actually feel at my own sins do not all correspond to what my reason tells me about their comparative gravity...."[13] As the psalmist says in Psalm 107:17, "Fools, because of their transgression, and because of their iniquities, were afflicted."

Suffering helps us put our sinful habits in perspective. Because of the pain we encounter, we decide to yield the sinful part of our lives to God's grace and not repeat the sin any longer. Peter recalls that the readers of his Epistles spent considerable time living in sin. He identifies the people he addressed as former Gentiles who were now set "free" from the empty way of life handed down to them from their pagan culture. They were living in debauchery, unbridled lust and lawlessness, having a complete disregard for any restraints, immorality and drunkenness. We may pray for a miracle deliverance from our present character flaws or sinful habits, but the miracle may come in the form of suffering that causes us to break free from our sins and find a new release of God's grace and life.

SUFFERING AND THE GRACE OF GOD

A young woman named Cammie has written a letter that vividly portrays the truth of the mystery of suffering and the grace of God. At the age of two, she was diagnosed with cancer and her parents were told that she probably would not live. But she did live, only to face the specter of cancer again as an adult. She wrote a letter to her family and friends explaining how she viewed the mystery of her personal suffering in light of the grace of God.

Fredrick Beuchner's belief is that every little detail of our lives can be thought of as the vowels and sibilants that God uses to speak to us. When our ears are carefully listening to the heartbeat of our loving God, He begins to spell out the beauty of His grace and majesty. Nothing becomes insignificant, and mysteries too deep for words begin their melodies right where question marks have thrived. "Why," we ask, "why would a loving God allow a little child to suffer? Why would He crush a dream, bringing barrenness to her, she who longed for her own children? How could He be truly good if pain is the cup we daily drink of?" And I was tempted, as we each are at one point or another, to harden myself within my unanswered questions.

I know there are many who have pitied my beginnings, thinking it tragic that I had to endure such traumas both as a child and throughout my life, but I confess that I have rather pitied those who have never tasted the bitterness of a trial "too severe." For how is one to appreciate the contrast of light's dawning hope if his soul has never trembled through the dark hours of a nightmare's watch? Or how can one prove God's faithfulness if he never is granted the privilege of wandering through a barren desert, where only pools of Christ's Presence can possibly provide survival?... We dare not steel ourselves against our trials, running away from the fires where our pruned branches crumble to ashes. For if we escape those flames, we will risk barrenness of soul and will miss out on the beauty that only is born through the ashes of yesterday's grief.[14]

Oh the maturity and beauty that were pressed into this woman's character through the suffering she endured.

I'd like to end this chapter with a poem written by Annie Johnson Flint entitled "Pressed." May it speak to you as it has to me.

Pressed out of measure and pressed to all length;
Pressed so intensely it seems beyond strength;
Pressed in the body and pressed in the soul;
Pressed in the mind till the dark surges roll;
Pressure by foes, and pressure by friends;
Pressure on pressure, till life nearly ends.
Pressed into loving the staff and the rod;
Pressed into knowing no helper but God;
Pressed into liberty where nothing clings;
Pressed into faith for impossible things;
Pressed into living a life in the Lord;
Pressed into living a Christ-life outpoured.

The only life worth living is to live it for God.

Notes

1. Elisabeth Elliot, *A Chance to Die* (Grand Rapids: Fleming H. Revell Company, 1987), p. 221.
2. Paul Billheimer, *Don't Waste Your Sorrows* (Fort Washington, PA: Christian Literature Crusade, 1987), p. 20.
3. Ibid.
4. http://www.gatewaycathedral.org/The_Gateway/2001/1-200/gw/InYourBoat.htm.
5. Swindoll, unable to locate the source of this quote.
6. Bill Gothard, *Institute of Basic Youth Conflicts* (Oak Brook, IL, 1994).
7. Saint Augustine, *Confessions and Enchiridion* (Christian Classics; www.ccel.org). Book 4, verse 9. 24 July, 2003.
8. Randy Bectyon, *Does God Care When We Suffer?* (Grand Rapids: Baker Book House, 1988).
9. Robert McAnally Adams, ed., "Christian Quotation of the Day" (CQOD Compilation Copyright 2003). www.gospelcom.net/cqod/. 27 July, 2003.
10. Paul Billheimer, *Don't Waste Your Sorrows* (Grand Rapids: Bethany House, 1983), p. 21.
11. Edith Schaeffer, *Afflictions* (Grand Rapids: Baker Book House, 1978), pp. 85-86.

12. Joni Eareckson Tada, *When God Weeps* (Grand Rapids: Zondervan Publishing, 2000), p. 231.

13. Robert McAnally Adams, ed., "Christian Quotation of the Day" (CQOD Compilation Copyright 2003). www.gospelcom.net/cqod/. 1 June, 1998.

14. Cammie Van Rooy, quoted by Robert McNally Adams, ed., "Christian Quotation of the Day" (CQOD Compilation Copyright 2003). www.gospelcom.net/cquod/. 6 August, 2002.

12

Miracles In You and Through You

MOTHER TERESA (1910-1997), founder of the Missionaries of Charity, which ministers to the poorest of the poor in Calcutta, lived a life of and left a legacy of sacrificial service to all people at all times. She considered her life to be simply "a little pencil in the hand of a writing God, who is sending a love letter to the world."[1] She said, "Let us touch the dying, the poor, the lonely and the unwanted according to the graces we have received. And let us not be ashamed or slow to do the humble work."[2] When asked by a young man, "How can I live a life of miracles such as yours?" Mother Teresa responded, "Find your own Calcutta."

You have a place in this world where you can be used as a channel for God's miracles. God has chosen to work through your human weaknesses, flaws, shortcomings, doubts and fears—but you must be available in your Calcutta.

I find it absolutely amazing that God has chosen people—yes, people like you and me—to be His pipeline to those in need. Sometimes we are aware that God is using us; other times we are completely oblivious to the whole matter. We are to live life with a servant's heart that is ready to be used by the Holy Spirit. David Brainerd (1718-1747), missionary to the native Indians of America, wrote in his journal, "As long as I see things to be done for God, life is worth living. But O how vain and unworthy it is to live for any lower end."[3]

George Müeller, the great man of faith who established orphanages in England during the nineteenth century, witnessed God's provision again and again for the many orphans under his care. One morning the daughter of a close friend was visiting the Müeller's. When she came down for breakfast, George Müeller took her hand and said, "Come and see what our Father will do." As he pushed open the door to the dining room, she saw long tables set and ready for the meal, but there was no food. No food and no money and a house full of children—what would Müeller do?

He prayed, "Dear Father, we thank Thee for what Thou art going to give us to eat." Immediately, a knock came at the door. The local baker stood there a bit sheepishly, "Mr. Müeller, I could not sleep last night. Somehow I felt you didn't have any bread for breakfast, so I got up at 2:00 A.M. and baked some fresh bread—and here it is." Müeller thanked the baker and gave praise to God. Soon, a second knock was heard. It was the local milkman whose milk wagon had just broken down in front of Müeller's orphanage. The man offered all his milk to Müeller so he could have his wagon hauled to the nearest shop.

These were not planned miracles by the baker or the milkman. Neither man may have had any idea that it was God nudging him toward becoming a channel of His divine plan. I believe God continually uses people as channels for miracles, even when they are least aware of it.

I'm reminded of a time when God used a stranger to become our pipeline for a miracle. Sharon and I left for Eugene, Oregon, to plant our first church with 18 other people. Eugene and its sister city, Springfield, were both mill towns that were hit hard by the economic crunch facing the lumber industry. Interest rates were at 11 percent and we simply could not afford to finance the new building. Our devoted congregation, many of whom were unemployed, squeezed their financial reservoirs till they ran dry, but we still lacked the amount needed to secure the property. The Sunday before our real estate transaction was to close, a visitor, who was not part of our church and never became part of our church, dropped a check in the offering for $8,000—the exact amount we still needed to complete our purchase that following Monday morning.

Like this giver, we must be prepared at all times to be conduits, pipelines and channels of God's power.

You Are a Channel for Miracles

Our faith has settled our hearts to believe in and contend for the supernatural in and around us, and our perspective is a pivotal point in our battle for God's miracles to be released among us with signs, wonders and healings. It is right to want God to use you in powerful and useful ministry. Second Corinthians 4:7 says that "we have this treasure in earthen vessels, that the excellence of the power may be of God and not of us." You have divine deposits in you: Kingdom treasure. You are anointed by the Holy Spirit to pour out your faith and your gifts upon all who are around you. Reach out and touch a person in need today. Reach out and believe for the supernatural to break forth into a world of lost, hurt, broken and confused people.

Second Corinthians 1:21 explains that you are anointed by God for miracles, "He who establishes us with you in Christ and has anointed us is God." The works of God—miracles, signs and wonders—performed through Christ and those performed through believers cannot be separated from one another. They are the work of God. We are channels established and anointed for His works to flow through.

We are empowered by God to do more than we exercise.

God has given the same power to us as He gave to His disciples. Luke 9:1 says that "He called His twelve disciples together and gave them power and authority over all demons, and to cure diseases." He hasn't taken the power back. It's still here, and it's still available. Christ hasn't changed; He still does today what He did back in New Testament times. Remember, He is the same yesterday, today and forever.

You are Christ's disciple now. Wherever you are, whatever you do, whoever you are, you are appointed and anointed to be a disciple of Christ. Mark 3:14,15 says that "He appointed twelve, that they might be with Him and that He might send them out to preach, and to have power to heal sicknesses and to cast out demons." We are now recipients of Christ's authority to pray for the sick, to cast out demons and preach the kingdom of God (see Luke 10:9,17). Jesus reproduced His Kingdom ministry in and through His disciples, in and through His Church. Today's disciples are people with spiritual authority to do what Jesus did when He was on earth.

If you are not moving out regularly to minister grace and hope to those around you, the well inside of you may dry up.

And speaking of a disciple with spiritual authority! Aimee Semple McPherson (1890-1944), founder of the Foursquare denomination, was asked to preach at a boxing match in San Diego during one of the fights. She had but a few minutes as she was center stage on the elevated boxing ring, fenced in by ropes. She had no choir, no worship and no atmosphere of expectation. She was scared and showing it physically by her shaking hands and limbs. The crowd spilled into the aisles with people who were drinking, smoking, yelling, cursing, coughing—hardly a crowd to preach to. In those days a woman of any level of character would not be speaking at a boxing match. But in she went with this attitude:

> We feel our weakness and shake our heads in doubt, but just with that the Spirit whispers, "Not by might, nor by power, but by my Spirit saith the Lord." Why yes Jesus, that's so, please forgive us, we cry. Neither man nor woman, with all their power has been able to move this sinful city. It is only You, dear Lord, by Thy power we can do it now. Make us clean and empty channels through which Thy power may flow. Yes, yes! Dear Lord, we

know You've never lost a battle! We do—we do trust Thee. Only keep us very yielded in Your hands, and give us strength and wisdom for such an hour.[4]

The night ended with the crowd standing, clapping and cheering for this little woman who became a channel of God's grace into a very unlikely crowd. You can be God's channel, too. Pray Aimee's prayer and move out into the deep. If you have to, do it afraid—but move out.

We are empowered to do more than we expect.

Expectation is an attitude of faith. Second Corinthians 4:13 says that "since we have the same spirit of faith, according to what is written, 'I believed and therefore I spoke,' we also believe and therefore speak." And yet sometimes our sense of expectation may be lower than it should be. Our expectation to be used mightily by God may be pushed back because of our own spiritual stagnation, lack of personal prayer and neglect of feeding on the Word of God.

If you, as a channel of God's power, have nothing flowing through the pipes, your expectation level may be nonexistent. If you are not moving out regularly to minister grace and hope to those around you, the well inside of you may dry up. Sir Walter Scott puts it this way:

One hour of life, crowded to the full with glorious action and filled with noble risks, is worth whole years of those mean observances of paltry decorum, in which men steal through existence, like sluggish waters through a marsh, without either honor or observation.[5]

John 7:37-39 tells us that "on the last day, that great day of the feast, Jesus stood and cried out, saying, 'If anyone thirsts, let him come to Me and drink. He who believes in Me, as the Scripture has said, out of his heart will flow rivers of living water.' But this He spoke concerning the Spirit, whom those believing in Him would receive; for the Holy Spirit was not yet given, because Jesus was not yet glorified."

You are empowered by the Holy Spirit to do great things for God— but the key to releasing your flow into your world is the spirit of faith, and the spirit of faith is experienced through an attitude of expectation.

Do you have more faith, power and expectation when you are around certain believers with strong faith? Do you lose confidence when those positive, faith-building people are absent? If you answered yes to these two questions, it could be that you are sipping out of the power-well of someone else's faith instead of filling your own.

Start right now with an attitude adjustment and ask the Lord for a new spirit of expectation. Expect God to do something through you today and every day. Expect miracles to happen in you, around you and through you.

I've had the privilege of watching God work incredible miracles to provide for the needs of His Church. Years ago, when we finally outgrew our first church plant in Eugene, we set out to purchase a huge parcel on the outskirts of town that required what was for us an enormous sum of money. Again we found ourselves in a financial dilemma.

On one particular day, a Catholic man, new to our congregation, who owned several Taco Bells, stopped by my office for what I thought was a rather weird conversation. He rambled on and on about a certain number of people, servants, horses and camels listed in Ezra 2:3-67. I tried to be polite, but I must tell you that I did not quite get his drift. That is until he told me that he had added up the amount of people and animals and decided to donate a check for the same amount to the church to buy the property. As I recollect, the amount was around $58,000. My jaw dropped, but my faith soared. It was beyond what I had expected God to do through one individual, and I've often wondered whether he himself had expected to write such an enormous check on that day! God truly provides for what He guides, and He can use the most unlikely people to sponsor His Kingdom plans.

Miracles demonstrate the presence of God's Kingdom. Expect miracles for those in need. Miracles build your faith and the faith of everyone in your sphere of influence. Exodus 14:31 says that "Israel saw the great work which the Lord had done in Egypt; so the people feared the Lord, and believed the Lord and His servant Moses." Expect God to use you as a faith person to unlock miracles for other people in need. "You will find, as you look back upon life, that the moments that stand out are the moments when you have done things for others."[6]

John 14:12 is a great verse to pray daily, asking the Holy Spirit that it be fulfilled in and through your life:

> "Most assuredly, I say to you, he who believes in Me, the works that I do he will do also; and greater works than these he will do, because I go to My Father."

Professor C.H. Dodd of Cambridge translated John 14:12 as follows:

> "I assure you, he who has faith in Me will do the works I am doing, and because I am going to the Father, he will do greater works still."[7]

Dodd then points out that the "works" are the miraculous works of Christ. Christ will continue His mighty works through His disciples of all ages and generations.

We are empowered to do more than we have experienced.

You are a messenger of believing and freedom. In Mark 9:23 Jesus said, "If you can believe, all things are possible to him who believes." And then in 2 Corinthians 3:17 we read, "Now the Lord is the Spirit; and where the Spirit of the Lord is, there is liberty [freedom]."

Don't let your lack of experience with miracles dictate how you will pray and speak about miracles. Your personal experiences are not the basis for your faith or for your message to others. You and I are to preach Christ and His accomplishments, His cross, His resurrection and His Holy Spirit. Second Corinthians 1:9 says that "we had the sentence of death in ourselves, that we should not trust in ourselves but in God who raises the dead."

In 2 Corinthians 3:5 the apostle Paul gives a clear life philosophy for how we should see ourselves:

> Not that we are sufficient of ourselves to think of anything as being from ourselves, but our sufficiency is from God.

Our sufficiency is not in and of ourselves, but in and of God. We have His treasure in us. We have His grace, His power and His Holy Spirit. We do not preach to others our experience or lack of it, but God's Word. This truth is confirmed in 2 Corinthians 4:5, which says that "we do not preach ourselves, but Christ Jesus the Lord, and ourselves your bondservants for Jesus' sake."

If you have never experienced a miracle, you still have the authority through the Word of God to testify of God's power to work miracles and to encourage others to receive God's miracles for their lives. Remember, our faith is not based on our good or bad experiences.

If you have had a prodigal child, you may find it difficult to encourage a parent who is going through the same difficult experience. You may think, *What can I say? My experience with my child takes away my authority to speak faith and encouragement.* This is wrong thinking. What are you preaching to that parent—your experience or God's Word? Where does the hope for the situation rest—in your experience or God's Word?

The same scenario works when praying for those in need of a physical healing. Your thoughts may ruminate with dialogues such as, *Have you ever been healed? Well, no, I guess not. Then why are you praying for people to receive this miracle when you have no faith for yourself?* This thinking is not the Holy Spirit talking to you. It's the enemy of your soul. What are you building your faith on—your experiences or the Word of God? If you never get healed from a sickness or disease, if you never see God heal anyone you have prayed for, you are still to have total faith and confidence in the Word of God, not in your experiences.

Numbers 23:19 says that "God is not a man, that He should lie, nor a son of man, that He should repent. Has He said, and will He not do? Or has He spoken, and will He not make it good?" God is not a liar. God is not double-minded. God has given you His truth in His Word. God is teaching us that the worst conditions cannot suppress the spirit of faith, because faith creates its own atmosphere.

Of course you will be stretched as you face the hopelessness and the no-faith attitudes of people. You will be challenged to rise in faith when you see the great needs of people around you. But as Howard R. Macy writes in *Rhythms of Life,* "The spiritual world...cannot be made suburban. It is always frontier, and if we would live in it, we must accept and even rejoice that it remains untamed."[8]

FACING POTENTIAL POWER SHORTAGES AND FAITH CRISES

A story in the Gospel of Mark serves as a backdrop to understanding our challenges as we desire to become channels for God's power to work miracles in us, around us and through us. Let's read Mark 9:14-18 together so that we might carefully examine the challenges presented in this passage:

> And when He came to the disciples, He saw a great multitude around them, and scribes disputing with them. Immediately, when they saw Him, all the people were greatly amazed, and running to Him, greeted Him. And He asked the scribes, "What are you discussing with them?" Then one of the crowd answered and said, "Teacher, I brought You my son, who has a mute spirit. And wherever he seizes him, he throws him down; he foams at the mouth, gnashes his teeth, and becomes rigid. So I spoke to Your disciples, that they should cast him out, but they could not."

Negative Theologians and Doubting People

The disciples were trying to be channels of God's power while surrounded by negative theologians and doubting people—not exactly an atmosphere you want to be in when miracles are needed. Nevertheless, it is the atmosphere you will often encounter if you want to pursue a miracle lifestyle and a "believe-all-things-are-possible" attitude.

Mark 9:14 says there was "a great multitude around them, and scribes disputing with them." The disciples were no match for the scribes. The scribes were the educated elite of the day. The word "scribe" means to write, order or count. The scribes were students of the law and official interpreters of the law. But there were two kinds of scribes—good scribes such as Ezra (see Ezra 7:6-12) and bad scribes (see Jer. 8:8) whose false pens converted the law into a lie by using false interpretations.

The Disciples Encounter a Power Shortage

The disciples were not educated in the official use of the law and Old Testament Scriptures; they were intellectually out of their league. They were proclaiming the power of God to heal and work miracles, expecting to have the results that happened when Jesus would go public and work miracles. However, there was a slight problem—they had a power shortage, a faith crisis. Their faith malfunctioned, and the scribes had a great time arguing with them and criticizing their efforts.

The disciples were out of the closet and into the public with their faith. There was nowhere to hide, no excuses they could use. The disciples had to produce, but they were unable to flow in God's channel of power at that moment for that specific need. The boy's father said in Mark 9:18, "I told your disciples to cast it out and they could not do it." They lacked the power; they were unable; they failed; they could not produce.

Facing People Situations When Defeat Has Been Long and Deep

In Mark 9:21 Jesus asks the boy's father, "How long has this been happening to him?" And he said, "From childhood." The Bible describes what happened when the demon seized the boy as "tearing at him." In other words, the boy was thrown into such violent convulsions that it seemed as if he would be torn into pieces. The demonic power would tear, shake and roll the boy back and forth.

Imagine the sight! As the father wrings his hands in despair, the convulsing boy is being thrown around like a rag doll. The helpless disciples are commanding the spirit, "Stop!" and desperately praying that something, anything, happens. On the sidelines the scribes are nudging each other and pointing their fingers, laughing and mocking at the futility of the disciples' prayers. Perhaps some of them are criticizing, blaming the disciples for the torment of the child, "Why didn't you just leave the demon alone? The boy wasn't this bad before you started."

How many years had the father flushed with embarrassment as his son became the brunt of public humiliation? How many times had he helplessly tried to hold his convulsing son, praying his boy would live through the torment? How many times had his heart anguished as he watched his wife weep over her son? Jesus asked the question, "How long?"

> Many people do not understand that the length and depth of defeat and despair have absolutely no bearing on Christ's ability to perform a miracle.

Defeat and Despair

Like the father in this passage, many people do not understand that the length and depth of defeat and despair have absolutely no bearing on Christ's ability to perform a miracle. No bearing whatsoever!

The boy had been tormented for years. The father and his son could have been visiting a neighbor, shopping in the market, walking down the street. Anywhere. Everywhere. Without warning the boy would suddenly be thrown to the ground with violent convulsions that seemed as if they would pull him to pieces. He foamed at the mouth and gnashed his teeth. After years of this torture, the boy looked like a skeleton, emaciated, his arms and legs wasted to skin and bones. His parents had no social life. After all, how could you visit friends or family if you knew they would have to watch your son writhe in such a grotesque manner. The whole family was drained. They could never leave the boy alone— he might fall into a fire or into a river during his convulsions. Their lives were controlled by the boy's illness.

"How long?"

"Since childhood."

Jesus knew the answer, but he wanted to hear the father say it. No doubt this worn-out parent had tried every other means available to him—local physicians, synagogue priests, sacrifices, prayers, anything, everything. But all was for nothing! Disappointed each time, the father now approached the disciples of the Miracle Worker. Perhaps this dad allowed himself to hope that maybe this time.... Instead he faced the same disappointment, the same despair, the same hopelessness. Nothing happened. Nothing worked.

If You Can, Do Something

The disciples were unable to fix the problem. It was a humiliating and embarrassing situation for them as the scribes mocked and a father's eyes pooled with tears of despair. Yes, the father had suffered a long and deep season of defeat, but Jesus was not finished. The disciples had also suffered a setback as they prayed for a miracle, but the setback was not a defeat. They would learn once again that Jesus was the power and the source and that Jesus could overcome any demon. The disciples would remember this event even after the Ascension when Jesus was no longer with them physically. They would use His name, His authority and His power to do great and mighty works.

"If You can do anything, have compassion on us and help us," the father pleaded. Long-term defeat in peoples' lives often gives rise to an "if You can" attitude, fostering a stronghold of discouragement.

Because He Can, You Can Be a Channel of God's Miracle Power

In Mark 9:23, Jesus explains to the father, "If you can believe, all things are possible to him who believes." The key to miracles begins with believing.

Jesus gently addressed the weakness of the father's faith. Then, the father shifted the focus to Christ's power—"If You desire, You can do anything"—and to the lack of power in the disciples. But Christ turned the focus back to the father and asked him to look at his own faith, graciously speaking words to strengthen the man's faith. "All things are possible." He encouraged the father to believe that the miracle-working power of God was available at his point of need. Do you dare to believe for the impossible?

The key to believing is an honest confession and a sincere plea, "God I believe, help my unbelief!" The boy's father responded openly and honestly. He was fully aware of his imperfections and he earnestly desired a greater faith. He began with "I believe" and ended with "I believe that You can do anything; help me believe." He recognized that his level of faith was not what it should have been and therefore cried out for more.

God will do nothing in our favor without faith. It is right to have confidence in God. And if we have confidence, it is easy for God to do the impossible. The problem is not God's power; it is our faith in His power and His ability to work. The boy's father felt the implied adjustment to his faith in the language Jesus used, and he was grieved that he could be destitute of faith. He deeply felt the need for his son's healing, and he did what you and I would do. He wept.

Nothing can be more touching or natural than this man's response. An anxious father, distressed at the condition of his son, having appealed to the disciples in vain, now came to Jesus. Unsure if he had the qualifications to be a man of faith, he wept.

Can you identify with this father as you reach out and touch the hurting world around you? Can you hear the words, "If you could believe, all things are possible"? Can you feel the tension, the sorrow and the realization that something might not happen because of your lack of faith? Can you feel the emotions, tears welling up inside of you? "O God, I need faith. Please help my unbelief." Jesus did not turn the weeping father away—and He will not turn you away.

Jesus can flow through you and meet the needs of people around you.

Mark 9:25-27 says that "when Jesus saw that the people came running together, He rebuked the unclean spirit, saying to it, 'Deaf and dumb spirit, I command you, come out of him and enter him no more!' Then the spirit cried out, convulsed him greatly, and came out of him. And he became as one dead, so that many said, 'He is dead.' But Jesus took him by the hand and lifted him up, and he arose."

Jesus through you can meet every need of the people around you. All things are possible. Every problem can be solved by the miracle-working power of God. Jesus is always ready to help people through you. You are His hands, His feet, His mouth and His eyes.

In Acts 3:6,7 Jesus worked through Peter and John, "Then Peter said, 'Silver and gold I do not have, but what I do have I give you: in the name of Jesus Christ of Nazareth, rise up and walk.' And he took him by the right hand and lifted him up, and immediately his feet and ankle bones received strength." The miracle was released as Peter and John were ready to believe, to speak the word and to take the lame man by the hand and lift him up.

In Acts 9:11,12 we read, "So the Lord said to him, 'Arise and go to the street called Straight, and inquire at the house of Judas for one called Saul of Tarsus, for behold, he is praying. And in a vision he has seen a man named Ananias coming in and putting his hand on him, so that he might receive his sight.'" God could have healed Saul of Tarsus without the help of Ananias. In fact, Ananias preferred that God do it without his help! But God chose to use him as a channel of His power (see Acts 22:12,13).

It is possible! Anything can happen if you will only believe. The one who has faith can be the recipient of any and all kinds of miraculous benefits. It is possible! It's okay to say it: "Help my unbelief. Cast out my unbelief. Help me, Lord, where I lack in belief."

Will you pray the following with me:

Lord, help me to believe more in the face of impossibility. Help me when I waver because of what I see and cause me to turn my eyes upon You. Help me when I run out of strength to persevere in my praying. Help me when I don't see results. Help me to stay the course and keep my eyes on the Author and Finisher of my faith. Please Lord, help me to have more faith, more hope, more possibility-thinking, more of Jesus.

Someone has said that "faith is like a boomerang; begin using what you have and it comes back to you in greater measure." Sow in faith and you will reap a harvest of miracles.

Notes
1. James B. Simpson, comp., *Simpson's Contemporary Quotations* (Boston: Houghton Mifflin Company, 1988), http://www.bartleby.com/63/93/4293.html.
2. Mother Teresa. QuoteDB (www.quotedb.com). 27 July, 2003.
3. Mark Water, *The New Encyclopedia of Christian Quotations* (Grand Rapids: Baker Book House, 2001).
4. Aimee Semple McPherson, *This Is That* (Los Angeles: Foursquare Publications, 1923), p. 248.
5. Mark Water, *The New Encyclopedia of Christian Quotations* (Grand Rapids: Baker Book House, 2001).
6. Henry Drummond, quoted by Mark Water, *The New Encyclopedia of Christian Quotations* (Grand Rapids: Baker Book House, 2001).
7. J. I. Packer, et al., *The Kingdom and the Power* (Ventura, CA: Regal Books, 1993).
8. Quoted by Ken Gire, *Windows of the Soul* (Grand Rapids: Zondervan, 1996), p. 53.

13

Miracles Hidden in God's Providence

Benjamin Franklin (1706-1790), statesman and inventor, said, "The longer I live, the more convincing proofs I see of this truth, that God governs in the affairs of men."[1]

I never really thought much about the word "providence" until I'd been a Christian for a few years and realized that God was controlling my life in ways I had never discerned before. Things just seemed to fall into place, even in what I thought to be casual decisions or lucky choices. Somehow, I always found myself in the right place at the right time. Eventually, I began to see a pattern of God's sovereign hand involved with my jobs, the people I met, the friends I developed and the schools I attended. Looking back on the past 35 years of my Christian journey, the providence of God is clearly stamped all over my life. I agree with Elizabeth Elliot (1936-), the great missionary whose husband was martyred, "God never does anything to you that isn't for you." What a great definition of providence.

Providence is the overseeing care and guardianship of God for all His creation. His constant care and guardianship stand at the very heart of

God's nature, and they are confirmed repeatedly in Scripture. God loves and cares for individual people, one person at a time. God not only directs nations, but He also directs and cares for every single individual believer with a personal involvement, planning his or her life, providing for that person with masterful wisdom and love.

YOU ARE THE FORESIGHT
AND FORETHOUGHT OF GOD

Matthew 10:29,30 assures us, "Are not two sparrows sold for a copper coin? And not one of them falls to the ground apart from your Father's will. But the very hairs of your head are all numbered." God in His providence is concerned with everyone of His children—from the least to the greatest. No one is left out; no one is overlooked; no one is unimportant. It's unbelievable, isn't it?! Can you even start to grasp how God has directed your life since you became a believer, providing everything you have needed, even when you didn't ask for it? Even when you didn't notice what He was doing, God was busy making a way for you.

The Greek word for providence is *pronoia*, meaning foresight or forethought (see Acts 24:2). As applied to God, it expresses His unceasing power exerted in and over all His works. It is the opposite of chance, fortune and luck. God is in control of all things concerning your life and controls all things for the highest good of His plan and purpose. If the telescope reveals the immense magnitude and countless hosts of worlds that He has created and sustains, the microscopy shows that His providence is equally concerned with the minutest issues of your life.

Miracles are works of God's providence in and around you. They are not luck, chance or unplanned blessings. Miracles are foreordained for your life according to God's foreknowledge and forethought about you. The anomalies apparent now—the temporary sufferings of the righteous and the prosperity of the wicked, the failure of good plans and the success of bad ones—confirm the revelation of the judgment to come that will rectify these anomalies.

God is in control over all the contradictions we face, and He holds the keys for understanding life as we see it. Providence is not superficial optimism, looking through rose-colored glasses at a world with no problems, no pain, no suffering and no unpleasant surprises. Not at all! Providence is a right perspective of the big picture.

THE GOD WHO WORKS BEHIND THE SCENES

Proverbs 16:33 says that "the lot is cast into the lap, but its every decision is from the Lord." What seems like coincidental is not accidental, but is God's providence secretly and quietly working. How you moved to a certain country and went to a certain school to meet a certain person who became your spouse—was it chance or was it providence? How you happened to meet a person in college who became a friend who later became your business partner who helped you create a successful business—chance? Providence! (See Amos 9:9; Ps. 104; Acts 17:28.)

A young lady in our church went to the doctor for a minor ailment. During the examination, the physician found a tumor that resulted in her undergoing several surgeries and chemotherapy. How was God working in this woman's circumstance? Normally that type of cancer is not found until it has spread to other organs, leading to a very low survival rate. As her doctor said after her ordeal was over, "You were extremely lucky that we found the tumor. Someone upstairs must like you." Luck? No, it was the providential hand of God that guided her steps in seemingly insignificant ways to bring about a miracle of healing.

Through providence God controls the universe (see Ps. 103:19), the physical world (see Matt. 5:45), the affairs of nations (see Ps. 66:7), man's birth and destiny (see Gal. 1:15), man's successes and failures (see Luke 1:52) and the protection of His people (see Ps. 4:8). God's providence is unlimited. It includes all things and all creatures in respect to all that takes place in the universe (see Ps. 145:9-17). Great and small miracles are all the same to God. Things of seemingly slight importance are under His overruling power just as much as the life-changing events that leave us standing in awe (see 1 Kings 22:34; Esther 6:1; Matt. 6:26; 27:19; Luke 12:6-7; Acts 23:16).

The particular steps in God's divine process of guiding, protecting and providing usually go unnoticed by us and are incomprehensible when we do notice them. But they are all miracles of God working in us, around us and through us, miracles of God working quietly, slowly and powerfully.

Think about providence for a moment. Think of yesterday. What happened in your life yesterday? What was God doing in the background? How was He working? There are providential miracles working out right in front of you that you cannot see, or perhaps have not discerned yet.

During World War II, John and Celia, missionaries to China, saw the providence of God firsthand as God moved them from place to place, always ahead of the bombings. Sometimes God woke them in the middle of the night and told them to move. Other times natural circumstances provoked them to leave a village, but they were never in a village while it was bombed. "Oh sure," you might say, "it's easy to see the providence of God working in their situation."

Promise plus hope equals expectation, which becomes the atmosphere for experiencing miracles.

But what do we do with the story of Darlene and her daughter? Missionaries to Indonesia during the same war, they were captured and herded into a concentration camp where they spent more than four years. While John and Celia never saw violence, Dorothy lived with it daily. She watched friends die and hid in trenches as bombs fell. Yet she, too, would tell you amazing stories of God's providence—of how bombs fell into trenches just after she left them and how bombs that did fall into her trench did not explode. God was working miracles in the lives of both families, and they had eyes to see it. God grant that we would have eyes to see His hand at work in our lives!

Miracles of providence! What a great way to live life! It's seeing nothing as accidental and nothing as outside of God's concern or care. Nothing is luck or fortune. Perhaps we need to change our view of life and our view of waiting for miracles. Maybe they are already here and we just haven't seen them yet.

Miracles may be viewed as aspects of God's extraordinary providence. They can be seen as events manifesting divine activity that is out of the ordinary processes of nature. In performing a miracle, God (who oversees and governs all things) acts in a supernatural manner. He goes beyond ordinary sequences in the order of life and acts on your behalf. God has extraordinary and providential things planned for you. You are special. You are not only the creation of God, but you are also blood bought, redeemed by the sacrificial blood of Christ and filled with the Holy Spirit. You are a person of destiny and importance, and God is working providentially on your behalf to seal your destiny (see Gen. 33:5; 48:9; Josh. 24:3-4; 1 Sam. 1:27; Job 10:18; Pss. 71:6; 139:15,16).

SIMEON'S MIRACLE OF PROVIDENCE

Consider with me the destiny of a man named Simeon. According to Luke 2:21-24, the parents of Jesus were doing what the law required. After the days prescribed for purification, they brought Jesus to the Temple. A man who had waited his whole life for this one day was about to embrace a miracle of providence. Simeon is called a righteous and devout man, a man who was filled with the Spirit and eagerly expecting the fulfillment of a God-given dream. He had been waiting for the coming Messiah his whole life. Luke 2:25 says that he was looking for the consolation of Israel. He was a special man with a special word because he believed what Luke 2:26 said, "And it had been revealed to him by the Holy Spirit that he would not see death before he had seen the Lord's Christ."

Some learned men, who have been conversant with the Jewish writers, find that during that first century there was a man of great stature in Jerusalem named Simeon. His father was the famous Hillel, the first man given the title of "Rabban," the highest title bestowed upon their doctors, and this title was only given to seven men. Simeon succeeded his father, Hillel, as president of the college that his father had founded and as president of the great Sanhedrin.

Jewish history says that Simeon was endued with a prophetic gift and that he was removed from his position as president because he stood against the common opinion of the Jews that the kingdom of the Messiah would be an earthly one. But Simeon set himself aside in the Temple with prayer and fasting, waiting for his secret word to be fulfilled—that he would not die until he had witnessed firsthand the promised Christ. He would see God's Son. And a miracle of providence was in the making!

God begins some miracles with a promised word—a dream.

Simeon had received a revelation from the books of the Old Testament and from the Holy Spirit that God would send Jesus in the fullness of time. But Jesus was a long time in coming, and those who believed He would come continued to wait, desiring and hoping with faith and patience. Simeon also received a private, personal visitation of the Holy Spirit about this hope. A word of promise was given to him. The Holy Spirit was upon him not only as a spirit of holiness, but also as a spirit of prophecy.

Have you ever received a special, quickened word from God through the Scriptures or through prophetic utterances? Have you received a dream from the Holy Spirit that would require a miracle?

God directs our paths to cross with miracles.

Simeon entered the Temple on that providential day, not knowing that this would be the day Scripture would record about his life. Though Simeon lived many years on this earth, God had the writers of Scripture record that one special day. His path crossed with providence and miracles at the same time and created a point in history that we all remember.

Perhaps today is your day. Perhaps there are some providential miracles in the making right now that are about to cross your path. God has premade, predestined, sovereign miracles for you and me that are to be intermingled with our lives. These miracles will meet us on the way, at prescribed times and places. We're not meandering randomly through life, living by chance and luck. Our steps are ordered by the Lord. Our path is directed by the sovereign hand of God. "We travel an appointed way."[2]

Simeon had come into the Temple at the right time, on the right day. Luke 2:27 tells us that "he came by the Spirit into the temple" just when Joseph and Mary brought the child to be registered in the Temple book as their firstborn. He did not come by chance or luck, but by the direction of the Holy Spirit. The same Spirit that had provided for the support of his dream now provided for the fulfillment of that dream.

God fills our hearts with hope and expectation for miracles.

Deep in his heart Simeon was filled with hope of the dream of seeing the Christ child. We, too, are filled with hope and expectation for the promised words, dreams and visions that God has and will bring to pass with the working of His providential miracles. Promise plus hope equals expectation, which becomes the atmosphere for experiencing miracles.

God speaks to us by His Spirit, nudging us into a place to receive miracles.

If Simeon had disobeyed the divine voice of the Holy Spirit on that very special and providential day, he could have suffered the loss of his dream. Ignoring divine impulses can mean missing providential miracles. He heard a whisper in his ear, "Go to the temple now. Don't hesitate. Go now, and you will receive your heart's dream" (see Luke 2:25-27). We must be people who are divinely inspired, overshadowed and protected by the power and influence of the Holy Spirit. Luke 2:26 says that "it was revealed to him." Simeon was divinely informed; he had an express communication from God concerning the secret of the Lord. He probably had knowledge of Malachi 3:1, "And the Lord, whom you seek, will suddenly come to His temple." Simeon may have put his trust in this Scripture when the Holy Spirit said, "Go. Now. Go to the temple."

What is the Holy Spirit saying to you today about when or where you should go to see the dream of your heart fulfilled and to meet with the miracle God has prepared for you?

God sustains our latter years to reveal some of His greatest miracles.

I don't know anyone who really likes old age. Our latter years come with trials and risks, yet they also bring incomparable privileges. Those of us who have reached a certain level of maturity have a storehouse of precious memories whereby we can testify to the younger generation of the many miracles we have experienced. A good old age does not come accidentally. To live beyond the age of activity, independence, importance and admiration, to be reminded daily that you are the survivor of a past generation, causes many aging people to end their lives in sorrow and unbelief, simply existing rather than participating in life. Simeon rejected that kind of thinking and believed instead that miracles would be activated in his latter years.

No matter what your age, God still has miracles that He wants to activate through your faith. Will you believe?

RECEIVING HIDDEN MIRACLES PROVIDENTIALLY PREPARED FOR YOU

First Corinthians 2:9 heralds the message that "eye has not seen, nor ear heard, nor have entered into the heart of man the things which God has prepared for those who love Him." You may not have the ability to imagine the miracles that God wants to bring into your life, but be assured that they are prepared for you. They are packaged and on their way to the right place for the right time.

Receive your miracle of a healed past and a happy future.

In Genesis 13:14-18 we read that "the Lord said to Abram, after Lot had separated from him: 'Lift your eyes now and look from the place where you are—northward, southward, eastward, and westward; for all the land which you see I give to you and your descendants forever. And I will make your descendants as the dust of the earth; so that if a man could number the dust of the earth, then your descendants also could be numbered. Arise, walk in the land through its length and its width, for I give it to you.' Then Abram moved his tent, and went and dwelt by the terebinth trees of Mamre, which are in Hebron, and built an altar there to the Lord."

Abraham had just left Lot. The relationship had been damaged and now Abraham was left alone. He had done the right thing by taking the humble leftovers and offering Lot the privilege of choosing the best land. Abraham had yielded over his right of control and choice in the matter. He trusted God, knowing that God always does better for those who trust Him than they can do for themselves. We lose nothing when we choose meekness and yieldedness.

Our enemy can be a person, a habit, or any human emotion, but if we trust God to change us rather than our circumstances, we will find the hidden treasure He has prepared for us in the "present" of that enemy.

The word of the Lord came to Abraham at that providential moment. It looked as though he would be the lesser person, have the inferior land and would not have as great a future as Lot. But the word for him was to "lift his eyes." God wants to bring a miracle of new vision into your life right now. In the midst of your present struggles and present limitations, lift your eyes. Look from where you are spiritually. You may be discouraged about your job, your marriage, your lack of relationships, your dreams and your destiny. But with the help of the Holy Spirit, you can lift your eyes of faith and see what the Lord has for you—and it is much broader, much deeper and much more exciting than what you might expect.

Look from where you are emotionally. Abraham was feeling low. His nephew had left him and the relationship had been fractured. But God chose that difficult time to speak a fresh, new word to him about his future—and you, too, can know that God is with you and wants to speak something new into your life when you are hurting the most. Here are a few considerations to ponder the next time you feel your life skidding into a lonely valley:

- God's voice is more distinctly heard in solitude.
- The valleys of life cause us to need a renewed sense of divine approval.
- The divine promises are more clearly apprehended in the valley.
- We are freer to survey the greatness of our inheritance during times of need.
- We gain an enhanced idea of the divine resources when we have no one to turn to but God.

So lift up your eyes and see the miracle of a new beginning for your life. Let your past pass. See by the Spirit and in the Spirit that the Lord has good and mighty things planned for you. Your future is bright. Put your past under the blood of Christ's cross and release your past to God. The past can never be relived, so refuse to keep reliving it in your mind. The past is not the prophet of your future (see Gen. 41:51; Phil. 3:13)— so focus forward with expectation for tomorrow's miracles and refuse to preserve yesterday's losses (see Gen. 19:17,26).

Receive your miracle of hidden wells of refreshing in hard times.

Genesis 21:16-20 says that "she went and sat down across from him at a distance of about a bowshot; for she said to herself, 'Let me not see the death of the boy.' So she sat opposite him, and lifted her voice and wept. And God heard the voice of the lad. Then the angel of God called to Hagar out of heaven, and said to her, 'What ails you, Hagar? Fear not, for God has heard the voice of the lad where he is. Arise, lift up the lad and hold him with your hand, for I will make him a great nation.' And God opened her eyes, and she saw a well of water. And she went and filled the skin with water, and gave the lad a drink. So God was with the lad; and he grew and dwelt in the wilderness, and became an archer."

How did the well happen to be there just when Hagar needed it? The shepherds only dug wells for their own flocks, not for wandering travelers. And yet, God in His providence guided the steps of Hagar to intercept her hidden miracle. Life is filled with hidden wells of stored-up blessings. They are ready at the right time and the right moment to supply for those who are in the trials and testings of a spiritual wilderness.

Look for the hidden table of divine provision that God has promised to you in the presence of your enemy.

Psalm 23:4,5 promises, "Yea, though I walk through the valley of the shadow of death, I will fear no evil; for You are with me; Your rod and Your staff, they comfort me. You prepare a table before me in the presence of my enemies; You anoint my head with oil; my cup runs over."

> Roy Anthony Borges is a prison inmate who, becoming a Christian, had some hard lessons to unlearn. All his life he had been taught to hate his enemies, particularly within prison walls. One of his most vexing enemies was Rodney, who stole his radio and headphones one day while Roy was playing volleyball in the prison yard. It was an expensive radio, a gift from his mother. The earphones had been a Christmas present from his sister. Roy was angry and wanted revenge, but as he prayed about it, it seemed that God was testing him.
>
> Day after day, Roy wanted to respond violently, to knock the wisecrack grin off Rodney's face, but Romans 12:20,21 kept coming to mind: Paul's instruction to avoid vengeance, leaving it to God to settle the score. Roy began to look at Rodney through God's eyes and have compassion on him. He began praying for him. He began trusting God to accomplish something in Rodney's life.
>
> By and by, Roy's hatred for Rodney began fading and he found himself helping his enemy and telling him about Jesus.

Then one day, Roy later wrote, "I saw Rodney kneeling down next to his bunk reading his Bible, and I knew that good had overcome evil."[3]

Our enemy can be a person, a habit, an attitude or any number of human emotions, but if we trust God to change us rather than our circumstances, we will find the hidden treasure He has prepared for us in the "present" of that enemy.

Look for your hidden water of refreshing from unusual resources.

First Corinthians 10:4 says, "And all drank the same spiritual drink. For they drank of that spiritual Rock that followed them, and that Rock was Christ." God may draw from many unusual sources to give you refreshing. Your spiritual drink could come in the form of a telephone call from a person with whom you have had little or no contact, or it could come from a book someone drops into your hands. God knows both your address and your phone number, and He will make sure that you receive just what you need when you need it most.

Look for your hidden well of strange providences.

Sometimes its difficult to understand why we end up in larger-than-life circumstances. Surely David must have wondered. First Samuel 17:17 and 23 say that "Jesse said to his son David, 'Take now for your brothers an ephah of this dried grain and these ten loaves, and run to your brothers at the camp.' Then as he talked with them, there was the champion, the Philistine of Gath, Goliath by name, coming up from the armies of the Philistines; and he spoke according to the same words. So David heard them."

And what about Stephen's martyrdom and the impact it had on Saul, who became the great apostle Paul. In Acts 7:58 we read, "And they cast him [Stephen] out of the city and stoned him. And the witnesses laid down their clothes at the feet of a young man named Saul."

Sometimes God hides His treasures in dark places. They are not sinful or evil places, but dark, unusual, unexpected places—even painful places. We wonder how anything good could possibly come from that source. Even the struggles of prayer can become a hidden well and a secret source of strength, joy and wisdom in a time of testing.

There are no accidents in the life of the believer. God overrules even the most bizarre or weird things that come our way and brings them under His hand, making them serviceable to His people. As I mentioned earlier, when Christopher Columbus ran aground at a place not of his choosing, he realized that the Lord wanted him to start a settlement there. So many good things came of that work that he called the disaster a significant blessing in disguise.

God often accomplishes His purposes by taking a course in direct contradiction to what our narrow views would prescribe. He brings a death upon our feelings, wishes and prospects when He is about to give us the desire of our hearts. God is already at work to fashion the miracles of providence for your unusual life, using unusual means, unusual people and unusual circumstances.

- Settle in your heart that God is a miracle-working God—yesterday, today and forever.
- Settle in your heart that God has miracles for you. They may be hidden, delayed or resisted by the enemy, but they won't be stopped. Faith is the key for opening your miracle door.
- Settle in your heart that you have enough faith for miracles. It only takes a little faith to release great works of God into your world.
- Settle in your heart that you are loved, you are accepted, you have a destiny, you have miracles coming your way right now—beginning today, small, greater, mind-boggling miracles.

Don't settle for less!

Notes

1. Ward & Trent, et al., *The Cambridge History of English and American Literature* (New York: G.P. Putnam's Sons, 1907—21; New York: Bartleby.com, 2000 (www.bartleby.com/cambridge/). 30 July, 2003.
2. Robert J. Morgan, ed., *Nelson's Complete Book of Stories, Illustrations & Quotes*, quote of A.W. Tozer (Nashville: Thomas Nelson, 2000), p. 651.
3. Roy Anthony Borges, "Love Your Enemies: One Prisoner's Story of Risky Obedience," *Discipleship Journal*, Issue 107, pp. 42-43.

14

Miracles and the Omnipotence of God

"HOW CAN YOU BELIEVE THAT?" exclaimed a university student coming upon a classmate reading the Bible. "Don't you have difficulty with such a miracle as the dividing of the Red Sea?"

"Yes, I have difficulty with the Red Sea," was the reply, "but my difficulty is not how it was divided, but how it was made. For certainly He who made it could divide it."[1]

Our understanding of the nature and attributes of God will have a direct affect upon our faith to believe in miracles. Everything about our lives—our attitudes, motives, desires, actions and even our words—are influenced by our vision and knowledge of God. Is it possible for a mere human, less than a tiny speck on a pebble of a planet in the midst of a vast galaxy, to know the God who created everything? Yes, absolutely! Is it possible to know God well enough to trust Him with the most sensitive areas of our lives? Yes, yes, yes! Is it possible to believe in God's attributes, expecting them to be expressed today in your life? It absolutely is. Can you or I expect the omnipotence of God to matter in our lives? Unequivocally YES.

Not everyone in culture or in our Christian churches believes the same things about God. Worldviews other than the biblical worldview control their thinking. Those believing in "naturalism," for example, say that God does not exist and that physical matter is all there is. Their belief structure—which includes that of the secular humanists and the evolutionists—has no room for miracles.

"Pantheism" says, "All is one, one is all, and all is God." This belief structure is strong in parts of the world where Hinduism and Buddhism are embraced. The New Age movement in the United States fits comfortably into this belief system. People of this persuasion have difficulty believing in a God of the Bible who does miracles.

"Polytheism" is the idea that we must appease and please many gods, goddesses and spirits in order to have a reasonably good life. Again, miracles are almost nonexistent in this worldview. "Relativism," on the other hand, is reluctant to commit to any one particular belief system as relativists prefer to pick and choose what they like about various religions. They are not concerned about whether or not the ideas contradict each other, thus they are not supportive of the Christian belief that the Bible is the inspired Word of God, the final truth—nor do they accept the God of Scripture as being the only true God. God-given miracles are not part of their expectations either.

The Biblical Worldview

Christianity says that only one God is supreme and sovereign. While He is transcendent (above and beyond us), He is also and simultaneously imminent (right here among us). He created everything—the universe and the world in which we live. Furthermore, He did it with absolutely nothing. He didn't rearrange some eternal substance to form the world. He created.

His crowning creation was humanity—man and woman. We are made in God's image. When we die, we will either go to be with Him or be separated from Him forever. There's no coming back to try to get it right. And because sin prevents us from getting it right, God sent His Son, part of Himself, to redeem and justify us. According to the Scriptures, Christ died for all our sins, He was buried, He was resurrected on the third day, and He is alive now!

The God of miracles is the God of Creation, the all-powerful, all-knowing, eternal, immutable God. Because this is our God, it is easy to believe in miracles and for miracles. He is the only God, and miracles are part of His nature. In Jeremiah 9:23,24 the Lord says, "Let not the wise man glory in his wisdom, let not the mighty man glory in his might, nor let the rich man glory in his riches; but let him who glories glory in this, that he understands and knows Me, that I am the Lord, exercising lovingkindness, judgment, and righteousness in the earth. For in these I delight." (See also Job 23:3; Hos. 4:1,2; 6:6; Acts 17:22,23; Heb. 1:1-3; 2 Tim. 3:14-16.)

Because our God is the Creator God, nothing is too hard for Him. Listen to what Scripture says about the greatness of our God:

Jeremiah 32:17-19: Ah, Lord God! Behold, You have made the heavens and the earth by Your great power and outstretched arm. There is nothing too hard for You. You show lovingkindness to thousands, and repay the iniquity of the fathers into the bosom of their children after them—the Great, the Mighty God, whose name is the Lord of hosts. You are great in counsel and mighty in work, for your eyes are open to all the ways of the sons of men, to give everyone according to his ways and according to the fruit of his doings.

Psalm 33:6-11: By the word of the Lord the heavens were made, and all the host of them by the breath of His mouth. He gathers the waters of the sea together as a heap; He lays up the deep in storehouses. Let all the earth fear the Lord; let all the inhabitants of the world stand in awe of Him. For He spoke, and it was done; He commanded, and it stood fast. The Lord brings the counsel of the nations to nothing; He makes the plans of the peoples of no effect. The counsel of the Lord stands forever, the plans of His heart to all generations.

The Scriptures build our faith to believe in an awesome God who is mighty, sovereign, and for whom nothing is impossible. Our belief system is a miracle belief system. Psalm 147:5 says that "great is our Lord, and mighty in power; His understanding is infinite." And Jeremiah 32:17 says, "Ah, Lord God! Behold, You have made the heavens and the earth by Your great power and outstretched arm. There is nothing too hard for You." Our God is a God of unlimited power who is willing and ready to work on your behalf, on my behalf. Ephesians 3:20 tells us that He "is able to do exceedingly abundantly above all that we ask or think, according to the power that works in us." (See also Pss. 21:13; 59:16; 147:5.)

God Is All Powerful and Unlimited

Our God is omnipotent and all-powerful. He has unlimited power, authority and influence. Our God never needs to ask permission. He is unrestrained, indescribable, has infinite power and His abilities have no parameters. Blaise Pascal, a seventeenth-century philosopher said, " The greatest single distinguishing feature of the omnipotence of God is that our imagination gets lost thinking about it."[2] "The simple idea of the omnipotence of God is that He can do without effort and by volition whatever He wills, this is the highest conceivable form of power. It is that which is clearly presented in Scriptures. God can do whatever He will. He wills and it is done."[3]

"God is the all-powerful One; nothing is too difficult for Him to accomplish. Nothing is beyond His capability. God declares about Himself, 'Is anything too hard for the Lord.' God is the God of omnipotence, both in actuality and possibility. There are virtually no limitations with God. He has all power (see Ps. 62:11)."[4] Millard J. Erickson says in his book *Christian Theology*, "What all of this means is that God's will is never frustrated. What He chooses to do, He accomplishes. He has the ability to do it. As Psalm 115:3 says, our God is in the heavens. He does whatever He pleases. However, God is wise so that He knows what to do. He is good, and thus He chooses to do the right. He is powerful and therefore is capable of doing what He wills to do."[5]

GOD IS ALMIGHTY—HIGHEST IN AUTHORITY

God is almighty, possesses all power, is a being of unlimited might, and has boundless sufficiency (see Gen. 17:1; 28:3; Pss. 91:1; 97:1; Rev. 1:8; 4:8). God is mighty, very powerful, having great command and is very strong or great in power (see Gen. 49:24; Deut. 4:37; 9:29; Neh. 9:32; Ps. 24:8; Eph. 1:19). God is powerful, having great power, forcible, mighty, strong in extent of dominion, potent, possessing or exerting great force or producing great effects (see Exod. 15:6; 1 Chron. 29:11; Pss. 29:4; 59:16; Matt. 6:13). God is great, chief, vast, extensive, superior, preeminent (see Deut. 7:21; 10:17; Neh. 1:5; 4:14; 8:6; Pss. 77:13; 86:10). He is supreme, highest in authority, holding the highest place in all creation; He is unrestricted, not limited in any way or confined in any way!

It's easy to believe in miracles when you understand the magnitude of our God. Yes, we are limited, confined, powerless and restrained, but with God these limitations are changed.

GOD USES HIS POWER PURPOSEFULLY

God, who is almighty, is the God whose character is also holy, loving, merciful, faithful, truthworthy and just. Therefore, He does and will do only those things that are in harmony with who He is. When we speak of the omnipotence of God, we mean His ability to do whatever He wills, but because His will is submitted to His nature, God does everything in harmony with His attributes. Bill Bright adds that, "God uses His power purposefully. God has unlimited power within Himself and does what He wants with it. God is not a tyrant or a monster God. He is a father God, a wise God. He uses His power to fulfill His purpose in us and in the world."[6] (See Job 34:12; Rev. 15:3; 16:7.)

By His power, God created the heaven and earth (see Gen. 1:1; Jer. 27:3; 32:17; 51:15), created man out of the dust of the ground (see Gen. 2:7; Job 32:8; 33:4), created woman out of a rib from Adam (see Gen. 2:21-23), and sustains the whole universe by the Word of His power (see Heb. 1:3). God has power over nature and all creation (see Exod. 14:22; 2 Kings 6:5-7; Job 10:17-19; Mark 4:35-41), over all nations, kingdoms and kings (see Exod. 15:6; Isa. 40:45; Dan. 4:35; Acts 17:26), over death (see 2 Kings 4:18-36; Acts 2: 24; 1 Cor. 15:26,54,55; Eph. 1:19,20; 2 Tim. 1:10), over both the barren womb and the virgin womb (see Exod. 23:26; Isa. 7:14; Matt. 1:23; Luke 1—2; Luke 1:7), over all sicknesses, diseases and infirmities (see Matt. 9:6-8; Mark 3:15; Luke 5:22-26; 6:19; 8:46; Acts 10:38) and over the devil, demons, evil spirits and hell (see Matt. 8:28-32; John 16:11; Rom. 16:20).

GOD SHARES HIS POWER WITH BELIEVERS

The power of God has been committed to those who, on becoming believers, are empowered and indwelt by the Spirit of God and will execute His power accordingly. The inscription on the Reformation monument in Geneva reads, "One man with God is always in the majority."

One person with God can make a huge difference in today's world, and you are that person. You are God's connecting rod for releasing miracles through. You received a portion of God's power at salvation. Romans 1:16 says, "For I am not ashamed of the gospel of Christ, for it is the power of God to salvation for everyone who believes, for the Jew first and also for the Greek." (See also 1 Cor. 1:18; Eph. 1:19; 1 Thess. 1:5.)

After salvation you can receive more of God's spirit through the baptism of the Holy Spirit. R.A. Torrey said, "I was baptized with the Holy Spirit when I took Him by simple faith in the Word of God."[7] Acts 1:8 says, "But you shall receive power when the Holy Spirit has come upon you; and you shall be witnesses to Me in Jerusalem, and in all Judea and

Samaria, and to the end of the earth." (See Acts 4:7; 4:33; 6:8.)

The believer can walk and live in the power of the Holy Spirit. Then, powerful things will happen and miracles are possible (see Luke 9:11; 2 Pet. 1:3).

I still remember the first time I sensed the Holy Spirit's power flowing through me. I was about 17 years old and decided to step out in faith to teach a Bible Study with approximately a hundred kids attending. I was scared spitless! But as I began to speak, God's anointing surged through me—and like fuel through the engine of an airplane, I suddenly realized that I was soaring above my natural talent, above my natural intelligence and wisdom. God's power was pouring through me to fulfill His purpose so that those who heard were not merely listening to me, but they were hearing God's heart and love through a human vessel. I was at that moment hooked by the Lord to become a pastoring fisher of men.

If God can fashion the mountain, if He can keep the sun in its orbit, if He can split a sea and dry the ground beneath it, do you doubt God can work miracles in your life?

Another time during my teens I sensed God's power impressing me to go to the home of a woman I barely knew. When I arrived, the woman was in the middle of a crisis with her son. I prayed with her and God turned the situation around. She later said, "Frank, you were like an angel of the Lord sent here by God." Of course, we all know that I was only following the One who has the power to change every situation, but one person can make a difference when he or she is submitted to God's power—no matter how young or old that person happens to be.

As already mentioned, one of God's great believers in miracles was Kathryn Kuhlman, now in the Lord's presence. Kathryn made history with her miracle crusades in the 1960s and 1970s. When asked about her success and where the miracles came from, she responded, "The Holy Spirit is the secret of the power in my life. All I have to do is surrender my life to Him."[8] Scripture promises that the Holy Spirit is in us, around us and works through us. We need Holy Spirit power.

As a matter of fact, here's a simple acronym for "power" to help you:

P - Partner with the Holy Spirit.
(Mic. 7:8; Rom. 15:13,19; 2 Cor. 4:7; Eph. 6:10)
O - Order your heart to align with faith.
(1 Cor. 2:5; 4:20; Eph. 3:20; 2 Thess. 1:9)
W - War against destructive thoughts and habits.
(Rom. 8:11; Col. 5:16-18; 2 Tim. 1:7)
E - Exchange your weakness for Christ's strength.
(Isa. 40:29; 2 Cor. 12:9-10; 13:4; Col. 1:21)
R - Replenish daily through prayer and the Word.
(Pss. 85:6; 119:25; Isa. 57:15; Eph. 6:18)

God's omnipotence means that instead of collapsing into your weakness, you can learn to change the orientation of your mind. If God can fashion the mountain, if He can keep the sun in its orbit, if He can split a sea and dry the ground beneath it so an entire nation can cross, do you doubt God can work miracles in your life? Do you doubt that He can break your ingrained bad habits or stop a sin pattern so that you can walk and live in His miracle-working power? God gives us His power in our weakness. (See Appendix B for "A Biblical View of God's Power and the Healing Ministry.")

WAITING ON THE LORD

Psalm 46:10 says that we are to "be still, and know that I am God; I will be exalted among the nations, I will be exalted in the earth!" Be still—that's quite an accomplishment in today's culture. To be still is to be quiet, to wait upon the Lord. If you desire miracles of power, you must learn to wait.

The most important and frequent use of the word "wait" is to define the attitude of a soul toward God. It implies a listening ear, a heart responsive to the wooing of God, a concentration of a person's spiritual faculties upon heavenly things, the patience of faith. Waiting is an eager anticipation and yearning for the revelation of His power and His miracles (see Pss. 62:5; 69:3; Prov. 20:22). *Webster's Dictionary* defines "waiting" as "to stay or rest in expectation, to stop or remain stationary, to wait for the arrival of some person or event, to rest in expectation and patience."[9] *Nelson's Bible Dictionary* defines "wait" as "to be in readiness or expectation."[10] In Scripture the word "wait" typically suggests an anxious, yet confident expectation by God's people that the Lord will intervene on their behalf.

WAITING, THE WORKING OUT OF HOPE

Waiting on the Lord is having a heart that drinks life from God's presence. James G.S.S. Thompson says, "Stillness of heart is an important and essential factor in our waiting before the Lord in prayer."[11] G.Campbell Morgan puts it this way:

> Waiting for God is not laziness; waiting for God is not going to sleep; waiting for God is not the abandonment of effort. Waiting for God means, first, actively under command, second, readiness for any new command that may come, third, the ability to do nothing until the command is given.[12]

Waiting on the Lord is one of the keys to receiving and releasing the power of God in our own personal lives. Waiting is not a welcome part of our culture; we cram more in, start earlier, work later, take work home, make phone calls in the car, use laptops in airports, we don't wait much for anything. Waiting at the stop light, waiting at the doctor's office, waiting for a spouse, waiting for the mail—waiting isn't easy. Just thinking about waiting can make us anxious!

But waiting on the Lord is a biblical principle taught clearly in Scripture. God rewards those who wait on Him. Isaiah 40:31 says that "those who wait on the Lord shall renew their strength; they shall mount up with wings like eagles, they shall run and not be weary, they shall walk and not faint."

We need to be filled and refilled with the manifold presence of God daily. The omnipotence of God is made real to us when His presence saturates our whole being. The power of God for working miracles is found in the manifest presence of God. Isaiah 25:9 says that "it will be said in that day: 'Behold, this is our God; we have waited for Him, and He will save us. This is the Lord; we have waited for Him; we will be glad and rejoice in His salvation.'"

Waiting on the Lord involves the spiritual discipline of prayer and, at times, prayer and fasting. When we wait upon the Lord, we should prepare our hearts to receive. And we receive most when we understand that there are many different ways of waiting on Him.

Waiting Passionately

Passionate waiting is opposite of "whatever will happen will happen. I'm here if You want me. Use me if You want to." That is an attitude of indifference, lukewarmness and status quo. Psalm 34:4 says, "I sought the Lord, and He heard me, and delivered me from all my fears." Your passion is activated by engaging your prayers, being ready to hear the Holy Spirit speak. It is activated when you pray your heart out before God, go through the Word with pen in hand, ready to hear, ready to write down, ready to obey. Be ready to move out in faith and be a channel for miracles. That is passionate waiting (see 2 Chron. 15:15; Ps. 119:10).

Waiting Patiently

Waiting patiently means having an attitude that holds out and waits for God's timing and God's will. Bill Gothard has said that it is accepting a circumstance from God without giving Him a deadline for removing it. Psalm 40:1 says, "I waited patiently for the Lord; and He inclined to me, and heard my cry." Waiting patiently means that I am committed to standing my ground and remaining firm, even under pressure. I have planted my feet and will not be moved, no matter how long I must wait. I believe God is my source and everything is in God's hands, I realize that I cannot make anything happen; only God can. I know that He is omnipotent. I know that He can do anything, but I am obligated to wait upon His timing and His ways. I know that it is in God's power to grant or to withhold and that my only hope is in Him. I wait. I wait patiently (see Heb. 12:2; Isa. 26:8). Joshua Webber describes waiting patiently as "worry-free waiting."

A story is told of a speedboat driver who survived a racing accident. He said he'd been at near top speeds when his boat veered slightly and hit a wave at a dangerous angle. The combined force of his speed and the size and angle of the wave sent the boat spinning crazily into the air. He was thrown from his seat and propelled deeply into the water—so deep, in fact, that he had no idea of which direction the surface was. He had to remain calm, without worry, and wait for the buoyancy of his life vest to begin pulling him up. Once he discovered which way was up, he could swim for the surface.

Sometimes we find ourselves surrounded by confusing options, too deeply immersed in our problems to know which way is up. When this happens, we too can remain calm, waiting for God's gentle tug to pull us in the proper direction. Our "life vest" may be other Christians, Scripture or some other leading from the Holy Spirit, but the key is recognizing our dependency upon God and waiting upon Him until He shows us the way up.[13]

Waiting Purposefully

This kind of waiting acknowledges that God is in control, that God has a plan, and that God is working out all the details of His plan. Waiting purposefully means that I rededicate my life to the sovereign power of God and the sovereign will of God. I wait for His purpose to be worked out. I purpose in my heart to align my thinking to His thinking, my emotions to His emotions and my purpose to His purpose. I wait with spiritual intensity. I build my altar and call on God's name, knowing that He is my God and that He works all things according to His plan and purposes (see Gen. 26:25; Ps. 42:1; Rom. 8:26-28).

Waiting Prayerfully

Prayerful waiting offers prayer in and through the Holy Spirit. This kind of waiting communes with the Holy Spirit. Second Corinthians 13:14 says, "The grace of the Lord Jesus Christ, and the love of God, and the communion of the Holy Spirit be with you all." Waiting with prayer means that I pray in the Spirit, praying with my spiritual language and with my understanding. I must develop my inner spiritual man to move out into spiritual realms. An undeveloped spirit will hinder my ability to hear God, to wait on God and to follow God. To wait on the Lord is to receive His holy power and the Holy Spirit's direction (see Isa. 28:11,12; Matt. 3:11; Rom. 8:26-27; 1 Cor. 14:4,14,15; John 7:38,39). Let us wait on God with prayers of thanksgiving, praise, intercession, petition, dedication, communion and worship.

Waiting Persistently

Waiting persistently means to wait with endurance of faith and hope, refusing to give up. Don't give up on the miracles you are believing for. Don't give up on the prayers you are praying. If the answer doesn't come right away, keep waiting. Persistence requires an attitude of trusting God and knowing that He will act when He is ready—just keep on trusting Him. Waiting with persistence puts iron into your soul, feeds your inner nature with a new boldness and single-mindedness, giving you the holy determination you need to see your miracle come to pass (see Ps. 25:5; Rom. 8:25).

> You don't wait for a train at the bus station, and you don't wait on the Lord in front of a television set.

Rich and Angela, a young couple in our church, gave the following testimony about waiting persistently:

What we discovered about waiting is that we can't dictate when the wait is over. Like any other couple starting out in marriage, we began to plan a family. Our plan was to have our children close in years with the hope that they would also grow close in relationship. After having our first son in September of 1991, we felt that we were right on track. At that time we couldn't have foreseen that our second wouldn't arrive until October of 2002.

During those 11 years of waiting, we struggled between being content with what we had and with the feeling that we were incomplete. All we could do was give our desire for more children to God. We had to continually put that desire in His hands. Sometimes we wondered if we were done, but something in our spirit told us we weren't. We never felt released to give up.

Our eleven-year-old began praying for a sibling at the age of five, and it has been exciting to watch his faith have the opportunity to grow so significantly. We have seen him become very patient in prayer for his friends and family who need salvation. He simply sees it as a matter of time.

After carrying the desire for more children for so many years, we know that it is more than coincidence that we conceived during a season when our church body began to press in for miracles. Having a second son added to our family has truly been God answering our prayers. More than anything, we know that this was a miraculous addition to our family. We now feel that we are complete. Good things truly do come to those who wait upon the Lord.

Waiting Expectantly

Waiting expectantly is waiting on the Lord with a revived spirit that is filled with Holy Spirit expectation. This kind of waiting implies a confidence and assurance that God will reveal Himself and that He will accomplish His Word. God's omnipotence is to be expected. Let us expect more of God, more of His Word and more of His miracles. Expect God's power in the unexplained circumstances of life. Be ready. Watch. Be looking expectantly. Fix your eyes on God. Wake up and stretch out your faith. Miracles are on their way. Miracles come to those who expect God to do the impossible.

Waiting on the Lord is both a decision and a discipline. And with the choice to wait comes choosing the right place to get serious with God— a prayer closet, a prayer mountain, a place where you have time in the quietness of your soul to hear from God. You don't wait for a train at the bus station, and you don't wait on the Lord in front of a television set. Find the right place to wait on the Lord (see Jer. 33:3; Ps. 37:4).

We all want to see new levels of miracles, new levels of God's power in our lives and in the world around us, but we must wait upon the Lord, be refreshed, refilled and refocused. The Lord calls us to stop, to unplug from the normal flow of life and to intentionally give ourselves to waiting upon Him. Let's be like Mary who chose the better part (see Luke 10:41,42). Let's wait with the abiding faith of an Arthur and Wilda Matthews.

When the communists came to power in China, the western missionaries were forced to flee for their lives. Arthur and Wilda Matthews and their small daughter were trapped for two years until the government finally agreed to release them. In those two years they seldom had enough food, their toddler almost died and they suffered at the hands of the Communists. Against that backdrop, Arthur wrote the following poem:

In waiting I'm waiting for You, blessed Lord,
Though encompassing foes threaten ill.
My weak, trembling faith clings fast to Your word
And trustingly waits Your will.

In waiting I'm waiting for You, Lord, alone—
Not deliverance from dangers without—
But for You, Lord, to come and claim my heart's throne
And self's lesser hopes put to route.

In waiting I'm waiting, my hope, bruised and sore,
Murmurs, Lord, at Your "tarrying yet."
You plan a harvest where death locks the door,
Then grant, Lord, my faith never forget.

In waiting I'm waiting Your fire, Lord, to burn
The base metal that quails neath Your hand.
To be still and know—through Your fire would I learn
You are God when I can't understand.

You are God when I can't understand.[14]

OUR STORY

Lest you think that we, the Damazio family, are immune to the anguish of needing a miracle and having to wait on God, I'd like to share a personal story.

Shortly after I decided to embark on a series of teachings on miracles in our church, my wife and I were taken aback to learn that our precious 11-year-old daughter, Jessica, was diagnosed with Level 1 diabetes. This life-threatening kind of diabetes is not hereditary but a solitary, isolated condition. We thought the timing, the emotions and the processing to be so relevant that I decided to clarify a few things for our congregation—and now, I want to share some of these same things with you.

First, how do we feel? Suffering is part of the life we face in a fallen world with sin, sickness, disease, etc. We understand that no one is exempt, no one.

Who is in charge, God or the devil? God is! He is our protection. He is our refuge. Nothing happens without God's knowledge, and He is in control.

Is this a direct attack from the enemy because we are preaching on miracles? Maybe! It really doesn't matter because our focus is upon God's goodness, not the enemy's evil ways. We are not at the enemy's disposal for him to do with us as he wishes.

Our faith is not shaken at all. We are parents. And like any other parents, we have had tears, felt overwhelmed at times, had questions and, of course, we as a family are now facing a huge lifestyle adjustment.

Our hearts are thankful that the doctors discovered this problem and treated it quickly, a small miracle for which we praise God. We believe early detection was God's protection. Our faith for miracles is the same. We believe that God desires to work mightily, and we are in pursuit of Kingdom power but...whether we see a healing according to our time table or not, whether we see prayers answered or not, God will not be blamed. He will be honored, and we will give Him rightful place. He is God.

The doctrines of Scripture are not evaluated based on yours or my experiences. The Word of God is true. We will stand on the Word and the faithfulness of God.

Pray for us as you would anyone else, but don't make us a special case. Let this not cause you to be discouraged or sidetracked. Stay focused on the big picture: God is still the same—yesterday, today and forever—and He has a miracle that's earmarked for you.

Notes

1. Walter B. Knight, ed., *Knight's Master Book of New Illustrations*, "Point of View" taken from *Christian Digest* (Grand Rapids: Wm. B. Eerdmans, 1956), p. 404.
2. By Blaise Pascal, http://www.christianglobe.com/Illustrations/a-z/o/omnipotence.html.
3. Charles Hodge, *Systematic Theology* (Grand Rapids: Wm. B. Eerdmans, 1960), Vol. I, p. 407.
4. J. Rodham Williams, *Renewal Theology* (Grand Rapids: Zondervan Publishing, 1996).
5. Millard Erickson, *Christian Theology* (Grand Rapids: Baker Book House, 1998).
6. Bill Bright, *God: Discover His Character* (Orlando, FL: New Life Publications, 2002).
7. R. A. Torrey, *The Holy Spirit: Who He Is and What He Does* (Grand Rapids: Fleming H. Revell Company, 1927), pp. 199-200.
8. Kathryn Kuhlman, *Prayer* (Speak the Word Church) <http://www.speaktheword.com/quotes/prayer.html>. 11 January 11, 2003.
9. *Webster's 1828 Dictionary*, http://www.christiansoup.com. (Independence, MO: Christian Technologies, Inc., 2002).

10. *Nelson's Illustrated Bible Dictionary* (Nashville: Thomas Nelson Publishers, electronic edition from Biblesoft, 1986).

11. James G. S. S. Thompson, *The Praying Christ* http://www.backtothebible.org/knowgod/worship.htm.

12. By G. Campbell Morgan, http://www.christianglobe.com/Illustrations/a-z/w/waiting on God.html.

13. Craig Brian Larson, ed., *Illustrations for Preaching & Teaching* (Grand Rapids: Baker Books, 1993), p. 174, adapted.

14. Isobel Kuhn, *Green Leaf in Drought Time* (Chicago: Moody Press, 1957).

Appendix A

Healings in the New Testament

Seeing the healings and miracles of Christ arranged in a simple manner, we can easily see how He functioned: His methods, the people He healed and the results.

Healing	Matt.	Mark	Luke	John	Method
1. Man with unclean spirit		1:23	4:33		Exorcism, word
2. Peter's mother-in-law	8:14	1:30	4:38		Touch, word; prayer of friends
3. Multitudes	8:16	1:32	4:40		Touch, word; faith of friends
4. Many demons		1:39			Preaching, exorcism
5. A leper	8:2	1:40	5:12		Word, touch, leper's faith and Christ's compassion
6. Man sick of palsy	9:2	2:3	5:17		Word, faith of friends
7. Man's withered hand	12:9	3:1	6:6		Word; obedient faith
8. Multitudes	12:15	3:10			Exorcism, response to faith
9. Gerasene demoniac	8:28	5:1	8:26		Word, exorcism
10. Jairus's daughter	9:18	5:22	8:41		Word, touch; faith of father
11. Woman with issue of blood	9:20	5:25	8:43		Touching His garment in faith
12. A few sick people	13:58	6:5			Touch (hindered by unbelief)
13. Multitudes	14:34	6:55			Touch of His garment, friend's faith
14. Syro-phoenician's daughter	15:22	7:24			Response to mother's prayer, faith
15. Deaf and dumb man		7:32			Word, touch; friends' prayer
16. Blind man (gradual healing)		8:22			Word, touch; friends' prayer
17. Child with evil spirit	17:14	9:14	9:38		Word, touch; faith of father
18. Blind Bartimaeus	20:30	10:46	18:35		Word, touch, compassion; faith
19. Centurion's servant	8:5		7:2		Response to master's prayer, faith

HEALING	MATT.	MARK	LUKE	JOHN	METHOD
20. Two blind men	9:27				Word, touch, men's faith
21. Dumb demoniac	9:32				Exorcism
22. Blind and dumb demoniac	12:22		11:14		Exorcism
23. Multitudes	4:23		6:17		Teaching, preaching, healing
24. Multitudes	9:35				Teaching, preaching, healing
25. Multitudes	11:14		7:21		Proof to John Baptist in prison
26. Multitudes	14:14		9:11	6:2	Compassion, response to needs
27. Great Multitudes	15:30				Faith of friends
28. Great Multitudes	19:2				He healed them
29. Blind and lame in temple	21:14				He healed them in the temple
30. Widow's son			7:11		Word, compassion
31. Mary Magdalene and others			8:2		Exorcism
32. Woman bound by Satan			13:10		Word, touch
33. Man with dropsy			14:1		Touch
34. Ten lepers			17:11		Word; faith of men
35. Malchus's ear			22:49		Touch
36. Multitudes			5:15		He healed them
37. Various persons			13:32		Exorcism, and not stated
38. Nobleman's son				4:46	Word; father's faith
39. Impotent man				5:2	Word; man's faith

In the Early Church, being saved was not a prerequisite to experiencing miracles. On the contrary, the majority were not believers when they were healed. Of the miracles listed here, eleven unbelievers were healed and four believers.

REFERENCE	PERSON(S)	AFFLICTION	BELIEVER?
Acts 3:1-10	Beggar at Beautiful	Congenital paralysis	No
Acts 5:12,15	Crowds of "the people"	Various	No
Acts 6:8	"The people"	Various	No
Acts 8:6-7	Samaritans	Demons/paralysis/etc.	No
Acts 9:17-18	Saul of Tarsus	Blindness	Not yet
Acts 9:32-34	Aeneas	Paralysis	No
Acts 9:36-42	Dorcas	Unknown, but fatal	Yes

Reference	Person(s)	Affliction	Believer?
Acts 14:3	People at Iconium	Various	No
Acts 14:8-10	Man at Lystra	Congenital paralysis	No
Acts 16:16-18	Fortuneteller at Philippi	Demon possession	No
Acts 19:11-12	People at Ephesus	Various, including demons	Unknown
Acts 20:7-12	Eutychus	Accident	Yes
Acts 28:3-6	Paul	Snakebite	Yes
Acts 28:7-8	Publius's father	Fever/dysentery	No
Acts 28:9	Other Maltese	Various	No
Phil. 2:25-30	Epaphroditus	Unknown, but serious	Yes

In the Old Testament, five times the people healed were followers of God and four times they were not followers of God.

Reference	Person(s)	Affliction	Believer?
Num. 12:10-15	Miriam	Skin disease (leprosy)	Yes
Num. 21:4-9	Desert complainers	Snakebite	Yes
1 Kings 13:1-6	King Jeroboan I	Sudden hand paralysis	No
1 Kings 17:17-24	Widow's son at Zarephath	Unknown, but fatal	No (v. 24)
2 Kings 4:17-37	Shunammite's son	Possible sunstroke	Yes
2 Kings 5:1-19	Naaman	Skin disease (leprosy)	No
2 Kings 13:20-21	Israelite soldier	Fatal battle wound	Unknown
2 Kings 20:1-11	King Hezekiah	Severe carbuncle?	Yes
Isa. 38:1-8	King Hezekiah	Severe carbuncle?	Yes
Job 2:1-8;42	Job	Painful sores	Yes

Another interesting aspect in Scripture is that godly people were not always healed.

Reference	Person(s)	Affliction
Gen. 48:1; 49:33	Jacob	Unknown, but fatal
1 Kings 1:1; 2:10	David	Possible circulatory problem
2 Kings 13:14-20	Elisha	Unknown, but fatal
Gal. 4:13-14; 2 Cor 12:7-10	Paul	"Thorn in my flesh"
1 Tim. 5:23	Timothy	Stomach disorder
2 Tim. 4:40	Trophimus	Unknown

Appendix B

A BIBLICAL VIEW OF GOD'S POWER AND THE HEALING MINISTRY

In pursuing a biblical view of God's power and the healing ministry, it is necessary to read and to ponder the Scriptures, especially those that deal with miracles. Our desire is to seek a balanced, yet powerful, ministry of healing and to see this ministry fully recovered for today's Church. Please read these Scriptures, which are foundational to our teaching on miracles and healing. Note their references to power, healing, signs and wonders.

- **The miracle ministry of Jesus:**

  Luke 4:18: "The Spirit of the Lord is upon Me, because He has anointed Me to preach the gospel to the poor; He has sent Me to heal the brokenhearted, to proclaim liberty to the captives and recovery of sight to the blind, to set at liberty those who are oppressed."

- **The miracles of Peter and John at the temple gate:**

  Acts 3:1-10: Now Peter and John went up together to the temple at the hour of prayer, the ninth hour. And a certain man lame from his mother's womb was carried, whom they laid daily at the gate of the temple which is called Beautiful, to ask alms from those who entered the temple; who, seeing Peter and John about to go into the temple, asked for alms. And fixing his eyes on him, with John, Peter said, "Look at us." So he gave them his attention, expecting to receive something from them. Then Peter said, "Silver and gold I do not have, but what I do have I give you: in the name of Jesus Christ of Nazareth, rise up and walk." And he took him by the right hand and lifted him up, and immediately his feet and ankle bones received strength. So he, leaping up, stood and walked and entered the temple with them—walking, leaping and praising God. And all the people saw him walking and praising God. Then they knew that it was he who sat begging alms at the Beautiful Gate of the temple; and they were filled with wonder and amazement at what had happened to him.

- **The miracles of power by Philip, the evangelist:**

Acts 8:6-8: And the multitudes with one accord heeded the things spoken by Philip, hearing and seeing the miracles which he did. For unclean spirits, crying with a loud voice, came out of many who were possessed; and many who were paralyzed and lame were healed.

- **The miracle of the paralyzed man:**

Acts 9:32-35: Now it came to pass, as Peter went through all parts of the country, that he also came down to the saints who dwelt in Lydda. There he found a certain man named Aeneas, who had been bedridden eight years and was paralyzed. And Peter said to him, "Aeneas, Jesus the Christ heals you. Arise and make your bed." Then he arose immediately. So all who dwelt at Lydda and Sharon saw him and turned to the Lord.

- **The miracle of raising Tabitha from the dead:**

Acts 9:36-43: At Joppa there was a certain disciple named Tabitha, which is translated Dorcas. This woman was full of good works and charitable deeds which she did. But it happened in those days that she became sick and died. When they had washed her, they laid her in an upper room. And since Lydda was near Joppa, and the disciples had heard that Peter was there, they sent two men to him, imploring him not to delay in coming to them. Then Peter arose and went with them. When he had come, they brought him to the upper room. And all the widows stood by him weeping, showing the tunics and garments which Dorcas had made while she was with them. But Peter put them all out, and knelt down and prayed. And turning to the body he said, "Tabitha, arise." And she opened her eyes, and when she saw Peter she sat up. Then he gave her his hand and lifted her up; and when he had called the saints and widows, he presented her alive. And it became known throughout all Joppa, and many believed on the Lord. So it was that he stayed many days in Joppa with Simon, a tanner.

• **The miracle of Peter's shadow bringing healing:**

Acts 5:12-16: And through the hands of the apostles many signs and wonders were done among the people. And they were all with one accord in Solomon's Porch. Yet none of the rest dared join them, but the people esteemed them highly. And believers were increasingly added to the Lord, multitudes of both men and women, so that they brought the sick out into the streets and laid them on beds and couches, that at least the shadow of Peter passing by might fall on some of them. Also a multitude gathered from the surrounding cities to Jerusalem, bringing sick people and those who were tormented by unclean spirits, and they were all healed.

• **The unusual miracles of Paul:**

Acts 19:11,12: Now God worked unusual miracles by the hands of Paul, so that even handkerchiefs or aprons were brought from his body to the sick, and the diseases left them and the evil spirits went out of them.

• **The miracle of raising the dead boy:**

Acts 20:7-12: Now on the first day of the week, when the disciples came together to break bread, Paul, ready to depart the next day, spoke to them and continued his message until midnight. There were many lamps in the upper room where they were gathered together. And in a window sat a certain young man named Eutychus, who was sinking into a deep sleep. He was overcome by sleep; and as Paul continued speaking, he fell down from the third story and was taken up dead. But Paul went down, fell on him, and embracing him said, "Do not trouble yourselves, for his life is in him." Now when he had come up, had broken bread and eaten, and talked a long while, even till daybreak, he departed. And they brought the young man in alive, and they were not a little comforted.

- **The miracles of Paul with his preaching:**

Romans 15:18,19: For I will not dare to speak of any of those things which Christ has not accomplished through me, in word and deed, to make the Gentiles obedient—in mighty signs and wonders, by the power of the Spirit of God, so that from Jerusalem and round about to Illyricum I have fully preached the gospel of Christ.

- **The miracle power of the Cross:**

1 Corinthians 1:17,18: For Christ did not send me to baptize, but to preach the gospel, not with wisdom of words, lest the cross of Christ should be made of no effect. For the message of the cross is foolishness to those who are perishing, but to us who are being saved it is the power of God.

- **The demonstration of the power of God:**

1 Corinthians 2:4,5: And my speech and my preaching were not with persuasive words of human wisdom, but in demonstration of the Spirit and of power, that your faith should not be in the wisdom of men but in the power of God.

- **The kingdom of God is power:**

1 Corinthians 4:20: For the kingdom of God is not in word but in power.

- **The exceeding great power that works in the believer:**

Ephesians 1:18-20: The eyes of your understanding being enlightened; that you may know what is the hope of His calling, what are the riches of the glory of His inheritance in the saints, and what is the exceeding greatness of His power toward us who believe, according to the working of His mighty power which He worked in Christ when He raised Him from the dead and seated Him at His right hand in the heavenly places.

- **The believer's might is in God's power:**

Ephesians 6:10,11: Finally, my brethren, be strong in the Lord and in the power of His might. Put on the whole armor of God, that you may be able to stand against the wiles of the devil.

- **The gospel is the power of God:**

1 Thessalonians 1:5: For our gospel did not come to you in word only, but also in power, and in the Holy Spirit and in much assurance, as you know what kind of men we were among you for your sake.

- **The power of God expressed in prayer:**

James 5:14-18: Is anyone among you sick? Let him call for the elders of the church, and let them pray over him, anointing him with oil in the name of the Lord. And the prayer of faith will save the sick, and the Lord will raise him up. And if he has committed sins, he will be forgiven. Confess your trespasses to one another, and pray for one another, that you may be healed. The effective, fervent prayer of a righteous man avails much. Elijah was a man with a nature like ours, and he prayed earnestly that it would not rain; and it did not rain on the land for three years and six months. And he prayed again, and the heaven gave rain, and the earth produced its fruit.

- **The healing power of Christ's cross:**

Isaiah 53:5: But He was wounded for our transgressions, he was bruised for our iniquities; the chastisement for our peace was upon Him, and by His stripes we are healed.

- **The delivering power of God:**

Matthew 8:16,17: When evening had come, they brought to Him many who were demon-possessed. And He cast out the spirits with a word, and healed all who were sick, that it might be fulfilled which was spoken by Isaiah the prophet, saying: "He Himself took our infirmities and bore our sicknesses."

- **The power signs of the apostles:**

2 Corinthians 12:12: Truly the signs of an apostle were accomplished among you with all perseverance, in signs and wonders and mighty deeds.

- **The deceiving signs of power by the antichrist:**

2 Thessalonians 2:9: The coming of the lawless one is according to the working of Satan, with all power, signs, and lying wonders.